ROUSSEAU'S HAND

Rousseau's Hand

The Crafting of a Writer

ANGELICA GOODDEN

OXFORD
UNIVERSITY PRESS

OXFORD

UNIVERSITY PRESS

Great Clarendon Street, Oxford, OX2 6DP,
United Kingdom

Oxford University Press is a department of the University of Oxford.
It furthers the University's objective of excellence in research, scholarship,
and education by publishing worldwide. Oxford is a registered trade mark of
Oxford University Press in the UK and in certain other countries

First Edition published in 2013

Impression: 1

Published in the United States of America by Oxford University Press
198 Madison Avenue, New York, NY 10016, United States of America

British Library Cataloguing in Publication Data

Data available

ISBN 978–0–19–968383–3

As printed and bound by
CPI Group (UK) Ltd, Croydon, CR0 4YY

Acknowledgements

I am very grateful to St Hilda's College, Oxford, and the Faculty of Medieval and Modern Languages at the University of Oxford for granting the term of sabbatical leave during which I was able to start work on this book; to the two anonymous readers for Oxford University Press, whose comments on my original typescript were exceptionally helpful; to my former students Joe Smith and Hannah Wroblewski for helping me with typing when time was especially pressing, as well as to all the other students at Oxford with whom I have been able to study and discuss Rousseau over the years; and for everyone in the editorial and production teams of Oxford University Press for their efficiency and forebearance.

Contents

Introduction

BOOK AND HAND

'Les habitans du monde enchanté font generalement peu de livres, et ne s'arrangent point pour en faire; ce n'est jamais un métier pour eux.'[1] Rousseau had a theory about proper writing that condemned its opposite. Wordsmiths and pen-pushers,[2] so he thought, led disenchanted lives, their efforts drudgery, their making books as different from writing them as craft from art, or chalk from cheese. The work that really counted came from sudden revelation, like the vital moment in 1749 that showed Rousseau what he had to say to save mankind (or at least to win the Dijon essay prize), an instant causing 'effervescence'[3] of the heart and mind that laid bare truths which simply had to be expressed. In more normal circumstances wordlessness seemed preferable.

So when his books were banned and burnt Rousseau kept himself in other ways, mostly as a scribe who copied scores for music lovers, not an author setting down inflammatory thoughts. He would, no doubt, have written more but for the censoring of *Emile* and *Du contrat social* and the persecution they invited; we hardly think of him as wordless, though, this author of confessions, essays, novels, treatises, and plays: they said the things he had to say, and so he said them, then withdrew. If wordsmiths in that fertile age wrote endlessly, they never changed the world as Rousseau did. Yet after writing he went back to doing what he said he always should have done, working as a craftsman in the little world of those who make things patiently by hand.

For his were still a maker's times, although they ushered in an age of manufacture where technology and automation would replace the older,

---

[1] Jean-Jacques Rousseau, *Dialogues (Rousseau juge de Jean-Jacques)*, in *Œuvres complètes* (henceforth *O.C.*), ed. Bernard Gagnebin and Marcel Raymond, 5 vols. (Paris: Gallimard, 1959–95), I.672–3. All references to Rousseau's works are to this edition.
[2] Or 'livriers' (Rousseau's coinage), those who write professionally for money (*Dialogues*, I.840). We might liken them to Mercier's 'écrivailleurs' and even to Voltaire's 'canaille'.
[3] *O.C.*, I.673.

manual skills[4]—skills that once sustained both mind and body, not the deadening abstractions of the 'clever' world that followed them.

For these and other reasons, there is nothing strange in Rousseau's having been, as Derrida describes him,[5] a writer who mistrusted writing: the *Dialogues*, or *Rousseau juge de Jean-Jacques*, sounds the note it does because it mirrors times of pain and disarray. Yet his choice of silence, and with it the adoption of a manual means of self-support, was not simply caused by persecution; he gladly reembraced techniques based on materials,[6] not material*ism* (that byword of the loathsome Godless *philosophes* as well as the obsession of the covetous). Certain truths he glimpsed that day in 1749 had given him a sense of purpose, clarity about the kind of work he had to write and publish: his language must be honest as the *Discours sur les sciences et les arts* defined the word, free of specious eloquence and forthright as the case demanded. The *Discours* presents other contrasts to confirm this missionary intent, oppositions that became definitive of Rousseau: fiction and reality, sentiment and reason, poetry and prose, and many more.

For he, born to a family of watchmakers, had let the solid substance of his father's world offset the different spheres imagined in and by the books he read in boyhood; as an adult, equally, he published serious works on statecraft and morality together with less weighty things, stories, plays, and operettas that in turn were followed by an educational treatise masquerading as a novel. Lastly came an urge for self-disclosure, less righting of the world than writing of and on the self, otherwise the shaping of Jean-Jacques. For a self-declared 'oisif'[7]—a word that seems at variance with *homo faber*'s universe—it is a formidable tally.

The following account is mainly a discussion, loosely but essentially chronological, of how the writer Rousseau came to readopt in middle life a form of handwork he had first engaged in as an adolescent, then returned to writing in his last decade; what made the artisan become a theorist of

[4] However, Anne Deneys-Tunney, *Un Autre Jean-Jacques Rousseau. Le paradoxe de la technique* (Paris: Presses universitaires de France, 2010), persuasively qualifies the casual view of Rousseau as an out-and-out enemy of technology.

[5] Jacques Derrida, *De la grammatologie* (Paris: Editions de Minuit, 1967), part II, especially chapter 1. See also his *Le Toucher, Jean-Luc Nancy* (Paris: Galilée, 2000).

[6] Among works discussing the tangible fabric of eighteenth-century European life, see especially the writings of Dena Goodman cited in the Bibliography, though her concern is not with such matters as craft's relation to the practical world of writers like Rousseau.

[7] See Pierre Saint-Amand, *The Pursuit of Laziness*, trans. Jennifer Curtiss Gage (Princeton and Oxford: Princeton University Press, 2011); Roland Mortier, 'Paresse et travail dans l'introspection de Rousseau', in *Rousseau and the Eighteenth Century: Essays in Memory of R. A. Leigh*, ed. Marian Hobson, J. T. A. Leigh and Robert Wokler (Oxford: Voltaire Foundation, 1992), pp. 125–34; Paul Audi, *Rousseau, éthique et passion* (Paris: Presses universitaires de France, 1997), p. 230.

statecraft who would also practise other very different crafts, those dependent on dexterity and fine aesthetic judgement. It seeks to offer insights into social issues linking eighteenth-century practices with later ones, focusing on Rousseau's hand as a tool of craftsmanship as well as authorship, on the 'making' of a writer who also made a range of *things*. His practice in this light is placed on a continuum stretching from the ancient world, with its views on how the thinker and the maker are related to each other, through Renaissance writings on artificers who marry thought and craft, to theories of art and artisanship in the seventeenth and eighteenth centuries that culminate in the 'Enlightened' rehabilitation of skilled labour, and leading in turn to the development of various movements for the arts and crafts that still inform the Slow and Green philosophies of the present day. It is tempting to read the eighteenth century in general, and Rousseau's life in particular, through the Industrial Revolution, Marxist theories of alienation and labour, and the problematic mechanization of modern existence; but if we are historically determined by his example as we are, according to Foucault, by the Enlightenment itself,[8] we should also see how Rousseau's hand was shaped by long-formed habits in both folk and intellectual tradition.

HOMO FABER'S FAITH

If those who live in the enchanted world professedly write little, what of others? How, and when, do they create? Their universe may seem ruled by capital and calculation, the world Schiller called degodded[9] and Weber would associate with disenchantment,[10] an arid space in which materialists

---

[8] Michel Foucault, *Qu'est-ce que les lumières?*, ed. Olivier Dekens (Rosny: Bréal, 2004). Daniel Brewer, *The Enlightenment Past: Reconstructing Eighteenth-Century Thought* (Cambridge: Cambridge University Press, 2008), also describes the formulation of an Enlightenment philosophy that defines important aspects of our present political and social life.

[9] 'Entgöttert': Schiller, 'Die Götter Griechenlands'.

[10] 'Entzauberung': Max Weber, *Wirtschaftsgeschichte* (Munich and Leipzig: Duncker and Humblot, 1923). Weber argues that rationalism caused disenchantment, so establishing modern science, the rule of technology, and the rise of capitalism (p. 308). See also Jeffrey Green, 'Two Meanings of Disenchantment', *Philosophy and Theology*, 17 (2006), pp. 51–82, p. 56: in Weber's use 'Entzauberung' designates a sociological concept based on three world-historical processes, secularization, the development of modern science, and a psychological condition of disillusion born of a crisis of meaning. There are further useful discussions in Marcel Gauchet, *The Disenchantment of the World*, trans. Oscar Burger (Princeton: Princeton University Press, 1997); Dorinda Outram, 'The Enlightenment Our Contemporary', in William Clark, Jan Golinski and Simon Schaffer (eds.), *The Sciences in Enlightenment Europe* (Chicago and London: University of Chicago Press, 1999), pp. 32–40; and, more generally, Theodor Adorno and Wilhelm Horkheimer, *Dialektik der Aufklärung* (Amsterdam: Quesido, 1944), whose description of the world as disenchanted is evidently indebted to Weber.

might scrabble after substance[11] as the project of a rationalistic, Godless, and Enlightened world took shape. Others, it is true, regarded the material sphere more positively, thinking that it offered solid stuff to work on, to adapt and carry forward into human space: the plates accompanying the *Encyclopédie*'s many volumes body forth this vision, with images that naturalize what otherwise might seem bizarre or monstrous. Barthes calls them all surreal but for the human factor figured in the random hands they show[12]—amputated hands that steal (into) the printed space, fluttering detached above machinery and gadgets, linking them with human enterprise, tracing a materialist poetics that unites the world of craft and artisanship with technology. Hands circumscribe the vastness of this project, measuring the range of manufacture that belies its manual origin, the building of machines which, capable of crushing man, instead embrace and are embraced by him. Such unions seem to celebrate the power of reason, illustrating, in Barthes's formulation, the 'faire tout-puissant de l'homme, qui de rien peut faire tout'.[13] Even Rousseau, while opposing progress for the sake of progress, hoped to find a way of reconciling morals with this ingenuity. Yet he also knew how difficult the task would be.

He knew, for instance, that what seemed emancipation and control by living creatures actually marked subordination to more doubtful fruits of human rationality,[14] just as clever robot arms in modern life sew beads and sequins onto fabric made by toxic chemicals. (A century before Rousseau, Descartes, contrastingly, had seen the universe's 'grande machine' as governed by the deity.) Eighteenth-century common man might think he mastered matter, but in truth he lacked the knowledge to invent machines and the wealth required to exploit the power and freedom they offered. As Weber would remark, implicitly endorsing Rousseau's view, the savage understood his tools far better than does civilized man his own more

[11] See Charles Taylor, *A Secular Age* (Cambridge, MA, and London: The Belknap Press at Harvard University Press, 2007), pp. 28–9.

[12] Roland Barthes, 'Image, raison, déraison', *L'Univers de l'Encyclopédie* (Paris: Les Libraires associés, 1964), pp. 11–16, esp. p. 12.

[13] While Barthes comments on the happy look of the workers in these plates, others see them as joyless automata: see, for example, William H. Sewell, Jr, *Work and Revolution in France* (Cambridge: Cambridge University Press, 1980), p. 277; also Simon Shaffer, 'Enlightened Automata', in Clark et al., *Sciences in Enlightenment Europe*, pp. 126–65, esp. pp. 126–9, and the *Lettre à d'Alembert*'s comments on the Montagnards' workshops (*O.C.*, V.56–7) discussed in Chapter 4.

[14] See his letter of 20 April 1751 to Mme Dupin, *Correspondance complète* (henceforth *C.C.*), ed. R. A. Leigh, 52 vols. (Geneva, Madison, Wisconsin, Banbury, Oxford: Voltaire Foundation, 1965–89), II.142–4.

complex instruments.[15] In any case, if simple implements can symbolize for us a world in which modernity has not quite blurred the interface between technology and humanness, they may still foretell a future in which digital evangelists, mistaking mere mechanical advance for human progress, unsettlingly win the day.

These urgent and symbolic hands tell us, then, of human origins we must remember: yet what of function? While plates depict inertia, mechanisms move: to capture successivity as language does, these printed images would need to blend and blur like limbs in motion, skittling like weavers' shuttles as they shoot across the warp, like the other cycles set in train in craftsmen's workshops, or the legs of horses that, galloping, seem not quite to be there, disappearing in a haze of speed. Movement needs an icon, but can the engraved hand or the flying shuttle quite supply it? Surely not.

Rousseau's hand was never animated by this quickened impulse, so he says—lingering by the loom at a cousin's textile factory, he let the mechanism catch and bruise his fingers[16] in an accident we may read symbolically. How can it be that touch appears so fleeting yet so permanent, so apt at summarizing our whole character? (Hands gain this certain knowledge by an art of touch and movement, as Diderot's *Lettre sur les aveugles* of 1749 observes; blind men say they need to feel God to believe in him, deaf ones that they 'hear' the sound of music when they sense an instrument's vibrations.[17]) Rousseau's hand is more deliberate than this, too slow to let him write down all the truths his life-transforming vision let him glimpse in 1749; a writing hand that strains against its limitations. Often, though, the measuredness is meant; it marks the conscientious scribe he is for those who hire him as their copyist or secretary, careful as when setting down his own creations: drafts of work he calls illegible are generally easy to decipher. The apprenticeship with an engraver he began in adolescence would have taught him, had it ever been completed, how to shape and scrape the letters onto stone or metal as if carving for eternity, with a slow and calligraphic care; even though unfinished, it still showed him how to make script beautiful, how to ink in words with passionate, deliberate exactness, as he later copied out his presentation volumes of *La Nouvelle Héloïse*. Writing as inscribing or as copying was a

---

[15] On this general principle, see James Schmidt and James Miller, 'Aspects of Technology in Marx and Rousseau', in Teresa de Lauretis, Andreas Huyssen, and Kathleen Woodward (eds.), *The Technological Imagination* (Madison, WI: The Coda Press, 1980), pp. 85–94, esp. pp. 90–2.

[16] *Rêveries du promeneur solitaire*, *O.C.*, I.1036.

[17] On Diderot's *Lettre* in general, see Kate E. Tunstall, *Blindness and Enlightenment: An Essay* (London: Continuum, 2011).

form of imitation, obedience to a higher power, something based on skills that summed up craftsmanship: following, then doing, what could not be taught by words, the lesson that was slowly shown, as masters show apprentices, by practical example.[18]

The same unhurriedness beset his brain, said Rousseau, but as affliction, slothfulness, paralysis, exposing him to punitive authority, prey to those who chased him from his homeland, making everything he wrote an agony of effort[19] even though the sentences and paragraphs were weighed and sifted in his mind for hours on end, over countless sleepless nights.[20] This slowness, too, so he maintained, had stopped him shining in the social world, at gatherings where what seemed to count were wit and brilliance, not the speaker's honour and sincerity. Matters were quite different in the fever of creation: then the author-scriptor wrote like one inspired, his thoughts now tumbling out and racing on beyond the speed of human hand (this, at least, is how he describes the writing of Fabricius' prosopopœia in the first *Discours*), spinning words so fast they almost had to squeeze between the lines, curl around the punctuation marks, cram the margins in what seemed a perfect froth of spontaneity.

Barthes calls what Rousseau practised 'un pur geste d'inscription',[21] a kind of sensory innocence, a literal feel for beauty; yet it was in truth far from transparent. What he gave his readers as their copyist or scribe was clarity or legibility with an extra factor: not authorship (except in isolated cases), but fingerprint or signature, the Rousseau touch, a touch not light enough to be invisible, not wanting to be quite unseen, bearing a discreet yet evident identity. That makes him more than Barthes's 'scripteur', however, someone born together with the text; Rousseau is more camera than painter, yes, but he somehow states his individuality even in another person's work.[22] We shall soon see how and why.

Rousseau's chosen trade of musical transcription during and beyond the period of his greatest literary fame did more than save him from the pitfalls of imagination, though it managed that to a degree. Copying, while involving penmanship, was obviously distant from the creative

---

[18] See Pamela H. Smith, *The Body of the Artisan* (Chicago and London: University of Chicago Press, 2004), pp. 7–8, for a related idea.

[19] *Confessions*, *O.C.*, I.114.

[20] Or nights that Rousseau claimed were sleepless, a claim others disputed. See, e.g., *C.C.*, XX.323 (d'Escherny's report of a botanizing expedition with Rousseau).

[21] Roland Barthes, 'La Mort de l'auteur', *Le Bruissement de la langue* (Paris: Seuil, 1968), pp. 61–7, esp. p. 64.

[22] This might also be linked with the theory of ornament outlined in Michel Foucault, *Les Mots et les choses* (Paris: Gallimard, 1966), p. 64, and with his concept of the *signature* that marks similarity and difference between things of divergent origin, or the distinction between creation and copy.

issuing of words: copying simply meant transcribing signs that made up passages of sound, not sentences with all their power to mimic and betray. (Sometimes, though, as he himself admitted, his own use of language was dictated by the timbre and form of words in preference to strict grammaticality: music of the ear and eye, not strains of lucid logic.) Its real importance was that it returned him somewhere close to where he started out, to a line of makers who since the early 1600s had earned their living in Geneva as horologists, masters of a skilled and useful craft that stood in contrast to the needless trade, as Rousseau saw it, of professional writers, the 'livriers' he despised. What he himself would write was different, he knew, done not for others' pay but for their moral benefit; so, having written, he would publish fearlessly, guileless as his then friend Diderot, thrown in jail for heresy, learned not to be. In *Tristes Tropiques* Lévi-Strauss describes this signature as Rousseau's motive force, his true vocation.[23] And Rousseau would be proud of never having sold his pen: the enchanted world demanded certain principles, he thought. When writing was curtailed, another kind of handwork seamlessly took over.

THE CRISIS OF MODERNITY

The plight of moderns, he insisted, was their alienation, their sense of having once lived in a charmed, enchanted place now lost beyond retrieval, lost, at least, to all but those who dared to speak against the rotten values of the present, and were criticized for blocking out reality. Hating the techniques of mastery that distanced man from deeper forms of sustenance, Rousseau blamed his age for offering salvation through machinery and secular invention, things that lessened tactile and related forms of vital sensory experience. His own doctrines, partly born of disaffection with modernity, would in turn be ridiculed as superstition, their adherents all dismissed as madmen, freaks with Rousseau's kind of lunacy, crazy hermits properly cast out from social life. On such principles were he and his most 'infamous' works, built on radical perceptions of the destiny of man, removed from France and Switzerland.

Yet his abiding Protestant faith prescribed a kind of disenchantment too.[24] The practicality of the Reform discouraged faith in ghosts and

[23] See also Christopher Kelly, *Rousseau as Author: Consecrating One's Life to the Truth* (Chicago and London: University of Chicago Press, 2003), pp. 10–11, on Rousseau's determinedly living *as a writer*, making his authorship inseparable from his identity despite the perils of censorship.
[24] See Philip Benedict, *Christ's Churches Purely Reformed: A Social History of Calvinism* (New Haven and London: Yale University Press, 2002), especially p. xxi and pp. 533–4.

miracles, substituting for them creeds whose moral distillation could be found in little worlds of decent, craftsmanlike activity. These new creeds, admittedly, might make men want to master objects of the physical world in ways Rousseau criticized, urging as he did the mistrust of material culture that has marked the history of Western thought from its earliest days; but they also signalled something intimate, urging the believer to continue doing what skilled hands had done for centuries, crafting, copying, or moulding, working at the task of daily manufacture as the apprentice did in tracing numerals and letters or insignia on metal plate, then engraving them until perfection, and hence mastery, was reached. Rousseau never made the grade of master craftsman; mastery of writing was another matter.

The complex and in many ways mysterious connections between Calvinism and craft are hinted at throughout his writings, yet the problems they lay bare are many. Could anything as delicate as reenchantment be assured where pragmatism (if not materialism) held sway? Raynal's *Histoire philosophique des deux Indes* of 1770 would argue that for European nations craft gradually replaced warmongering as a primary means of self-enrichment, the liking for commodities developing man's taste for worldly things, not conquest.[25] Did this mean that everything might be a matter of degree, of healthy practicality, not 'bad' materialism? Whether or not, as some have argued, Reformation had itself encouraged forms of self-reliance fostering sins of covetousness that led to capitalism,[26] Rousseau would reject the greater part of money's goods, spurning cash and pensions offered by admirers such as George III of England and Frederick the Great of Prussia, proudly living with the humble sticks of furniture Bernardin de Saint-Pierre recorded seeing in his Paris tenement,[27] or staying

---

[25] Raynal, *Histoire philosophique des deux Indes*, 10 vols. (Geneva: J. L. Pellet, 1783), X.148.

[26] See Max Weber, *Die protestantische Ethik und der Geist des Kapitalismus* (Tübingen: Mohr, 1934); Hugh Trevor-Roper, *Religion, the Reformation and Social Change*, 2nd edn (London and Basingstoke: Macmillan, 1972), p. 4 and *passim*; Christopher Hill, 'Protestantism and the Rise of Capitalism', in F. J. Fisher (ed.), *Essays in the Economic and Social History of Tudor and Stuart England in Honour of R. H. Tawney* (Cambridge: Cambridge University Press, 1961), pp. 15–31; Hartmut Lehmann and Guenther Roth (eds.), *Weber's Protestant Ethic* (Publications of the German Historical Institute, Washington, DC, and Cambridge: Cambridge University Press, 1993); Herbert Lüthy, *Le Passé présent. Combats d'idées de Calvin à Rousseau* (Monaco: Editions du Rocher, 1965); Hartmut Lehmann and Guenther Roth (eds.), 'Variations on a Theme by Max Weber', in Menna Prestwich (ed.), *International Calvinism 1541–1715* (Oxford: Oxford University Press, 1985), pp. 369–90; Martin Malia, *History's Locomotives* (New Haven and London: Yale University Press, 2006), pp. 1–6; Gordon Marshall, *In Search of the Spirit of Capitalism* (London: Hutchinson, 1982); W. Fred Graham, *The Constructive Revolutionary: Calvin and His Socio-Economic Impact* (Richmond, Virginia: John Knox Press, 1971).

[27] Bernardin de Saint-Pierre, *La Vie et les ouvrages de Jean-Jacques Rousseau*, ed. M. Souriau (Paris: Cornély et Cⁱᵉ, 1907), p. 33.

in the 'cellule philosophique' that was his home on the île de Saint-Pierre,[28] like Heidegger in his Bavarian hut or Wittgenstein his empty Cambridge room. It seemed natural, then, that when the flow which generated *Emile*'s 'heretical' *Profession de foi* (a tract denying institutional authority as well as Christian revelation) and the irregular religious doctrine of *Du contrat social* was stemmed by censorship, he should earn a modest living from inscription of another kind, copying sheets of music and then, in exile and in old age, copying life, his own life.

Both these enterprises involved a kind of making, if in different ways, the first in adding what the *Confessions* in another context called 'indifferent' ornaments[29] to enhance the scores he copied (and which let him charge a price above the market rate),[30] the second in embroidering—harmlessly, he claimed—a range of past experiences as he set them down on paper. Although he would mistrust art's tendency to enhance material retrieved by memory, the self-account of the *Confessions* is so manifestly structured that its readers lose all concern with exactness of mimesis.[31] Rousseau both tacitly and openly declares his right to depart from cognitive truth, on the grounds that a 'felt' relation with the past is more trustworthy than a rationally demonstrable one.

As to non-literary forms of copying, he disliked most portraiture, including, famously, the picture Allan Ramsay did of him in London:[32] he thought that knowing man demanded skills of analytical investigation far beyond the power of painters (and most moralists), but which he deployed in various accounts despite the sense of personal inconsistency that never left him. Yet while believing that the task of tracing moods and other abstract states was worthwhile, sometimes vital, he still ranked it below the work of socio-moral exploration undertaken in the vital texts he published in the early 1760s, *Emile* and *Du contrat social* especially. Only after persecution did he turn to other matters, letting exploration of the self succeed the social theory.

There seemed, accordingly, to be at least two Rousseaus. First there was the moralist and prophet, writing on the basis of a semi-mystical experience that had changed him radically by showing him the cause and nature

---

[28] See Franz von Wagner, *L'Ile Saint-Pierre, ou l'île de Rousseau* (Berne: n. publ., 1815), p. 50.

[29] See I.5; also I.1035–6.

[30] See, e.g., Olivier de Corancez, *De Jean-Jacques Rousseau* (collected extracts from *Journal de Paris*, nos. 251, 256, 259, 261), an VI, p. 7.

[31] See Jean Starobinski, *Jean-Jacques Rousseau. Le transparence et l'obstacle* (Paris: Plon, 1971), and Ann Hartle, *The Modern Self in Rousseau's 'Confessions'* (Notre-Dame, Indiana: University of Notre-Dame Press, 1985).

[32] See Chapter 6.

of man's alienation, though in secular terms, and through which he had, as he declared, become another man. Then there was the plain and seemingly straightforward workman, *homo faber*, crafting safe and moderately useful objects for his fellows. The first Rousseau could offer hope, the second practicality; the first redemption, the second simple purposiveness. But there was a third Rousseau, a man of harmless inactivity (so he liked to think, at least) who pleased himself while hurting no one, living peacefully with others while not entirely of their world, one whose seeming disengagement from society made the works for which we may admire him most today. These are works that perfectly combine the other kinds, works of writer and of maker, where he uses pen and tool (or pen as tool) together. This Rousseau is both less and more than what his ancestors had been for generations, craftsmen he felt close to yet inevitably stood distant from: and he too resists easy patterning as he writes down vital human truths, capturing ideal lives in treatises and novels, yet reluctant to commit himself to all or even most of their demands. Practicality and sociability were not always, it appeared, precisely what he wanted.

FAITH AND MATERIALS

Yet the age in which Rousseau lived exalted practicality and thus craft. The subtitle of the *Encyclopédie* whose music articles he wrote ranks craft as equal with arts and sciences (or knowledge, the eighteenth-century meaning of the word 'science'): *Dictionnaire raisonné des sciences, des arts et des métiers*. The status of the crafts themselves had varied over history, damned by the ancient Greeks for their alleged discouragement of mental exercise, by the time of the Renaissance more comfortably associated with the various operations of the mind, then demoted once again by seventeenth-century rationalistic thought.[33] The craft-loving eighteenth century also worshipped rationalism, hence abstraction, even though all craft evokes the tangible and practical; yet Rousseau pits the (disenchanting) world of reason[34] against another vital impulse, the force of feeling that defined him as a man of sensibility and let him set the temper of his age. The matter is a complex one. On the side of reason we may note, besides his sharp dismissal of all miracles and revelation, his view that Christian faith and secular life exclude each other (the opinion that

[33] See Smith, *Body of Artisan*, pp. 6–7, and R. Hooykaas, *Religion and the Rise of Modern Science* (Edinburgh and London: Scottish Academic Press, 1972), pp. 80–90.
[34] See, more generally, Harvey S. Goldman, 'Weber's Ascetic Principles of the Self', in Lehmann and Roth, *Weber's Protestant Ethic*, pp. 165–72.

would lead to the proscription of the work proposing it, *Du contrat social*), even his republican dissent from principles of monarchy and aristocracy and the progressive notions of equality that went with it.[35] His conviction, too, that man alone, perverted from original goodness by a range of social pressures and the lure of the material, stood responsible for moral evil also fell within the bounds of rational thought, as did the link he posited between environmental spoliation and societal mismanagement. His faith in providence or a benevolent God rested on quite different principles, however. No more than others of his time and later could he see a 'meaning' in the Lisbon earthquake of 1755, yet his negative view of progress let him put the blame for Lisbon's massive loss of life on human agency, the piling-up of person upon person, storey above storey, in towering urban tenements (a view belonging to the sphere of what is now called human ecology). Materialist philosophers might simply point to the geological causes of such seismic shocks; but Rousseau's interest in the natural world did not extend that far, fond though he would later be of minerals and fossils.

The democratic, 'feeling' Rousseau mistrusted any rationalistic creed that cut short human freedoms by developing control techniques designed to guarantee political stability.[36] Censorship was one of these, and he suffered grievously from its effects; but Calvinism emphasizes the cult of self-denial to similar ends, if by different means (moral self-governance or conscience, in the main). This asceticism broadly suited Rousseau's character, though not, as his rebellious apprenticeship suggests, when it shaded into forms of disempowerment typical of inflexible hierarchical societies: this helps explain, indeed, why popular sovereignty on Geneva's pattern would appeal so strongly to him. Where he judged the power of rational control to be excessive, he often simply took his distance from those areas it governed, rather than challenging its legitimacy as others might have done. Yet rationalism, however ready to impose its rule, may itself be challenged by an inner power of conviction, the power Rousseau would call conscience (literally a matter of shared knowledge). Puritanism, both Calvinist and other, is the conscientious, ordered self par excellence, supporting the internal moral order even if reliant on collective wills to enforce it.

---

[35] See in general Jonathan I. Israel, *Radical Enlightenment* (Oxford: Oxford University Press, 2001).

[36] See Michel Foucault, *Surveiller et punir. Naissance de la prison* (Paris: Gallimard, 1993); also John Gray, *Enlightenment's Wake: Politics and Culture at the Close of the Modern Age* (London and New York: Routledge, 1995), p. 158, p. 178, on the 'will to power' in modern culture, which he contrasts with Heidegger's 'Gelassenheit zu den Dingen', relaxedness about things, letting them be. See Martin Heidegger, *Discourse on Thinking [1959]*, trans. John Anderson and E. Hans Freund (New York, Evanston, and London: Harper and Rowe, 1966), pp. 54–6; also p. 174, n. 42.

While this implies that personal freedom must to a degree be curbed, it still allows a strong self to emerge. Rousseau's character displays some of this self's variants: independence, self-sufficiency, devotion to some higher cause or value, all impulses that make up the campaigning spirit which prompted him to write his works of public doctrine, and which shaped the man of mission he would feel himself to be after his 'reform' in middle life, the calling he would live by in the world and out of it. They also marry up with aspects of the craftsman's work, whose essence contrasts sharply with non-Puritan art and luxury. The *Confessions* traces the development of Rousseau's sense of moral selfhood following on the mood of play that marked his adolescence and his early years in Paris, a seriousness that was counter-socialized to a degree (he would leave Paris on its account), and is so because reform requires a narrowing of personal focus for the sake of working out new schemes for structuring society. Anyone embracing such a doctrine may appear dehumanized, admittedly, more instrument than individual; but Rousseau kept his sense of self intact by living idiosyncratically, following principles of conduct that, while austere, were never depersonalizing. They did not, however, save him from the mockery of society.

If it is sometimes hard to see the part craft plays in such developments, that may be because craft's realm is practicality, not abstract principle. Notwithstanding this, craft *attitudes* are often highly moral, especially in societies (such as Rousseau's) also pledged to mechanization or material superfluity, or both: ecological principles attach to craft in industrialized economies, for instance, although aesthetic ones may figure in them too. Craft and luxury rarely go together except in societies that have developed further than Rousseau's own, and have, as it were, moved so far beyond craft's primitive reach as no longer to need it in practical terms, mechanization having taken over efficiently and comprehensively the functions it once performed. When that point is reached, the focus shifts from craft's utility to its integrity or beauty, the opposition its robust simplicity implies to all the complex ways of civilization. It possesses beauty of both form and function, a wholeness and wholesomeness that retain the literal sense of manufacture, handmade-ness. At this stage the craftsman's fingerprint is all-important.

The aim of comprehensive systems (the rational among them) to explain all aspects of experience may create antipathy or mistrust; thus the eighteenth-century Enlightenment is to some degree a hostile reaction to the 'esprit de système' associated with the seventeenth century, however clearly it continues many of the earlier period's rationalistic patterns. Diderot embodies all the flexibility or pluralism ensuing from such mistrust, his fondness for the dialogue form being often, and persuasively, associated with this bet-hedging disposition. Rousseau's constant references to the difficulty of thinking[37] show the same unease with philosophical rigour as with the professionalization of intellectual activity, helping to explain what drew him to the countervailing practicality of craft. Craft embodies rational precept and principle, certainly, and underlines the importance of obedience to the rule of method, but there is nothing abstract about it.

If craft depends on substance, furthermore, it is not associated with a corrupting kind of physicality, but rather with its opposite. The theory of craft suggests integrity of a kind that must exclude the mercantile extremes of capitalism—the 'hollow' materialism of the Enlightenment—and therefore limit the extent to which it will embrace technology: more and quicker, in the craft world, rarely signifies better, partly because of the importance craft assigns to principles of intactness (purity of substance, usefulness of application, faithfulness towards tradition). Yet rejecting technology outright, or affecting so to do, may be an option only in advanced societies whose development has bred a romantic attitude towards the past, just as nostalgia for the simpler modes of life, including more 'authentic' ways of making things, seems possible only from a position of comparative sophistication. Eighteenth-century nature worship and the 'hamlet' at Versailles suggest as much.

KINDS OF MASTERY

The concept of progress is clearly relative, if not simply for the reasons Rousseau gives in the *Discours sur les sciences et les arts* of 1750 and the *Discours sur l'origine de l'inégalité* of 1755. The efficiency of craft methods, for example, may be such that more advanced technologies can do little to improve them. Many tools have barely changed through centuries of manufacture[38] because a practical procedure combining rationality and 'feel' was at their origin: the craftsman's intimate familiarity with his materials let him see how best to handle and adapt them for a given purpose. Expert knowledge often yields simplicity of this kind, simplicity that hides great knowledge; it explains why craft apprenticeships last as long as they generally do. The craftsman's touch may look instinctive, but it is in fact supremely practised; a rational, or rationalized, process

---

[37] See, e.g., *Confessions*, I.403–5, *Discours sur l'origine de l'inégalité*, *O.C.*, III.138.
[38] See John Wyke, *Catalogue of Tools for Watch and Clock Makers*, ed. Alan Smith (Charlottesville: University Press of Virginia, 1978), p. 16; Richard Sennett, *The Craftsman* (London: Allen Lane, 2008), pp. 20–1, p. 37.

underpins it. We may readily understand Rousseau's attack on reason for causing estrangement or alienation from the sensory, from the physical as well as the moral world, but also see how it is tempered in reality.

Craft, then, is always more than a mechanical activity. At its highest levels it can match art as an independent and imaginative pursuit involving subjective discrimination and expertise throughout: the choice of a material (the deep knowledge of its properties that indicates its fitness for the task at hand), the aesthetic as well as practical judgement that determines what form it shall take, the working of the substance (the pressure of blade on stone or wood, the tension of threads on loom, the feel of clay on potter's wheel)—technology may have removed some of the manual knowledge that these moves once called for, so lessening the maker's input, but such forfeiture is always relative. Nowadays the craft product is often valued, as Rousseau's scores and the handwritten copies of his novel were in his own time, for manifesting an individual touch, even idiosyncrasy, that machine-made objects lack: the hands-on job has intrinsic worth in being original, a one-off, something that cannot be duplicated, no two versions being precisely identical. The case is wholly different with machine-made objects, however wondrous the ways and means in which and by which they are manufactured.[39]

So there is pride as well as mystery in the web of operations that hand and tool perform together, particularly when they are set against the novice's ineptness. The *Confessions* pitilessly details Rousseau's botched attempts at using the tools of his watchmaker grandfather, as Mme de Vandeul's 'life' lists Diderot's hapless efforts with his cutler father's; both stories underline the skill that making even mundane craft objects ordinarily requires, showing why we should admire those simple-seeming things that, because we use them every day, we often fail to value as we ought. *Emile* deconstructs the household object by giving its pupil access to the workshops where such things are made and attaching him to master craftsmen to discover principles at first hand. The pupil learns, coincidentally, the abstract lesson that the useful may (but may not always) be more highly valued than the merely beautiful, or perhaps that usefulness has inherent beauty.

While the difficulty of using small precision instruments provoked the boy Rousseau, mastering it later seemed to him a source of pride: so he came to describe horology as a quintessentially Swiss art contrasted

---

[39] On this, see Margaret C. Jacob, *The Cultural Meaning of the Scientific Revolution* (Philadelphia: Temple University Press, 1988), and Richard Holmes, *The Age of Wonder* (London: HarperPress, 2008).

with the workaday creations of Paris,[40] rather as we might distinguish the intricate skill of the Japanese netsuke maker from the broader adeptness of craftsmen in other cultures. Such skills are, perhaps, typical of insular nations that have rarely fashioned great art, though whether their possession made the Genevese artists rather than artisans, as Rousseau somewhere suggests, is a moot point. In the previous century, however, it might have been a purely semantic one, for the two words were often used interchangeably, though with time 'artiste' became specifically associated with the practitioner of those trades and crafts in which the product (such as the jeweller's or goldsmith's) possessed a certain monetary or other intrinsic value, and by 1762 the definition of 'artisan' as 'ouvrier qui travaille avec esprit et avec art' had become archaic.[41] The motherless Jean-Jacques spent hours with his father in the workshop, but there is no evidence that he learned anything useful as a craftsman from the experience, and much, as the fate of his grandfather David Rousseau's tools implies, to suggest that he did not. Horology could not be learnt in the way simpler kinds of making could. Even so, every kind of worthwhile learning, according to Rousseau, comes from doing as well as mentally absorbing, from praxis and doxa together.

His fragment 'Des mœurs' observes of the mechanical arts (otherwise called 'les arts oiseux') that 'à force de prévenir toutes nos incommodités, ils énervent le corps et asservissent les âmes et produisent d'autres maux plus dangereux'.[42] He does not specify which these ills are, but they must take manufacture beyond the stage that simple tools permit; for when we dominate nature, Rousseau thinks, we also risk denaturing ourselves,[43] weakened by dependency on alien processes that we fail to understand.[44] Having delegated them, after all, we scarcely need comprehension. *Emile* states the complementary view, that handling tools with confidence presupposes expertise, or the kind of praxis taught by formal training. Seizing materials heedlessly with tools one is not meant to use, by contrast, is a depersonalizing of craft by technology that may become fatal, like the manufacturing of instruments from materials not fit for purpose. The classical myths of Prometheus and Icarus respectively suggest that these have been perennial dangers in the history of culture.

---

[40] See his letter to Théodore Tronchin, *C.C.*,V.241 (26 November 1758).
[41] See *C.C.*,V.221, n. b(i).
[42] 'Des mœurs', *O.C.*, III.556.
[43] See *Emile*, IV.249; also *Du contrat social*, book 2, chapter 7.
[44] See, in general, Maxine Berg, *The Machinery Question and the Making of Political Economy, 1815–1848* (Cambridge: Cambridge University Press, 1980).

INDUSTRIAL TIMES

De Jaucourt's *Encyclopédie* article 'Industrie' claims that the free development of the mechanical arts inevitably leads to the greater wellbeing of society, an assertion no less familiar than its pre-Luddite reverse (that machinery creates unemployment by doing work formerly done by humans, as Montesquieu contends). If Diderot's celebrated entry 'Bas' adopts neither view explicitly,[45] the overall conclusion is de Jaucourt's: it is good that looms are now able to perform many tedious, repetitive operations once performed by hand. Machinery had in fact been used in textile production for hundreds of years: silk weaving, for example, was a highly mechanized trade in Italy from the thirteenth century, and went on gradually being refined until the seventeenth century. At this point the pace quickened over Europe, bringing social consequences of the kind de Jaucourt sweeps aside (such as political unrest in Holland when the use of automatic looms was being established there). In 1675 the ribbon loom similarly caused riots in London, though its products were still regarded as precious—precious enough, possibly, to have motivated that poignant theft described in the *Confessions*, Rousseau's false incrimination of the Turin servant Marion for stealing a ribbon he had in fact taken.[46] The fact that he describes it as an *old* ribbon may mean it was itself a handmade one, in which respect it perhaps resembled the silk 'lacets' he himself would later weave in Môtiers for young women suckling their babies, probably to serve as a primitive form of breast support. Did he subconsciously intend them as atonement for his accusation of Marion? The *Confessions* does not say. When he wove these ribbons, he would anyway declare, he felt like half a woman himself.[47] Not every woman liked his work, however: a Mme Sandoz of Neuchâtel so criticized its habitual roughness that he hesitated ever to touch a spindle in her company again, though others were more appreciative. A ribbon of white and gold silk he made and presented to Anne-Marie d'Ivernois as a wedding gift was cherished by her and her descendants over the years,[48] and may still be seen in the Rousseau museum at Môtiers. Equally, a presumably approving Mme

---

[45] See Jacques Proust, 'L'Article « bas » de Diderot', in Michèle Duchet and Michèle Galley (eds.), *Langue et langages de Leibniz à l'Encyclopédie* (Geneva: Droz, 1977).

[46] *O.C.*, I.84–5. A letter from Mme de Charrière to Chambrier d'Oleyres on 5 January 1790 mentions Rousseau's futile wish from beyond the grave that Marion (who if alive then would have been about eighty years old) might be found and offered financial support (*C.C.*, XLVI.160).

[47] See letter from Julie de Bondeli to Dr Johann Zimmermann, *C.C.*, XII.236 (21 August 1762); also *Confessions*, I.601–2, and p. 1572, n. 3.

[48] *Confessions*, I.1572, n. 4.

de Verdelin told Rousseau she would teach him cooking if he showed her how to use the spindle properly.

We should not, therefore, speak of craft activities being suddenly transformed by the incipient industrial age, for change was often gradual. It may be—in the absence of further details certainty is impossible—that the Marion episode, if not the story of the 'lacets', illustrates the way craft products acquire status precisely when machines that can make their equivalents more quickly and cheaply than is possible by hand take over the market, or take it over for all except those connoisseurs who recognize and prefer the handmade version. The latter's cachet partly rests, indeed, on the fact that most consumers see no significant difference between it and its mass-produced equivalent. The more the general public deems them identical, the greater the expert's pleasure at knowing they are not.

If writers of de Jaucourt's stripe—Mercier in *L'An 2440*, Volney in *Les Ruines*, Restif in *L'An 2000*—took the Utopian view that moral and political improvement was a guaranteed by-product of mechanical science, Rousseau's preference was for letting be, a state that stands in opposition to all calculative thought. True, he seems to have found little to criticize in certain forms of mechanization, such as that of the textile factory mentioned in the fourth Promenade of the *Rêveries du promeneur solitaire*; but the seventh protests at finding industry—cottage industry, admittedly—halfway up an alp. We may ask how this celebrated sufferer from *Weltschmerz* would ever have reacted to a more developed modern world where people interact with companionate machines, are nursed by robots, and socialize on digital networks, a world in which the more ordinary threads of community have become frayed beyond mending. For in showing how what seems to give control (technology) in fact controls us he is surely showing us our own society, one replete with those illusions that most weaken moral life. This is what makes handwork so important.

The objection voiced in 'Des mœurs' remains, then, not that machines disfigure virgin nature, but that in bypassing the body they enervate it, stopping it from doing what was once within its power. For the body's resources are immense, far greater than the incurious or unpractised think. *Emile* will comment, as the *Lettre sur les aveugles* had done, on our capacity to 'feel' the visible, or to have what is primarily a visual experience, by means other than the organ of sight, such as the ever-present sense of touch;[49] it is an observation that may make us regret Rousseau's planned but never written treatise on 'le matérialisme du sage', or 'la morale sensitive'.[50] The body attuned or alert, not the body benumbed or somnolent

---

[49] See *Emile*, IV.387, and the second and third additions to Diderot's *Lettre sur les aveugles*.
[50] See *Confessions*, I.409 and n. 1.

for want of practical engagement, can act like the human barometer described in the first Promenade of the *Rêveries*:[51] sensory praxis depends on habit, keeping the arm in. The Nephew does this too in Diderot's *Le Neveu de Rameau*, maintaining the suppleness of his trained hand however reluctant it may be to do his bidding and play the violin.[52] The danger with the Nephew, if not with the ordinary craftsman, comes when this organic alertness shades into mental or moral over-sensitivity, the first warnings of paranoia. We can hardly avoid drawing the parallel with Rousseau himself.

The unease that he as craftsman, or craftsman manqué, felt at the mechanization of life did not originate in his times, however. The 90th of Seneca's *Epistulae morales* had pointed out nearly two millennia earlier that mechanical tools were not necessarily deployed by wise men, or men wise enough to manufacture them knowingly, and argued the point with a comparison that seems to anticipate the seventh *Rêverie*: it was not man's wisdom, but his ingenuity, that caused technology to be developed, just as it was greed, not wisdom, that led him to discover mines of iron and ore and then extract their content from the earth. We are alienated from the processes of making by the mechanical means we use to obtain the substances we need: we 'out' them crudely, greedily, or otherwise, treating nature as a pirate might treat bullion. The more complex our tools and mechanisms, the further we stand from the substance we intend to mould, opening up the earth as we might do Pandora's box without knowing what will emerge. We might reflect here on the negative implications of the English words 'craft' and 'crafty', signifying a devious and often exploitative cunning. French, it is true, has nothing comparable.

In any case, the craftsman knows materials in a far truer and more profound sense, because he experiences and lives (with) them, sees them almost as extensions of himself: it is probable that no division of labour has distanced him from his creation, no substance been tooled by others or made ready to be passed on to them such that each hand receives it passively or otherwise detachedly. A grounding in (the) material is a prerequisite of his trade. Rousseau spent much of his childhood in the artisan district of Geneva, surrounded by watchmakers and other craftsmen, after his father had been forced to sell the family house in the

---

[51] *Rêveries*, *O.C.*, I.1000-1. See also Jan Golinski, 'Barometers of Change', in Clark et al., *Sciences in Enlightenment Europe*, pp. 69–93, at p. 70.

[52] Diderot, *Le Neveu de Rameau*, *Œuvres completes* (henceforth *O.C.*), ed. Herbert Dieckmann, Jacques Proust and Jean Varloot, 25 vols (Paris: Hermann, 1975–95), XII.97. Unless otherwise stated, references to Diderot's works are to this edition.

Grand'rue; he felt this intimate possession in his bones, and in later life tried to explain its hold on him. When the human factor disappears, craft dies.

Perhaps, then, the craftsman stands where labour intersects with art. Labour is travail, hence often painful, tiring, lacking dignity, 'purely' manual.[53] Rousseau found that he had to be a labourer, chopping wood to the point of exhaustion, for relief from the symptoms of a urinary condition he suffered from throughout his life, though such activity did not demean him in his own eyes; indeed, he felt it elevated him by showing his distinctness from the idle 'salonnistes' and 'académiciens' he despised. Of course a craftsman such as an engraver is raised above this level of pure physical exertion by the manual and mechanical devices he makes and uses, and by the mental grip craft presupposes: knowledge, practice, and creativeness are fundamental to his work. But does that make him a true artist? Not according to the scale of values that obtained in Rousseau's day, or not unless his profession was to engrave pictures rather than the dials of watches or clock cases (Rousseau's training had been in the latter trade); and even then, many engravers in the 'higher' mode reproduced the work of other artists more often than they created independently. The representational basis of aesthetic theory meant that the most academic of artists might still be seen as a mere copyist and hence be called a machinist or mechanic: Latour, whose pastel portrait of him Rousseau rather unexpectedly admired, is labelled a 'machiniste' in Diderot's *Salons*,[54] just like the ingenious engineer Vaucanson, midway between the artisanal and the artistic.

A carpenter such as Emile will become is certainly a craftsman, but may also be a 'machiniste' in a different sense, one who depends on tools as well as insight, making something practical as well as exercising 'feel' along with understanding. Rousseau did not object to living among artisans provided that his birthright as a citizen of Geneva was respected; but a Genevese watchmaker, he declared, was a great artist, a shoemaker merely an artisan. Even so, his letter to Dr Tronchin of 26 November 1758 announces that 'cet état des artisans est le mien, celui dans lequel je suis né, dans lequel j'aurais dû vivre, et que je n'ai quitté que pour mon malheur'.[55] (Surely he deceives himself.) The *Encyclopédie* entry 'Artiste' draws precisely this distinction,[56] emphasizing the lesser intelligence required by, and associated with, the artisan.

---

[53] See Sewell, *Work*, p. 24.   [54] Diderot, *Salons*, *O.C.*, XVI.241.
[55] *C.C.*, V.242.   [56] See also Sewell, *Work*, p. 249.

IDIOSYNCRASY

Yet the profession of music copyist Rousseau would adopt in 1751 seemed ideal for a man of his temperament. Copying let him work as journeymen craftsmen did, though not—advantageously for one of his independent spirit—as a mere hand in workshops, under a master. It gave him freedom to be the employee of many and the subject of none, involving work he did at his own speed, in his own time and space, and for just as long as he desired: when he had earned enough for his needs, he stopped. His success in attracting clients, as he freely admitted, was partly the product of his fame,[57] for Rousseau became a catch after the literary success of his *Discours sur les sciences et les arts*, and a score copied by him had cachet. (Even so, he must have proved far better at this job then than in his adolescence, when he worked so inattentively that every page he did was full of errors.) And whatever he might owe to clients, he felt at least an equal obligation to himself. It pleased him that he was a good enough musician to correct things silently, for example, or make good omissions to the score he had to duplicate, since it was in this respect as well as others that he could regard himself as better than the average penman, hence justify charging higher prices. Everything proclaimed the part he played in copying, from the coquettish artistic detail upwards. The Rousseau fingerprint was as difficult to suppress as to deny.

The larger issue this lays bare—his insistence on self-declaration even when a certain reticence seemed wiser—will be more fully treated further on. In life and in his inner person, he repeated, he was other than the man the public saw, and he did his greatest writing against the grain of popular perception. The personal works he wrote at the end of his career illustrate this mismatch between what others thought of him and what he knew he really was (hence the need to resume writing even though he had decided in his early fifties not to write again). His dislike of the painting done of him in England rested on the same belief, that any other person's vision must traduce him. There were other matters to consider too. We may, for instance, see in the convergence of scribe and man a bid to free himself from the impersonal sameness print had been imposing since Gutenberg's invention of the press,[58] as well as a more general, and typical, assertion of his selfhood.

---

[57] See his letter to Malesherbes of 12 January 1762, *O.C.*, I.1137.
[58] See Elizabeth Eisenstein, *The Printing Press as an Agent of Change*, 2 vols. (Cambridge: Cambridge University Press, 1979), II.661–2.

This Rousseau fought against the loss of personality implicit in the different types of standardization governing eighteenth-century social life, particularly that which stems from failing to respect or grasp the codes an individual follows, as those who operate machines may fail to understand the processes they set in train or supervise. The sameness of the parts, both living and man-made, that constitute consumer society seemed impoverishing to him, even though he witnessed just a tiny part of what they would become. The obverse of this picture is provided by the craft economy, whose goods are made by knowing, feeling hands, even if their moves seem automatic. Rousseau's hand is like the artist's or composer's fingerprint, the more-than-token signal of creativeness: such distinctiveness, his clients saw, was worth paying for, the precious, priceless touch of a master over and above the evident and endlessly repeated proofs of authorship in printed form, the multiple identical copies of bestsellers like *La Nouvelle Héloïse*.

Writing spelled danger for Rousseau, copying, safety: authorship, the forbidden (by the authorities, and hence by Rousseau himself), copying, the licit. Why should anyone regret his choice of copying when he had made his leaving literature so clear? Writing had been licensed in his own mind when, for all its prohibition by the church and state, it had been so evidently linked with real reform, with great and humane enterprise;[59] music might be pure expressiveness—though many in his age regarded it as imitative—and its aim sheer sensory delight, but 'serious' writing, at least until his last works, he thought of as a goal-directed enterprise, its purpose curative. Willy-nilly, language had become a matter of technique even for those, like Rousseau himself, whose lack of formal education, hence of training in the art of eloquence, made them mistrust clever discourse. Yet he knew even before the condemnation of his books that all types of art could be dangerous for their makers. Given art's false promises, its tempting of incautious imagination, it seemed wise to shut down thought completely, block out inspiration, switch to the uncontroversial motions of the scribe, develop in the absence of an orthodoxy, or one to which both he and the authorities assented, an orthopraxis that was limited and focused, like the actions of the master at his bench.

The goal of living life according to natural rhythms was paramount. Before the huge and falsifying power of consumerism carried man away, Rousseau aimed to *keep time* in the original sense of the phrase,[60] as in his

---

[59] See Christopher Kelly, *Rousseau's Exemplary Life* (Ithaca: Cornell University Press, 1987).

[60] For a related observation, see Frédéric Lefeyvre, 'Jean-Jacques Rousseau. Horloger malgré lui', *La Revue (Musée des arts et métiers)*, September 1998, pp. 35–41, esp. p. 35.

great passion, music: to keep a measured balance in his day-to-day existence that might bring contentment, even salvation. Yet all his origins had been in watching and keeping in a different, horological, sense, through the 'montre', the watch that guarded like a watchman as well as showed the time, and the 'horloge', the clock that lodged the hour. We need to understand how this transition came about.

*   *   *

The first chapter of this book is devoted to Geneva's tradition of making things by hand and the occupations of Rousseau's craftsman family over several generations, the second to his boyhood activities and acquisition of some rudimentary knowledge of different kinds of handwork. Chapter 3 explores his attitude towards art and the arts, specifically as these matters are addressed in the two *Discours*, and compares them with the artisan's practical activity, while the fourth chapter attends to Rousseau's writing on and of drama, an institution whose potential negative effects he sets against the moral benefits of small artisanal communities in Switzerland. Chapter 5 is focused on *Emile* and its treatment of themes such as wealth, handwork, and wellbeing. Chapter 6 describes Rousseau's dislike of Allan Ramsay's portrait of him, and his own contrasting efforts at a 'workmanlike' accounting of the self in words. Chapter 7, finally, considers how a rediscovered interest in botany alerts him to parallels between the pattern of the floral world and the structuring of human skills, before analysing his engagement with craft practices in old age. As a whole, the book treats Rousseau's hand in terms not of an authorial style but of an attitude towards the written word, offsetting it in various ways against the hand of craftsmanship: less how, than why, he wrote, then ceased to write, abandoning authorship for manual work.

1

The Business of Making

THE GENEVAN BACKGROUND

The story started, as it had to, in Geneva, in the world of Calvinism and horology. Why this inevitability, this profession, in that city? Why the link, especially, between exact timekeeping and the Protestant faith? Responsible attitudes towards time, particularly the appointing of specific hours for worship and devotion,[1] had long been associated with Godliness in general, and the Reformed faiths had no monopoly of such virtues. The link, rather, was with the tradition of Huguenot craftsmanship. While the Catholic cantons of Switzerland were largely agricultural, Protestant areas became centres of manufacturing, of textiles and machinery in general, but particularly of small precision instruments: what clocks had been to the medieval cloister, watches would become for the Reformed world of the merchant businessman. Horology seemed perfectly adapted to the sobriety and diligence of the Swiss Protestant character, making the country's limited stock of raw materials[2] less disadvantageous than might initially appear: nine tenths of the cost of a timepiece lay in the minute craftsmanship that had gone into manufacturing it, and the small quantity of imported metals and jewels required was relatively easy to transport over Swiss terrain.

Despite this emphasis on craft and practicality, however, the city into which Rousseau was born in 1712 found less to criticize in art's 'perversions' than Calvin had originally intended.[3] His terrifying doctrines of predestination and original sin became muted over time,[4] and with them the force of his thunderous attacks on various forms of earthly delight,

[1] See David Landes, *Revolution in Time: Clocks and the Making of the Modern World* (Cambridge, MA, and London: Harvard University Press, 1983), pp. 177–8.
[2] See Antoine Babel, *Les Métiers dans l'ancienne Genève. Histoire corporative de l'horlogerie, de l'orfèvrerie et des industries annexes* (Geneva: A. Jullien, Georg & Cⁱᵉ, 1916), p. 38.
[3] See Prestwich, *International Calvinism*, pp. 10–12.
[4] See Adriano Tilgher, *Work: What It Has Meant to Men through the Ages*, trans. Dorothy Canfield Fisher (London: Harrap, 1931), pp. 51–2; also Quentin Skinner, *The Foundations of Modern Thought*, 2 vols. (Cambridge: Cambridge University Press, 1978), II.6–12.

natural as well as manufactured.[5] If Christianity was still presented as stern, plain, and austere, the austerity had acquired what ordinary people thought reasonable limits. Calvin and his followers themselves rejected the Canon Law prohibition on earning interest, and also abolished restrictions on investment (a spirit of concessiveness that even stretched to the legal tolerance of usury).[6] This in turn was followed by the establishment of the Swiss banking system, one of whose most celebrated figures was Rousseau's contemporary Jacques Necker, the father of the future Mme de Staël. In *Du contrat social* Rousseau, mindful or not of these subtle shifts, praises Calvin the lawgiver,[7] though in the second of the later *Lettres écrites de la montagne* he criticises Calvinist theology,[8] partly, no doubt, because by that time his opinion of Geneva had been soured by its public burning of *Du contrat social* and *Emile*. Yet however stark the city's moral code seemed in Rousseau's time to those familiar with other cultures, Calvin's doctrine may not have been its only cause. A cult of self-control and self-denial predated his arrival in the city in 1536, with edicts having regularly been passed against fraud in commerce, usury, excessive luxury, prostitution, other sexual offences, and disorderly behaviour generally.[9]

The picture, then, was a mixed one, as the experience of Rousseau's family confirms.[10] Of immediate relevance to them, though the *Confessions* does not present it as such, is the fact that pre-nuptial conceptions rose markedly in late seventeenth- and early eighteenth-century Geneva.[11] For all the emphasis Rousseau lays on the unblemished morals of the aunts and uncles who brought him up after his mother Suzanne's early death and his father Isaac's move to Nyon following a skirmish, his maternal grandfather (not a priest, as the *Confessions* claims, though his brother was) had got a young woman pregnant outside wedlock, while Suzanne's brother Gabriel Bernard married the eldest of Isaac's sisters, Théodora, barely a week after she had given birth to their child. Less seriously, Suzanne Rousseau herself, as well as being summoned before the Vénérable Consistoire for going to

[5] See, in general, W. Deonna, *Les Arts à Genève des origines à la fin du XVIIIᵉ siècle* (Geneva: Musée d'art et d'histoire, 1942).
[6] See Ernst Troeltsch, *Protestantism and Progress* (Philadelphia: Fortress Press, 1986), p. 71.
[7] *Du contrat social, O.C.*, III.382.
[8] *Lettres écrites de la montagne, O.C.*, III.715.
[9] See John B. Roney and Martin I. Klauber (eds.), *The Identity of Geneva: The Christian Commonwealth, 1564–1864* (Westpoint, CT, and London: Greenwood Press, 1998), p. 4.
[10] Eugène Ritter's *La Famille et la jeunesse de Jean-Jacques Rousseau* (Paris: Hachette, 1896) remains a more informative source on Rousseau's early life than many more recent biographical treatments.
[11] See Linda Kirk, '"Going Soft": Genevan Decadence in the Eighteenth Century', in Roney and Klauber, *Identity of Geneva*, pp. 143–54, esp. pp. 144–5, on the atmosphere of comparative laxness in 18th-century Geneva.

the theatre disguised as a peasant, had to be cautioned three times against consorting with a particular youth, and Isaac more than once came up against the Conseil for causing or being involved in an affray. In the meantime Isaac's sisters, whom Rousseau calls virtuous and sage, had scandalized their neighbours by playing cards after the Sunday sermon. Jean-Jacques's paternal grandfather David Rousseau, finally, was reported to the Consistoire for giving a ball a few weeks after his wife's death.[12]

None of this gave the city a seriously repressive or killjoy atmosphere, however. David, for instance, had broken no ordinance in arranging the dance, because dancing was tolerated in Geneva for the sake of the foreign visitors who enjoyed it, a fact which suggests either that the little republic's economic wellbeing mattered more to its citizens than moral disapproval of certain social pleasures or, perhaps, that it saw dance as a positive force for social cohesion. Rousseau's *Lettre à d'Alembert* of 1758 supports this notion in its emphasis on the need to develop a folk culture capable of promoting the Genevan sense of communal identity, a culture that embraced the kind of country dancing typical of seasonal celebrations, and there is a similar observation in a letter of his from this time[13] attacking the society dancing master Marcel[14] for the mannered style he introduced, but defending dance that is free and natural in expression. It is not difficult to see how homespun recreation of this sort might have evolved as a way of reconciling the human desire for companionable pleasure with the moralistic urge to control the human passions.

Geneva's attraction for foreigners was not confined to its dance culture, however. Its willingness to take in refugees persecuted for their Protestant faith was of much greater significance, a generosity that other members of the Swiss federation such as Zurich and Berne were far from imitating.[15] By the time of the Revocation of the Edict of Nantes in 1685 Geneva itself had become too populous to admit most of those who sought refuge within its walls; but matters had been different in the previous century. Didier Rousseau, a Huguenot wine merchant who may also have been a bookseller, had moved there from Paris in the mid 1500s, possibly after contravening an edict of 1547 forbidding the sale of 'heretical' books blacklisted by the theological faculty of Paris,[16] and was formally admitted to the bourgeoisie in 1555: Calvin had just triumphed in the annual election of Syndics, the supreme magistrature of the Republic, and was

---

[12] See Ritter, *Famille et jeunesse*, p. 67.
[13] *C.C.*, V.212 (8 November 1758, to Lenieps).
[14] Also disparaged by Diderot in *Le Neveu de Rameau* and the *Salon* of 1765.
[15] See Miriam Yardeni, *Le Refuge huguenot. Assimilation et culture* (Paris: Champion, 2002), p. 17.
[16] See Ritter, *Famille et jeunesse*, pp. 19–20, p. 25.

attempting as a consequence to bolster a slender majority at the Conseil by admitting a large number of French refugees.[17] Although Didier was officially recorded as a bookseller in Geneva, he seems to have quickly resumed the sale of wine, opening an inn at the sign of the Epée couronnée. His grandson Jean was apprenticed to a watchmaker, thus inaugurating a line of horologist Rousseaus that reached down as far as Isaac and his first son François. The latter disappeared from view after completing his apprenticeship, however, and seems never to have practised his father's trade. Nor, as it happened, did his younger brother.

If many of the city's horologists were descended from Parisian craftsmen,[18] the status of the Genevese masters was well established in its own right by Rousseau's time.[19] His letter of 26 November 1758 to Dr Tronchin makes no bones about affirming their superiority:

[un] horloger de Genève est un homme à présenter partout; un horloger de Paris n'est bon qu'à parler des montres. L'éducation d'un ouvrier tend à former ses doigts, rien de plus. Cependant le citoyen reste; bien ou mal, la tête et le cœur se forment; on trouve toujours du temps pour cela, et voilà à quoi l'institution doit pourvoir.[20]

By 1685 Geneva had a hundred master clockmakers and 300 associated craftsmen manufacturing a total of 5,000 timepieces a year, along with eighty master goldsmiths and jewellers who employed another 200.[21] However unlikely the flourishing of any luxury trade must have seemed in Geneva's environment, there were obviously close links between horology and the art (or craft) of the goldsmith.[22] A goldsmiths' guild had been founded before the first influx of Protestant refugees, and managed to survive the passing of Calvin's sumptuary laws; when he banned the wearing of jewellery the goldsmiths simply joined forces with watchmakers, knowing that no horologist of ambition could dispense with using precious jewels and expensive metals. Indeed, the corporation of master watchmakers, given guild status in Geneva in 1601, stipulated that their products should be manufactured either in gold or in silver, an exception to the Calvinist rule that was said to have been made in part because Calvin's friend Thomas Bayard, who came to Geneva as his assistant in 1554, was himself a goldsmith.

[17] See Babel, *Métiers*, pp. 34–5.   [18] Babel, *Métiers*, p. 21.
[19] See Michel Launay, *Rousseau écrivain politique*, 2nd edn (Geneva and Paris: Slatkine, 1989), p. 29, p. 34.
[20] *C.C.*, II.212.
[21] See Gaspard Vallette, *Jean-Jacques Rousseau genevois*, 2nd edn (Geneva: A. Jullien; Paris: Plan-Nourrit, 1911), p. 20, n. 1 (quoting the historian Picot).
[22] Babel, *Métiers*, p. 37.

MAKING THE ARTIFICER

In the spirit of Rousseau's observation to Tronchin, Leroy's *Encyclopédie* article 'Horloger' comments on 'la différence qu'on doit faire d'un *horloger* qui n'est communément qu'un ouvrier, avec un *horloger* méchaniste qui est un artiste, lequel doit joindre au génie des machines, donné par la nature, l'étude de la géométrie, du calcul, des méchaniques, la physique, l'art de faire des expériences, quelques teintures d'astronomie, et enfin la main d'œuvre'. (Note the pairing of the 'méchaniste' with the 'artiste', and how the 'génie des machines' is called a gift of nature, not the product of study.) In the same spirit, Leroy's entry 'Horlogerie' emphasises the lowly status of the 'main d'œuvre' whose task is to manufacture the parts of a watch without properly grasping their function, contrasting him with the master whose elevated skills are required to put timepieces together. The training of the 'artiste horloger', according to this source, requires a comprehensive understanding of the principles of mechanics, geometry, metallurgy, and physics. Even so, Leroy continues, a lengthy apprenticeship and a due period of 'compagnonnage' were no guarantee of excellence, a true watchmaker being the 'architecte-méchanique' inspired by flashes of pure genius whose essence cannot be learnt or taught. In something of the same spirit d'Alembert had announced in the *Discours préliminaire* to the *Encyclopédie* that the inventors of such devices as the escapement, that irreplaceable part of the clock's or watch's mechanism, deserved as much esteem as great algebraists. Yet the guild status Paris watchmakers had attained in 1544 would not be granted to their Geneva peers until more than half a century later.

The French concern with developing a highly educated artisan class may be traced back to the seventeenth-century debates surrounding the creation of an Académie des sciences, itself evolving from discussions concerning two separate bodies, a Compagnie des sciences et des arts and a more general institution devised by Charles Perrault. For the first time the fine arts would be envisaged as separate from practical arts and what we now call the sciences,[23] a distinction crystallized in Colbert's statement that, just as the latter subject was taught by precept, so the practical arts must be both rationalized in terms of trade activity and promoted through 'true scientific method'. In other words, artisanship was to be elevated above blind traditionalism and perfected by theory leading to enlightened

[23] See Hahn, *The Anatomy of a Scientific Institution: The Paris Academy of Science, 1666–1803* (Berkeley, LA, and London: University of California Press, 1971), p. 55, pp. 67–8.

practice—a clear anticipation of eighteenth-century *Encyclopédiste* ideals. To this end, in 1675 Colbert instructed the body that later became the Académie de sciences to begin a description of the mechanical arts, an enterprise eventually resulting in the publication of a 27-volume *Description des arts et métiers* (1761–88) edited first by Réaumur and then by Duhamel de Monceau, and which was based on a repository of knowledge built up over decades by contributing members who patiently collected and collated information on the crafts.[24]

Insisting on the elevated status of watchmaking in his own city obviously mattered to Rousseau, and may be one reason why, in the dedication to the *Discours sur l'origine de l'inégalité*, he lists the serious books in his father's library almost as though they showed the craftsman's claim to be a practitioner of the liberal arts—'Je vois Tacite, Plutarque et Grotius, mêlés devant lui avec les instrumens de son métier'.[25] Whether this is true or not, we may assume that many of Isaac Rousseau's peers possessed, and probably also read, more serious works of literature than the novels his wife had left their sons, including authors Isaac himself was also said to own: Cicero, Virgil, Homer, Bayle, Locke, Machiavelli, Boileau, Pascal, Sallust, Seneca, and of course Calvin.[26] In light of this, Rousseau's insistence that he belonged by ancestral trade as well as birth to an elite of artisans, not so much separate from the 'peuple' as definitely distinct from the 'canaille', looks reasonable enough. Yet even though the 'peuple', made up of labourers, mercenary soldiers, servants, apprentices, and peasants, was guided in its political struggle against the aristocracy by the elite bourgeoisie, Rousseau's stated allegiance to the common folk sounds more romantic than sincere—as romantic, perhaps, as the educated founders of the British Arts and Crafts movement's urging working men in the late nineteenth century to read Plato,[27] or the weavers in Mrs Gaskell's *Mary Barton's* being encouraged to prop up Newton's *Principia mathematica* on their looms and read it as they worked.[28] The fact is that the originator of the artwork or artefact might be as distant from the working masses as was the horological 'genius' (etymologically linked with the *engineer*) contrasted in the *Encyclopédie* entry 'Horloger' with the mere 'main d'œuvre' assembling timepieces.[29]

---

[24] See Arthur H. Cole and George B. Watts, *The Handicrafts of France as Recorded in the 'Description des arts et métiers' 1761–1788* (Boston, MA: Harvard University Press, 1952).

[25] See Dedication to the Conseil général de Genève, *O.C.*, III.118.

[26] See Launay, *Rousseau écrivain politique*, p. 26.

[27] See Fiona MacCarthy, *The Simple Life: C.R. Ashbee in the Cotswolds* (London: Lund Humphries, 1981), p. 11.

[28] See Margaret C. Jacob, *Scientific Culture and the Making of the Industrial West* (Oxford: Oxford University Press, 1997), p. 7.

[29] See also n. 48.

Whether or not ordinary timepieces were necessary to the man in the street—if they were, according to the logic of Rousseau's *Discours sur les sciences et les arts*, they should sell for a moderate price—, the objects made by ambitious horologists could fetch enormous sums: hence, perhaps, the status of their trade as an art for aristocrats, even monarchs, to practise. Their products were often sumptuously decorated, ornately tooled and studded with priceless gems, and valued (as well as priced) accordingly. Had Calvin lived to see the revocation of the Edict of Nantes he might have found it deplorable not just in its leading to the renewed persecution of thousands of Protestants, but also in its directing so many makers of decorative objects to Switzerland against the grain of his own sumptuary prohibitions. For although the pious credentials of some craftsmen would be advertised by their manufacture of the special crucifix-shaped watches called 'montres d'abbesse', such pieces were eventually discontinued as too fanciful to suit austere Calvinist tastes.[30] The newcomers from France got round this prohibition, however, by creating richly ornamented timepieces of other kinds—speciality watches that looked like animals, flowers, or skulls (the second perhaps defensible on moral grounds as a symbolic *vanitas*, and the last similarly as an injunction to *memento mori*),[31] along with fantastically ornate and bejewelled artworks for the extremely wealthy, whether or not they had as pressing a need to keep time as the common man. The trade of Rousseau's forebears, in other words, acquired a note of luxury it would never lose. In this context it was natural that the master horologist should become a man of substance, often living in a style that ran counter to Geneva's frugal instincts, building grand houses, wearing expensive clothes, and enjoying lavish pleasures. Nor was it surprising that as time went by the monetary value attached to horology should be reflected in steep apprenticeship fees—at the start of the seventeenth century lower than those for goldsmiths, by its close considerably more.

Given that this evolution of horology and related crafts into luxury trades clearly offered tempting material prospects to those who worked in them, it might have been expected to inspire real staying power in the body of apprentices; but Rousseau himself was far from being the only deserter. Rather than determining to qualify as quickly as possible in order to start reaping the financial rewards available to master craftsmen, trainees often resented the treatment meted out to them, and escaped the discipline

---

[30] See Landes, *Revolutions*, p. 238.
[31] The Musée du Moyen Age (formerly the Musée de Cluny) in Paris has a death's head watch made by Jean Rousseau I in which the lower jaw separates from the upper to reveal the dial. See Eugène Jaquet and Alfred Chapuis, *Histoire et technique de la montre suisse* (Basel and Olten: Urs Graf Verlag, 1945), p. 24.

of the workshop as apprentices have always done. The master's view, contrastingly but predictably, was that the system greatly disadvantaged him for the first two years, when the apprentice was of little or no practical use, spoilt much of what he touched, and cost more than he was worth, factors that together explain why the employer's frustration should sometimes have found expression in acts of brutality towards his charge. The longer the trainee remained, however, the more valuable he became. Rousseau's failure to stay the course as an apprentice 'graveur pour l'horlogerie' doubtless owed as much to the ill treatment he received from his master Ducommun as to his own invincible love of liberty, referred to throughout his writings; but a lack of fixedness seems also to have been the norm rather than the exception over a range of trades, not just for apprentices, but also among journeymen. The latter's very name, indeed, may suggest short-term ambition and a habit of moving on.[32]

A tendency to uproot oneself and settle in an entirely different place was often regarded as a quintessentially Swiss character trait, reflected in the archetypal Swiss profession of mercenary soldier. Yet according to the rather reluctantly Swiss Mme de Staël, it was also a national characteristic to experience homesickness (*Heimweh*) with searing acuteness.[33] Even so, just as mercenaries were to be found fighting other nations' wars, so various types of Swiss professional were to be met with in foreign courts and lands, painting pictures, decorating ceilings, practising other trades, and moving to wherever money could be earned and talent appreciated. Austere Calvinist rectitude may have moulded many Genevese natures, but another side of the native character was the enjoyment of plenty, most morally satisfying in Swiss eyes, it is true, when it had been won by sustained honest effort—wealth bought by moving away, but with the proviso that it could be freely spent back in the mother country. Then there was the native landscape, which oppressed some as much as it exalted others. Mountains, which Rousseau called essential to his happiness, gave many the sense of being hemmed in, often fuelling the determination to escape to gentler locations, especially lakes (which Rousseau also adored) and rolling meadows.

It is, however, unlikely that any of these factors lay behind Isaac Rousseau's decision to seek work as a clockmaker in Constantinople between the birth

---

[32] See Philippe Minard, 'Trade Without Institution', in Ian A. Gadd and Patrick Wallis (eds.), *Guilds and Associations in Europe, 900–1900* (London: Centre for Metropolitan History, University of London, 2006), pp. 83–100, esp. p. 84.

[33] Mme de Staël, *De l'Allemagne*, ed. Comtesse Jean de Pange and Simone Balayé, 5 vols. (Paris: Garnier, 1958), I.159–60. See also the entry 'Musique' in the *Dictionnaire de musique* Rousseau finished in Môtiers (*O.C.*, V.924), and his letter to the Duc de Luxembourg of 20 January 1763 (*C.C.*, XV.52).

of his first son and the conception of his second. Before marrying he had been forced to travel by his future wife to test his constancy, and emerged with credit from the test:[34] he proposed to Suzanne Bernard on return and was accepted despite belonging to a far less wealthy family than hers (as the *Confessions* observes, he had nothing to his name but the title of master watchmaker, although he was, according to his son, very skilled at his trade). Having married and settled in the Bernard house on the Grand'rue, he decided within a year to leave his young family and work as a watchmaker to the Sultan's seraglio in Constantinople, partly, it seems, because Geneva was experiencing an economic slump. He would return only six years later, with Jean-Jacques born a predictable ten months thereafter.

The son would share some of Isaac's characteristics. Was a sense of practical detachment from the upbringing of children one of them? It may seem harsh to suggest as much in Isaac's case, at least from the fact of his removal to Turkey; he was, perhaps, simply doing what any responsible family man would do in difficult times. After all, there was a solid tradition of qualified craftsmen moving on from one location to another in search of new trade, the so-called 'wandering goldsmith' syndrome,[35] which overcame a prudent concern with maintaining one's position in the professional hierarchy and fed the urge to start afresh somewhere else. Rousseau's act in abandoning all his own children to the foundlings' home several decades later looks a great deal less defensible than his father's qualified abandonment. A specific tradition, besides, seems to lie behind Isaac's departure. There was a convention among Western powers of offering clocks to Eastern rulers as diplomatic gifts[36] (one appeared at an audience, as it were, with a clock under one's arm), for which purpose Isaac Rousseau's creations might surely serve as well as any other's. Although horology in the Turkish capital had previously been in the hands of a few masters from Blois, a famous centre of the craft, they were gradually displaced in the seventeenth century by a colony of Genevese masters who settled in Galata, a suburb and foreign quarter of Constantinople; it then became the practice for recently qualified masters to spend three to four years in Turkey before settling down back in the homeland.[37] This trade was dwindling, however, at the time Isaac Rousseau took his skills abroad, and although Galata's enclave of clockmakers lingered on for the first few years of the eighteenth century, it was slowly losing importance. Perhaps, then, it made good economic sense for him to return when he did, despite

---

[34] *Confessions*, I.6.   [35] See Sennett, *Craftsman*, p. 60.
[36] See Otto Kurz, *Clocks and Watches in the Near East* (London: Warburg Institute; Leiden: Brill, 1975), p. 60.
[37] Kurz, *Clocks and Watches*, p. 70.

the fact that the son attributes his homecoming in 1711 solely to Suzanne Rousseau's pleading (the *Confessions* suggests that the entreaties were connected with her sense of vulnerability, exposed to the advances of more powerful men during her husband's absence). Certainly it suited Jean-Jacques to stress her virtuous modesty; he had little else on which to base her characterization.

A footnote to this story of cultural enterprise is provided by Voltaire's commercial involvement in watchmaking from his fiefdom just outside the city gates of Geneva, where he established the so-called 'manufacture royale de Ferney' primarily for the export trade.[38] The venture had been prompted, he claimed to Frederick of Prussia, by the fact that the Turks had been importing Geneva-made watches for sixty years but were still unable to make or regulate their own (though how the Ferney enterprise might help end that state of affairs is unexplained). Whatever the case, it would be mistaken to conclude from this story that the clock, not the engine, was the true *moteur* of the continental Industrial Revolution. Besides, the Ferney business gradually declined in the 1770s, enjoying a brief resurgence when Voltaire died in 1778, but finally shrinking to the point where the clock- and watchmakers returned to practise their trade in Geneva.

ART AND CRAFT

Rousseau's letter to Tronchin on artisanship calls horology a median profession, exemplifying artisanal virtues of an essentially moderate kind: 'Partout le riche est toujours le premier corrompu, le pauvre suit, l'état médiocre [l'horlogerie] est atteint le dernier'.[39] Although this moderation seemed somehow associated with its utilitarian origins, *Emile* suggests that the view might be challenged: opinions on the usefulness of timepieces themselves varied according to the observer's angle of vision. For instance, to the child, whose situation of elemental need draws it close to the state of nature, time's passage is measurable by the need to eat or sleep, with duration defined purely in relation to such desires: the child 'joüit

[38] Voltaire, *Correspondance*, ed. Theodore Besterman, 107 vols. (Geneva: Institut et Musée Voltaire, 1953–65), LXXV.66 (Dupan to Freudenreich, 7 May 1770); LXXVI.117 (Voltaire to Chevalier de Rochefort d'Ally, 19 August 1770); LXXXV.127 (to Alexandre de Paule de Dampierre d'Hornoy, 6 June 1773); LXXXIX.52 (to Duc de Richelieu, 14 October 1774); LXXVII.127 (to Frederick the Great of Prussia, 1 March 1771); LXXXI.21 (to Catherine the Great of Russia, 14 January 1772); LXXXIII.120 (to Pierre Samuel Du Pont de Nemours, 9 November 1772). See also Jaquet and Chappuis, *Montre suisse*, pp. 75–6.
[39] *C.C.*, V.252.

du tems sans en être esclave', and 'ne fait pas [...] grand cas de l'horlogerie'.[40]
In this respect he perhaps resembles the savage described in *Du bonheur
public*, a being who lives in the present and therefore has nothing but an
'existence ponctuelle'.[41]

These illustrations make clear that, at least in such elemental conditions, horology cannot rank with activities bearing immediate relevance
to human survival. *Emile* develops this notion in terms we have already
encountered, but which are peculiarly relevant to the Swiss art of watchmaking. However tempting it may be to value manufactured objects in
proportion to the minuteness with which primary materials have been
adapted in making them, 'en chaque chose l'art dont l'usage est le plus
général et le plus indispensable est incontestablement celui qui mérite le
plus d'estime, et que celui à qui moins d'autres sont nécessaires la mérite
encore par-dessus les plus subordonnés, parce qu'il est plus libre et plus
près de l'indépendance. Voila les véritables régles de l'appréciation des arts
et de l'industrie; tout le reste est arbitraire et dépend de l'opinion'.[42] It is
only the logic of capitalism, in other words, that leads us to rate most
highly what involves the most labour and the most expensive materials,
and which is almost invariably the furthest from immediate need.[43] Rousseau's alternative view is based on the logic of utilitarianism: it may be an
ascetic system in comparison with that of capitalism, particularly as it will
appear in later (Marxian) economic and social theory, but its reach is
more extensive and more humane.

Craft processes that are least relevant to our needs, besides, are often
deliberately shrouded in secrecy, ignorance about their operations preserved for the sake of enhancing the monetary or curiosity value of their
products. Diderot's desire to expose these mysteries was an article of faith
that underpinned the whole *Encyclopédiste* enterprise. He hired the famous
horologist Jean Romilly, as well as Leroy, to contribute to the work, knowing that Romilly had, among other feats, presented to the Académie des
sciences an 'astounding' clock that ran for a week without needing to be
rewound.[44] (Romilly, incidentally, also made the watch Rousseau would
buy in 1765, despite the principles that had made him discard his original
timepiece at the start of his reform.)[45] In the volume containing plates of

[40] *Emile*, IV.459. [41] *Du bonheur public*, *O.C.*, III.509.

[42] *Emile*, p. 460. See also Philippe Besnard, *Protestantisme et capitalisme* (Paris: A. Colin,
1970), pp. 5–8, pp. 29–30 and *passim*.

[43] See Georg Simmel, 'The Metropolis and Mental Life', in *On Individuality and Social Forms*,
ed. Donald N. Levine (Chicago and London: University of Chicago Press, 1971), p. 328.

[44] See Lefeyvre, 'Rousseau horloger', p. 38.

[45] See Lefeyvre, 'Rousseau horloger', p. 41, and *Confessions*, I.363. Yet Rousseau will
claim in the *Dialogues* that 'le moment où il se défit de sa [première] montre fut un des plus
doux de sa vie' (I.845).

watch- and clockmaking processes Romilly comments on the secrecy the English preserved in such matters, and which, he claimed, made apprenticeship in the French system particularly desirable: 'ils [artisans] se perfectionnoient plus d'un an à Paris, qu'ils n'auroient fait en dix ans à Londres'. This may or may not have been true; Diderot's entry 'Bas' gives a more positive image of English modernity, at least in terms of general manufacturing developments in which they clearly enjoyed superiority to the French. But the fact that it was a superiority they allegedly defended by guarding trade secrets explains why the designs for modern English looms had had to be smuggled across the Channel by an industrial spy, Hindret, and covertly built for French use in Louis XV's stocking manufactory. This closedness remained the tradition in guild and craft circles, despite being challenged by a number of other publications in the eighteenth century. Yet even the most technical of these—such as the Minim Charles Plumier's encyclopaedic manual on lathe-turning (*L'Art du Tourneur*, 1701), a work of vast scope published in French and Latin[46]—fell short of overcoming the effective block on practical guidance so jealously preserved by guilds, as well as being hampered, like every such account, by the difficulty of evoking movement or process in words. It was a difficulty Diderot encountered when, as editor of the *Encyclopédie*, he visited workshops and asked workers there to explain what they did.

Instead of detailing the skills required in given trades, then, guild statutes referred to 'customs' or 'secrets', effectively insisting that knowledge should not be shared but remain the private property of master and initiate. The *Encyclopédie* did what it could to undermine these controls, on the principle that diffusing information on the most recent discoveries and developments in what are generally called the arts and sciences, and helping where appropriate to introduce them into the production process, would bring enlightenment and promote efficiency as never before.[47] (The *Description des arts et métiers* attempted to do much the same thing, and the *Encyclopédie* borrowed many of its plates.) With the fall of the monarchy, all academies and guilds in France were abolished because of their perceived association with discredited political and economic systems, if not for the secretive traditions—which might advantage members of the very classes the Revolution aimed to liberate—they embodied.

All of this must have seemed remote to the boy Rousseau, playing with his grandfather's tools after Isaac's departure for a new life in Nyon. The

---

[46] See Klaus Maurice, *Der drechselnde Souverän* (Zurich: Verlag Ineichen, 1975), pp. 106–8.

[47] See Antoine Picon, 'La Vision du travail des Encyclopédistes', *Recherches sur Diderot et sur l'Encyclopédie*, 13 (1992), pp. 131–47, esp. pp. 144–5.

Encyclopédie plates relating to watchmaking illustrate the enormous number of implements this craft demanded, an array that made the potential scope for devastation in unskilled and untrained hands enormous. And the description of Rousseau and his cousin Abraham's ruining David's instruments in the process of trying to make timepieces turns the *Confessions'* account into an ironic and probably deliberate antithesis of the convention in artists' 'lives' from Vasari onwards of showing a prodigy's genius emerging in his or her seemingly instinctive ability to use the tools of the trade—the painter's colours and brushes, the sculptor's chisel—without any training. Of course referring to tools in connection with the visual arts is far from signifying that what was being practised should properly be called a trade, as the cobbler's or the jobbing engraver's work would be even when done by skilled and trained hands; craft, conversely, never laid claim to the status of liberal art, though many *Encyclopédistes* thought it should do so. The fact that its duplicated processes were subject to rule rather than inspiration seemed to make the concept of genius inapplicable to it,[48] as did the mundane nature of its products, useful rather than 'essentially' beautiful, or both (though interpretations of the word 'essential' in this respect were always, as they remain, to a degree subjective). And the assumption of craft's inferiority to art generally persists, despite the revisionist efforts of the eighteenth-century *philosophes* and of the various arts and crafts groups active later on.

This situation superficially resembles that pinpointed in Diderot's words in the *Essais sur la peinture* on the classifying of different types of painting, a long-established tradition that continued into his own century, and which took historical works as the highest mode, making it the most expensive and prestigious, and genre painting (with still life) as the lowest,

---

[48] *Ars* in its classical usage itself stood contrasted with *ingenium*, the former merely a skill that could be learnt by rule or imitation, the latter an innate talent that could not. With the foundation of academies of art from the Renaissance onwards, it would be argued that such institutions were the guardians of *ingenium*, and the guild the home of 'maîtrise', mastery of a purely technical kind. Clearly, the status of art had evolved, being now associated with elevated perception and creativity. It is in this context that the later, Romantic, view of the artist as one who produced masterpieces (a significant word) by the light of inspiration rather than through technical knowledge and the application of rules may best be understood. However, it also entailed a reinterpretation of the role of all institutions that aimed to teach art, a development reflected in the artist David's complaints in the Revolutionary years about the hegemony of academies, no longer associated with *ingenium*, but rather with its reverse, a criticism that simply echoed the words of Diderot and others earlier in the eighteenth century to the effect that the rigid structure of these institutions, together with their assumption that everything to do with the promotion and appreciation of art could be brought within the scope of rational understanding and logical precept, was inimical to the free expression of genius. On the ancient world's denigration of art as well as craft, see *infra*, p. 45.

and therefore cheapest. In calling for this 'low' mode, exemplified in the canvases of Greuze and Chardin, to be ranked equally with the high,[49] and given the attention paid to various kinds of handwork in the *Encyclopédie*, Diderot is perhaps suggesting that there should be a similar revision in the case of (manual) craft relative to (liberal) art.

Certain issues relevant to these distinctions come to mind. One is the factor of repeatability. Part of the cachet, and hence the cost, of every type and quality of painting is its uniqueness, its absolute distinctness from the mass-produced or reproduced (if we leave aside the painting of replicas by the artist or the artist's studio). The craft object is unlikely to be unique in the sense that high and even low art is, despite the fact that each piece of handmade work is sui generis, not exactly resembling another of the same type by a single maker, always testifying to that maker's fingerprint as no machine- or factory-generated object can do. As its purpose is to perform a practical function as efficiently as possible, however, it must be available to all who need it for that function, which in turn usually entails multiple production. In such circumstances, the requirement for availability and cheapness as well as functionality may make the user prefer a machine-made and mass-produced version of the product to one made by hand, at least if the means of machine production exist; but in Rousseau's day the scale of industrial manufacture in Europe, if England is excepted, was relatively limited. Factory-made mechanical 'movements' for watches, for example, were not used in Swiss horology until the first half of the nineteenth century.

It may be thought a weakness of the work of art to be overtly or covertly functional rather than subject to what has been called the purely aesthetic attitude of 'disinterested interest'.[50] Is this a strong enough distinction to prevent the levelling the *Encyclopédistes* wanted, that is, both to prevent the mingling of high and low and to keep art separate from craft? In the eighteenth century functionality was not seen as necessarily compromising aesthetic effect; Rousseau fell in as enthusiastically as other writers of the time with the notion of art's potential utility (even though he more frequently accused it of promoting immorality). Nor was it counted a particular strength in art to be 'purely' beautiful rather than a mixture of the beautiful and the useful. The factor of individuality we assign to art may clarify the issue, but is perhaps less separate from those already considered than simply another version of them: craftwork can of course be quite as individual as art in manifestly bearing its maker's

---

[49] Diderot, *Essais sur la peinture*, *O.C.*, XIV.398–9.
[50] This definition of our apprehension of beauty is offered by Roger Scruton, *Beauty* (Oxford: Oxford University Press, 2009).

fingerprint, but fingerprint probably matters less than functionality. The related quality of originality or imaginativeness does not seem to be necessarily present to the same degree in craft as in art, since craft's chief purpose is to be purposive.

EVERYDAY WORLDS

Perhaps Rousseau himself wanted to address, if not resolve, these issues in devoting his last years of literary composition to the 'low life' story of a single man, himself; not the heroic lives he read about in Plutarch as a boy, nor the less heroic but still momentous ones peopling the novels he inherited from his mother, but a significant life none the less. Are his personal writings in this limited respect more like craft products than art, concerned with praxis rather than doxa, like the craft he had retreated to from literature after suffering persecution for his other kinds of writing, the doctrinal kind? This personal mode may look most like a humble verbal version of the still life or the genre scene in painting, a mode as free of the flowers of rhetoric as the 'sermo humilis' of ancient oratory.[51] Is craftwork their equivalent? We need to keep this possibility in mind for reconsideration later.

Rousseau knows that understanding a lived life comes when we return to it in practical as well as verbal ways. Part of how we know what we have been is through reexperiencing the different kinds of action we engaged in earlier: not simply through the various forms of memory we possess, but also, if such a thing is possible, by going back *in body* to those times. Walking and the dreaming he associates with it are potent means of rediscovery for Rousseau, but we cannot properly explore them yet. Examining the older self that generated the Promenades of the *Rêveries* and the other late works describing Rousseau makes us want first to attempt to grasp his younger self, place him back in time into all the moods and characteristic actions of the boy he was. That means finding out about the ways he used his body, how he saw and felt as well as played.

Play may seem to lack any settled purpose,[52] but its actions involve functions that, developed, help to clarify the world and through it clarify our place in life. An aqueduct Rousseau constructed as a boy at Bossey during his time lodging with Parson Lambercier is a case in point; it was made with Abraham, the son of an engineer then working on the city

---

[51] Erich Auerbach, 'Sermo humilis', *Literary Language and its Public in Late Antiquity and the Middle Ages* (London: Routledge and Kegan Paul, 1965), pp. 27–66.

[52] See John Huizinga, *Homo ludens*, first English edn, 1949 (London: Routledge, 1998).

fortifications in Geneva, and himself intended for his father's profession. Rousseau's stay at Bossey, he writes in the *Confessions*, restored him to the state of childhood that his love of reading had partly suppressed in Geneva; at Bossey, where he was obliged to study, play provided much-needed relief. Making the aqueduct involved diverting water from around a walnut tree Lambercier had planted to the willow the two boys positioned on the terrace a short distance away: it was a mere 'friponnerie',[53] and punished as such, for Lambercier, though he took violent physical action in dismantling their effort, could be heard laughing when he recounted the story to his sister.

Using tools would be to move one step beyond this basic form of doing. Belonging to the 'lesser' world of praxis, it stands as an attempt to create something out of (nearly) nothing, like the humble discourse or the lower modes of art; to make a concrete object from materials that on their own have little value. It is through doing, in other words, as Piaget describes it in his works of educational theory, simply repeating Rousseau's lesson in *Emile* (and referring to something much more intimate, more actively instrumental, than the actions of the modern child who 'makes' a bear simply by ordering certain processes on a computer: knowing *that* rather than *how*). Such exploratory bricolage often appeals more to the child than does playing with things designated as toys, so working as a bridge between infantile curiosity and adult manufacture. Rousseau, who says in the *Confessions* that he never quite outgrew his childhood, was a maker throughout life, fabricating things at a material level (herbaria, copies of music scores), at an abstract but creative level (political systems in particular, but also novels, plays, and works of social philosophy), and an intermediate one (the books he both hand-copied and published in the conventional printed manner). It is true that none of these, with the partial exception of the third, quite represents the physical act of crafting objects, though they may be closely linked with childlike and artisanal imagination. But whether or not he really thought he should have lived a craftsman's life, the habit of solitary making never left Rousseau; it was the combination of imagination and creativeness that came to haunt him.

Superficially, imagination may seem a quality no craftsman really needs to call on in the process of doing as the craft product has always demanded, with whatever modern adaptations he may think desirable. This partially explains why Rousseau came to regard craftwork as his only fixed and settled safety; but it also, more prosaically, accounts for the fact that so many implements have remained virtually unchanged over the ages of artisanship. As the *Encyclopédie* plates also suggest, the prototypes had been conceived

---

[53] *Confessions*, I.24.

so effectively that the same craft tools served a range of different activities[54]—horology, joinery, wood carving, engraving, metalwork, and no doubt others—all reflecting the fundamental similarity of moves made by humans in turning matter of one form into another. Individualism comes from other things, from the grip or angle of a pencil or the pressure of a chisel as from the conceptual grip or angle of an idea; these distinguish the beginner from the master, whether writer, thinker, or maker. The concept of a stock of fundamentals, unchanging over time and reassuring in their integrity, may also be appealing to the modern Rousseauist, as to anyone made uneasy by our world of constant technological development and the attendant ceaseless obsolescence of things.

Yet man is a tool-making creature; Franklin pronounced him so, and Marx's *Kapital* agreed. Tools extend man's power over nature in often unimaginably transformative ways. Rousseau's *Discours sur l'origine de l'inégalité* examines their development in early society, stressing how primitive aids to support life were found as much as made to serve that end ('on trouva quelques haches de pierres dures, et tranchantes, qui servirent à couper du bois, creuser la terre, et faire des huttes de branchages, qu'on s'avisa ensuite d'enduire d'argile et de boüe').[55] It may be a mark of human intelligence to see only raw materials for manufacture in the world, but it is also the price we pay for 'consenting' to sideline instinct; for progress, as the second *Discours* makes clear, always demands that some price or other be paid. To say that man is an inventor is not simply to say that he is intelligent; it also suggests that his intelligence is expressed in his adaptive skills as well as in other ways. While animals apparently have at best only spontaneous drives to rely on in the service of staying alive, the capacities of the human brain free us from enslavement to fixed, unalterable actions. This is why man is both *homo sapiens* and *homo faber*.

Is it surprising that the boy who had identified himself with every classical hero he had encountered in books mentions none of the Roman engineers as models for building his aqueduct? Not when we consider that the source of his fantasies was Plutarch,[56] whose *Famous Lives* he read in Amyot's translation, and who has nothing to say about them. Still, Rousseau has moved on in terms of his models. Where previously he likened himself to Aristides and Brutus, his sense of glory as he grows older so outstrips their great achievements that at the age of ten 'j'en jugeois mieux [what he had done] que Cesar à trente'.[57] Later on, at the time of

---

[54] As is evident in Wyke, *Catalogue of Tools*, p. 1.   [55] *O.C.*, III.167.
[56] See Rousseau's letter to Malesherbes of 12 January 1762 (*O.C.*, I.1134), and *Dialogues*, I.819.
[57] *Confessions*, I.24.

his infatuation with a Swiss ragamuffin called Bâcle, he convinces himself
that there is money to be made by offering public displays of a 'Heron's
fountain', an apparatus invented by Heron of Alexandria for producing a
jet of water powered by compressed air: the device had often been used in
antiquity to mystify the layman, and Rousseau, who had been given one
in Turin, thought that it might serve as a stunt for earning bed and board
from gullible rustics en route from that city to Geneva.[58] This proved to
be a deluded judgement, though as a variation on the watery theme it
might have amused Lambercier. Later on the *Encyclopédistes* would investigate such hydraulic machines as examples of both simple and complex
functions, the moving and lifting of water being powered by the motions
of the water itself (as with the paradigmatic machine at the château de
Marly). Such activities epitomized the non-human forces and elements of
the physical world along with the human capacity to harness them that so
engaged the Enlightenment mind.

ON THE JOB

The time at Bossey would end—or so Rousseau dramatically describes
it—with another disillusionment marking the passage from childhood to
the adult world. If the aqueduct incident had been ambiguous in this
respect (the boy's development of a grown-up idea was, in the literal as
well as figurative sense, a *diversion*, both for him and, to Rousseau's surprise, for Lambercier himself), nothing positive could be said about the
incident of Mlle Lambercier's broken comb. The cry provoked by Rousseau's wrongful punishment for this breakage, 'Carnifex [butcher],
Carnifex, Carnifex',[59] may superficially have resembled Lambercier's 'Un
aqueduc [...], un aqueduc, un aqueduc!',[60] but it had quite other implications. Rousseau tells the aqueduct story after the one involving the comb
as though to mark a crescendo, yet it is the earlier incident that carries the
stronger negative charge. Along with Abraham's equally brutal punishment for some other dereliction,[61] its consequences mark what Jean-
Jacques describes as the end of childhood: 'Dès ce moment je cessai de
jouir d'un bonheur pur [...]. Nous y [at Bossey] fumes comme on nous
réprésente le prémier homme encore dans le paradis terrestre, mais ayant
cessé d'en joüir'.[62] Their country surroundings, he notes, mirrored the
Fall: 'La campagne même perdit à nos yeux cet attrait de douceur et de
simplicité qui va au cœur. Elle nous semblait deserte et sombre; elle s'étoit

---

[58] *Confessions*, I.101.   [59] *Confessions*, I.20.
[60] *Confessions*, I.24.   [61] *Confessions*, I.19.   [62] *Confessions*, I.20.

comme couverte d'un voile qui nous en cachoit les beautés'.[63] Gabriel
Bernard duly took the cousins back to Geneva.

Once there, it is true, Rousseau spent some months (if not the two to
three years he claims) still living with Abraham and still playing:[64] it was
at this time that they damaged their grandfather's watchmaking tools, but
also made things from scratch—cages, flutes, drums, houses, crossbows,
toy boats, and puppets. Yet a future involving real work could not be
evaded. There were discussions as to whether Jean-Jacques should be a
watchmaker, an attorney, or a clergyman (his preference was for the
church, because he loved delivering sermons), though for the time being
he continued his informal education, sharing Abraham's drawing lessons
and developing a taste for draughtmanship that he would later apply to
his work as craftsman and botanist.

When he did start a profession, however, it was as clerk to a notary,
M. Masseron. Why not an apprenticeship in the craft of his brother
(who had initially been trained by Isaac),[65] his father, and virtually all his
Rousseau forebears? Surely the butchery of his grandfather's tools could
not have influenced this decision, even though the eighty-three-year-old
David, still professionally active at that time, might have greatly resented
Jean-Jacques's actions. Isaac Rousseau, having already left for Nyon, was
perhaps uninvolved in the choice of his son's profession. For whatever
reason, Rousseau joined Masseron's office, where his employment was
brief and undistinguished, ending with dismissal for incompetence and
ignorance. Although he had been 'sold' to Masseron by Gabriel Bernard
on the pretext 'que je savois, que je savois', the truth was 'que je ne savois
rien'; 'qu'il lui avoit promis un joli garcon, et qu'il ne lui avoit donné
qu'un ane'. According to Masseron's clerks, 'je n'étois bon qu'à mener la
lime'.[66]

In certain contexts this taunt might not to have been as dismissive as it
sounds. As the *Encyclopédie* plates relating to horology suggest, the file (or
'lime')—eleven types of which are illustrated, along with tweezers, pincers,
and pliers—was an indispensible adjunct to the basic skills involved in
many crafts. Whether or not the watchmaker, for example, fashioned the
cogs, springs, escapements, and other parts of a movement himself, or
simply assembled what had been made by others, horological work
involved the delicate shaping of small pieces of metal, forging, filing, and
turning them, and acquiring the ability to gauge correctness or 'fit' independently of automation. The text by Romilly accompanying the *Encyclopédie* plates reveals the enormous complexity of these operations,

---

[63] *Confessions*, I.20–1.   [64] *Confessions*, I.24–5.
[65] See Ritter, *Famille et jeunesse*, p. 167.   [66] *Confessions*, I.30.

essential preliminaries to the difficult work of absorbing the theory behind
the manufacture. Despite the fact that machine fabrication of timepieces had already been established in England, Romilly's view was that
the structure of certain components was too delicate to be made otherwise than by hand. In this connection there was some debate about the
nature of the skills required in horology, in particular whether or not
watchmaking families—some of them virtual dynasties, like the Rousseaus—were simply born with the necessary aptitude or acquired it over
time. Romilly seems uncertain, initially implying that 'la pratique [. . .]
consiste [. . .] à *acquérir* le coup d'œil juste pour juger avec intelligence
de toutes les formes qu'on est obligé de donner à de certaines pièces,
dont la délicatesse ne sauroit être soumise à aucune mesure', then deciding otherwise: the good craftsman is one who 'peut joindre à un travail
assidu des dispositions naturelles, comme une bonne vue et un tact très-
délicat'.

The degree of difficulty involved in becoming a skilled craftsman may
partly explain why Rousseau's brother François had to repeat nearly two
years of his five-year apprenticeship before apparently abandoning horology as soon as he qualified. But the apprenticeship Jean-Jacques began in
April 1725 after the debacle at Masseron's, two months short of his thirteenth birthday, was with a 'graveur pour l'horlogerie', not a watchmaker
himself, and according to its terms he was to be bound for the entire
duration to the young master Abel Ducommun. This meant moving
downtown from the Bernard family house in upper Geneva to the Saint-
Gervais district.

Any apprenticeship presupposes obedience to a master as well as attentiveness to an object or objects, along with a lesson that is taught about
them; reproduction is the goal, the means of reproduction the object of
learning. The watch and clock engraver practises an applied art that is
limited in scope (as Rousseau complained),[67] and his training essentially
consists in learning, first, which instruments to choose in order to achieve
the best match of material and intended product, and, second, how to use
the instruments selected. Scope for originality and creativity is restricted,
as the horologist's is: creativity in both is subordinate to the demands of
function, in the engraver's case by that of legibility (the need for a watch
or clock to show the time clearly, for example), in the horologist's by that
of reliability (the need to tell the time dependably). If the engraver's job is
presentational, the watchmaker's is more directly functional; the former
deals with surface, the latter with structure. Function achieved, the scope

---

[67] *Confessions*, I.30.

for experimentation opens up. The maker decides on the instrument case, made with or without the input of a gold- or silversmith, and the engraver tools the dial and, depending on circumstance, the case as well, either to order or on his own initiative.

Even for the bookish boy Rousseau had been from earliest childhood, the draw of craft was its often delicate physicality; its essence, manual dexterity. The master craftsman was a tangible presence, the work of his moving hands an irreplaceable practical tool, one no verbal instruction could replace. To serve an apprenticeship was, in effect, to acknowledge the essential fact that craft is a hands-on activity. Although the *Confessions* says nothing about what practical lessons Rousseau could and did learn from Ducommun, it is not thereby suggesting that all the information needed by the horologist's engraver was contained in handbooks and pattern books: craft, a material occupation, is radically opposed to abstraction, that which cannot be seen or felt. The unseen may support its fabric, as the theory of watchmaking bridges abstraction and materiality, invisible and material time, but the craftsman deals essentially with things.

The manual focus of Rousseau's apprenticeship was not always as positive an activity as this may suggest, however; or, rather, hands were not always used in craftsmanlike ways. Ducommun's repeated violence, Rousseau claims, removed the dignity from the craft universe he and his apprentice were meant to be experiencing, though Ducommun would no doubt have laid the blame for this at the boy's door. In Rousseau's view, the master compromised his pupil's preferred world of work-and-play, the world he had known in childhood reading in his father's workshop: the hands that beat him defiled the dignity of making. The new workshop, unlike his father's premises, had suddenly become a place of either fear or drudgery, sometimes the two together, and the games Rousseau tried to play there were accordingly traduced as counterfeiting, a quasi-art predicated on materialism (the theft of money, in effect) rather than the purely material, the real substance of craft. Ingenuity of the kind the mature Rousseau came to disdain in the mechanical arts belongs to quite another world, the world, say, of the 'machinist' Vaucanson, with his clockwork flute-player and defecating duck.[68] Its form of wonder betrayed what Rousseau saw as the truer craftlike essence, a matter of honest effort and manual dexterity rather than something closer to craftiness or trickery. His view was both that work should be civilizing, not cheapening, and that the spirit of play and leisure should somehow infuse it—a view of

---

[68] On Vaucanson, see André Doyon and Lucien Liaigre, *Jacques Vaucanson* (Paris: Presses universitaires de France, 1966).

its enlightened times. Ducommun broke that pact, admittedly under provocation.

Rousseau writes in the *Confessions* that he had not disliked the craft he was meant to be learning per se: 'le jeu du burin m'amusoit assez', the *Confessions* laconically notes.[69] He even, so he claims, borrowed some of his master's tools to use in his spare time for the purpose of improving his skills, as well as feasting his eyes on Ducommun's best drawings and prints in a locked private room adjoining the workshop where the tools were kept, and to which he illicitly gained entrance. Since 'je croyois voler le talent avec ses productions',[70] his furtive pleasures seemed justifiable. The pleasure he took in the 'jeu du burin' is unsurprising, given his enjoyment of the drawing lessons he had shared with Abraham, since drawing, according to the *Encyclopédie*'s entry 'Gravure', was itself the basis for engraving, 'le germe du goût qui doit la vivifier. Nul sentiment, nul progrès en gravure sans une expérience consommée dans la pratique du dessin'.[71] This held as much for line engravers decorating dials, watch cases, and the like as it did for those who engraved pictures: the latter might enjoy greater prestige and the dignity that accompanied membership of the Académie royale de peinture et de sculpture, but trade engravers of banknotes, maps, and timepieces could earn considerably more. (Rousseau became a connoisseur of fine picture engraving in later life, building up a small but choice collection of portraits and genre scenes.) A sumptuously encased watch with an ornate dial in New York's Museum of Modern Art bears the signature of its maker, Rousseau's ancestor Jean Rousseau I,[72] and its decoration was probably done by one of the engravers attached to his workshop; there is a similar example in the Garnier collection at the Louvre. Such ornateness may have contravened the spirit of Calvinist asceticism, but workshops insisted that they were obeying its letter overall, watches being in essence practical instruments rather than idle adornments.

Engravers were often directly attached to a watchmaker's premises[73] (though Ducommun's workshop was apparently independent), sometimes even working there alongside other craftsmen. By Rousseau's time they had been made to form their own corporation, however, partly because of worries relating to counterfeiting. There is a reflection of this state of affairs in Rousseau's flogging by his master for illicitly making the medals

---

[69] *Confessions*, I.31. [70] *Confessions*, I.35.

[71] See also Liliane Mottu Weber, 'Les Conditions d'apprentissage à Genève au début du XVIIIᵉ siècle d'après les minutes de notaires (1701–1710)', licence de la Faculté des sciences économiques et sociales, Université de Genève, 1963, p. 46.

[72] See Jaquet and Chappuis, *Montre suisse*, p. 23.

[73] Jaquet and Chappuis, *Montre suisse*, p. 98; also Babel, *Métiers*, p. 101.

for an imagined order of chivalry, even though they were simply intended to decorate his friends and himself: bearing as they did the city arms of Geneva, they seemd to Ducommun to resemble false coin.[74] He beat his apprentice for other derelictions too—petty theft and reading on the job, in the main—, aberrations of which the former idol of his aunts and the mostly obedient schoolboy of Bossey could never have been guilty. If to Ducommun he seemed no better than a thief and timewaster, Rousseau insisted that he had been corrupted by being treated not as an equal but as a subordinate, ordered from the dinner table before dessert (which accounts, he says, for his theft of produce from vegetable garden and orchard) and humiliated daily.

The ancient Greeks he read about in his beloved Plutarch despised all the arts for robbing citizens of the leisure they needed for thinking, on the principle that thought was the proper engagement of the free. When Rousseau the apprentice spent time he owed his master on other activities, it was, at least initially, only to do craft-related things 'qui avoient pour moi l'attrait de la liberté'—engraving his medallions, for instance. The theft of time once committed, other thefts naturally followed, accompanied by new vices. What mattered in all this was the exercise of choice, a vital component in the liberty Rousseau had enjoyed as a child and regarded as his birthright. He later noted his 'mortelle aversion pour tout assujettissement', commenting that 'j'étais fait pour aimer l'indépendance et pour n'en abuser jamais'.[75] Clearly, this goal was not incompatible with the demands of practical training in a craft that made use of his 'gout vif pour le dessin' (which may remind us of his statement in the *Confessions* that 'une seule feuille de beau papier à dessiner me tente plus que l'argent pour en payer une rame'),[76] and where using tools was almost like a continuation of childhood play; but as he still felt like a child, he resented being plunged into the adult world of work, with all its implications of duty and obedience.

According to the terms laid down by the guild and specified in the documents relating to Rousseau's own apprenticeship, the master was to have charge not just of his apprentice's practical education, but of his religious and moral one as well, conditions that Ducommun seems to have been temperamentally unsuited to meeting. Craftsmen taking on apprentices generally acted *in loco parentis*, housing them as well as providing their craft training, though it was in practice possible for these duties to be split between parent and master, the one supplying bed and board for one to two years and the other finishing the term. In such cases the total dues obviously varied. Rousseau's contract, in the effective

[74] *Confessions*, I.31.   [75] *Confessions*, I.122.   [76] *Confessions*, I.36.

absence of a father, specified a single payee to whom three sums of a
hundred livres were due annually, along with an initial extra payment of
two louis d'or. There was an additional indemnity if the apprentice did
not complete his apprenticeship.[77] Rousseau ran away from Geneva
after being accidentally locked out of the city in spring 1728, three
months before his sixteenth birthday, which put him in breach of contract. He stayed away. Yet his taste for drawing had helped the apprenticeship start well, even though he was never very good at it. The
problem was not apprenticeship as such, much though he might have
preferred some more demanding type of engraving than the sort done
for watchmakers, but the degree of constraint he suffered under Ducommun and the latter's repeated acts of physical violence. His sense of
imprisonment, indeed, was such as to assume in Rousseau's eyes the
same proportions as the disenchantment at Bossey, to be repaired only
by flight.

Being locked out of Geneva became for him the radical exclusion it
did not represent for the friends who were with him, because it symbol-
ised the ultimate breach with essential freedom, to be turned to positive
account only by becoming the *way* to freedom—not the kind he had
known in Geneva before he was put to work, but a fresh start entirely. He
promised himself that he would again be as independent as he had been
in the apparently structured, but actually directionless, life of the Bernard
household, while by leaving Ducommun's workshop he would be resum-
ing the passionately Republican ways he says his upbringing and reading
of Plutarch and others had instilled in him. Promenade 6 of the *Rêveries
du promeneur solitaire* attempts to show why the sense of duty on which
much social and moral conduct rests was repugnant to him, even though
it seems an inevitable part of any work contract, formal or informal; he
returned to this theme in his old age precisely because it had struck him
so powerfully in adolescence. Traineeship on Ducommun's terms was tyr-
anny, something he was no more prepared to endure than his heroes in
antiquity had been. What mattered was the moral faculty of choice, not
coercion. When he returned from Bossey he might have taken advantage
of the laxness of his uncle ('homme de plaisir, ainsi que mon père')[78] and
the unworldliness of his devout aunt, but neither he nor his inseparable
companion Abraham acquired any of the bad habits leisure could have
tempted them into. He was far from being 'oisif'—he would have much
to say about 'oisiveté' in later life—, 'car de la vie nous ne le fumes moins';
the boys simply spent their time harmlessly, and perhaps productively,
playing.

---

[77] See Ritter, *Famille et jeunesse*, p. 183.   [78] Ritter, *Famille et jeunesse*, p. 25.

This responsible use of freedom contrasted with the libertinage he attributes to his brother François, given a similarly unstructured education, and matches the state he had experienced earlier in life when, instead of being sent to school, he somehow discovered reading.[79] It was a pastime he shared with his father in his workshop or at bedtime, never playing with other children outside, and never misbehaving apart from once using an old neighbour's stockpot as a 'pissoir'.[80] When not with his father he sat with his doting aunt Suzanne, who would die at the age of nearly ninety-three (only three years before her nephew), watching her embroider and listening to her singing, both activities that would stay with him:[81] he attributes his passion for music to these scenes from childhood, and the weaving of his ribbons was perhaps partly stimulated by the memory of her needlework. The need to keep his hands busy in some way or another was one that stayed with Rousseau throughout his life.

Later in his career, the 'jeu du burin' would be replaced by a 'jeu de la plume', one type of copying by another, the lettering the apprentice reproduced from pattern books giving way to the musical symbols he would earn his living transcribing. Here, as with craft apprenticeships, the beginner learnt his trade by imitation, and the practice remained invariable. Engraving was modest work that might, in its very limitation, either satisfy its practitioner or, if he was ambitious, seem less than fulfilling. Rousseau never became an official master as 'graveur pour l'horlogerie', yet it could have given him a lifetime's satisfaction, he later said. 'Rien n'étoit plus convenable à mon humeur ni plus propre à me rendre heureux, que l'état tranquille et obscur d'un bon artisan, dans certaines classes surtout, telles qu'est à Genève celle des graveurs.'[82]

It might easily have happened, too, had he been apprenticed to a better master. So Rousseau says, at least; but escape meant that he experienced the opposite of what he had imagined, that happy anticipated state when 'Bientôt oublié, sans doute, j'aurois été regretté du moins aussi longtems qu'on se seroit souvenu de moi.'[83] What separates our later view of Rousseau from his own perception here is one of scale: the sheer proportions of the life and work to come in the different, more creative craft of writing. Yet the physical act of writing or lettering in a traditional craftlike sense, doing as engravers did, would be a lifelong engagement in other ways he did not then foresee: the act of setting symbols down with equal beauty and a sense of lasting fitness, a different

---

[79] Ritter, *Famille et jeunesse*, pp. 8–9.
[80] Ritter, *Famille et jeunesse*, p. 10.
[81] Ritter, *Famille et jeunesse*, p. 11.
[82] Ritter, *Famille et jeunesse*, p. 43.
[83] Ritter, *Famille et jeunesse*, p. 44.

kind of craft from Ducommun's, but possibly as useful. This profession let him live in safety as doer rather than thinker, as (music) copyist, not creator, practising inscription in ways that seemed, at least to him, to outstrip by far what he had come to call the unfitness of all literary penmanship. The saving grace of scribal work was that it spared him persecution, blocking out the perils of free-ranging thought, bringing him a workaday fulfilment of the kind his craftsmen forebears knew. Its very limitation was a reassurance.

2

Writing (Down) Music

EARLY HANDWORK

The fixedness and ubiquity of print explain why Rousseau's enemies believed they had to burn or pulp his books to end his influence and destroy the heresies he advocated. They banished him as well, and thought their act entirely rational: for writers 'obviously' stood for what they said and wrote, unless (like Voltaire, often, and Diderot, sometimes) they signalled their ironic distance from it. So Rousseau would be punished comprehensively for writing, with sincerity, works that set a challenge to authority, anchored in the general mind by print and publication. A later age might view these matters differently. The electronic world that Rousseau would have hated makes every text seem transient, provisional, the 'processing' of words now rendering what we write impersonal, detached, with script's solidity put everywhere in question by the flickering screen, and cultivating 'hands', or owning fountain pens, seen almost as aberrancy, as quaint as tatting. Even terms like 'digital' and 'digitize' are close to losing the essential link with fingers etymology enshrines: if 'pen-pusher' and 'pen-pushing' keep it just alive, 'livrier' and 'escrivaillerie' cannot.

How many writers, then, will find it poignant that so little in the modern world is *felt*, felt tangibly as it is written, is so seldom set down with the agency of hands as Rousseau knew it? Who may call themselves attentive to the angle of the nib on the page, the finger's pressure on the pen or pencil, when processing a text requires the barest contact between hand and keys, so separating us from writing as a physical engagement, an intense material enactment? It may, of course, be sheer naivety to think that feeling different forms and substances with and in the hand, watching ink flow from the nib, or sensing paper's texture as we write upon it, can affect the way our thoughts themselves are formed; but it may not be. Perhaps it does not matter that this writing hand of ours is literally unique, as singular as a fingerprint on paper, and that we impoverish ourselves if we stop using it; but possibly it does. Can strings of words still seem like firm commitments that are weighed up, set down, and considered, with a sense of their integrity and lasting fitness for the expressive task we ask of them? Will electronic writing ever match that sense of rightness an engraver or calligrapher experiences in giving shape to script? Are we close to losing touch (a poignant phrase) with words as forms of physical and moral bond? Can I 'give' my word and ask that it be taken as a guarantee, if not for all time, then for longer than it takes to say or write it down?

What, indeed, have words themselves become when texts can be 'predicted' electronically as though transcendent powers were thinking and transmitting thought for us, where we possess a 'virtual' publication only as Proust said we may possess another person when we make love to them—at least if we are men—when actually we possess nothing? What would he or Rousseau make of the sheer 'virtualism'[1] of a world in which we take our leave of matter and material in favour of the pallid spectre of a 'knowledge' economy? Predictive text is just as distant from the substance of our wills and actions, inevitably undermining authorial independence; for writing that may be anticipated is a cliché, a *stereotype* in literal terms, the printer's dropping of a matrix onto molten metal to produce a fixed, unchanging form. Rousseau is far from granting anyone the freedom to supply or guess his discourse, so far from being predictive (or predictable), indeed, that he replaces the expected term or word with a more harmonious one simply for the sake of euphony, even at the cost of technical correctness. Predictive text impoverishes, as clichés do, by silencing the author's personal voice. Rousseau would have seen it as confirming all his reservations about modernity and progress.

The writer's hand, in all the ambiguity of the phrase, defines his nature. Yet *Emile* calls the teaching of handwriting trifling,[2] and the *Confessions* never tells us when its author learned to write: perhaps he does not know it, any more than he seems certain when he learned to read (apparently long before he began his only period of semi-formal education at the age of nine, at Bossey). The likelihood is that his father or his aunt Suzanne taught him the alphabet and thus manuscript. Much later he would claim that he wrote legibly only when he copied, which is far from true: the 'unreadable' annotations he apologized for making to a botanical book lent to him by the abbé de Pramont are far from indecipherable,[3] and even the most heavily revised drafts of his literary works may be read without much difficulty, particularly in contrast with the manuscripts of

[1] On this word, see Matthew Crawford, *The Case for Working with Your Hands* (London: Penguin/Viking, 2010), p. 3.

[2] *Emile*, O.C., IV.358.

[3] See A. Matthey Jeantet, *L'Ecriture de Jean-Jacques Rousseau* (Le Locle: Courvoisier, 1912), p. 28, to abbé de Pramont, April 1778; also Henry Cheyron, ' "L'Amour de la botanique". Les Annotations de Jean-Jacques Rousseau sur la *Botanique* de Régnault', *Littératures*, 4 (1981), pp. 53–95, esp. p. 54.

his disciple Bernardin de Saint-Pierre. But Rousseau did, on surviving evidence, have two or three distinct hands,[4] one rapid and compact, with the letters close to one another, another looser and more expansive, and a third, intermediate, style, mostly adopted in some letters he seems to have written reflectively and calmly, without the crutch of a preliminary draft. Although there are clear variations over time, no extant manuscript lets us, say, compare a Bossey hand with a later Paris one, though there are periods when his script relates to a more clearly established norm—the rather mannered flourish of the chancery style he had to use as secretary to the French ambassador to Venice in the early 1740s, for instance. Overall, though, Rousseau's hand may be called a fine round one, an 'écriture XVIIIᵉ siècle'.[5]

His aborted training meant he lacked the expertise to earn a secure living on the journey he began after being locked out of Geneva, and so required protection. For someone who would claim, as he declared throughout his life, that he had always been a child at heart, and remained one until old age,[6] the state of real or affected innocence mattered. So to his many protectors, in adolescence as later, he was 'Petit': his protectress Mme de Warens would give him the name (and he gave her that of 'Maman' in return),[7] worried that he was too young to go from Annecy to Turin alone; her counterpart in Turin, Mme Basile, though possibly reciprocating some of his feelings for her, and the Comte de Gouvon, who also looked after him in the city, called him a child, and he accordingly told them his 'petite histoire' and employed his 'petit talent' in their service. Yet 'mon enfance ne fut point d'un enfant'.[8] Does this explain why he would live his childhood later on? '[Q]uoique né homme à certains égards j'ai été longtemps enfant et je le suis encore à beaucoup d'autres',[9] he says in the Confession. Later on there is a shift, his mistress (later wife) Thérèse becoming his 'Petite' with whom he goes on 'petits promenades champêtres' and shares 'de petits goûtés'.[10]

The 'petits talens' he could advertise, like the 'petite histoire' he would recurrently relate to impressionable women on his travels, the 'petit babil'[11] he entertained them with, was appealing in its modesty, but insufficient for his long-term prospects. In Turin, '[je] songeai à mon ancien

---

[4] See Ritter, *Famille et jeunesse*, p. 186.
[5] See Matthey Jeantet, *Écriture*, pp. 10–11; Ritter, *Famille et jeunesse*, p. 28.
[6] See *Dialogues*, I.800.
[7] 'Maman' was the name often used in Rousseau's time for the mistress of the household (Ritter, *Famille et jeunesse*, p. 6, n. 1). Diderot's letters to his fiancée Toinette Champion also address her as 'Maman', however.
[8] *Confessions*, I.62.   [9] *Confessions*, I.174.
[10] *Confessions*, I.333.   [11] *Confessions*, I.73.

metier; mais je ne le savois pas assez pour aller travailler chez un maitre, et
les maitres n'abondoient pas à Turin'.[12] He struck lucky with Mme Basile,
who fetched him goldsmith's tools to execute the 'petit travail' he had
been given, engraving letters or devices on her silverware: 'petit', but all
the same important. Marking family plate in this way was not just a useful
precaution against theft, but also something that, done better than Rousseau
was capable of doing it, added value to the objects: crests and heraldic
motifs, for example, advertised a family's proud origins or the social progress
it had made. The brevity of Rousseau's apprenticeship may have saved him
from more mundane chores such as cutting names on tankards, whips, dog
collars, and so forth, but the time he spent in the Basile house was also too
short for him to move beyond the modest tasks his hostess gave him. Her
husband inopportunely returned and Rousseau was ejected.

The interest he later showed in commissioning engraved plates[13] and
vignettes for his books suggests that he might have relished further visual
and manual challenges as a craftsman engraver, doing as beginners did and
building up a notebook full of ornaments and scripts, coats of arms and
flourishes. By the time he told Tronchin about the craftsman's life he
should have led he may have quite forgotten all the drudgery it often
meant, remembering those early times with pure nostalgia, regretting all
the slow and careful work that at the time had seemed a tedious chore. The
greater goal was sacrificed when he fled Geneva.

Not that finishing his training would necessarily have made of him a
Ducommun, with or without the brutality. There were other possibilities.
He might have found himself a place in the busy milieu of a man like Rey,
his future publisher, selecting type or planning page layout, deciding
where to put the vignettes and the 'printer's lace' (or 'flowers'),[14] and in
what proportions, or settling the other aspects of design and execution
towards which Rousseau's correspondence shows his sensitivity. And
though his pupillage was broken off, it had still given him a grounding in
some basic skills that later would be carried over to his working life in
other spheres, as scribe to aristocrats in Turin, to ambassador in Venice,
and to *haute bourgeoisie* in Paris and at Chenonceaux, and, beyond all
that, the honest, needful work as copyist and author. The care with which
he made his calligraphic copies of *La Nouvelle Héloïse* for a pair of lady

---

[12] *Confessions*, I.73.
[13] On this matter generally, see Philip Stewart, *Engraven Desire: Eros, Image and Text in
the French Eighteenth Century* (Durham, NC, and London: Duke University Press, 1992),
and Nathalie Ferrand (ed.), *Traduire et illustrer le roman au XVIIIᵉ siècle* (Oxford: Voltaire
Foundation, 2011).
[14] See Juliet Fleming, 'How to Look at a Printed Flower', *Word and Image*, 22 (2006),
pp. 165–87.

readers had been bred in him, however casual his apprenticeship, by early training in the art of cutting numerals and letters in a substance (metal) that endured correction and revision less easily than the printed or hand-written page.[15]

When a guest of Mme Basile's offered to give Rousseau lessons in accountancy to make him useful in the family business, he reacted with the scornful pride he subsequently showed the Comte de Montaigu, whose secretary he rather reluctantly became in Venice. The affinity he later described himself as feeling with the 'peuple', whose sweated labour made the goods that fed an idle, pampered world, is not much evidenced by his own activities in early life, from engraving plate to serving in what he regarded as a degrading capacity in a Turin patrician's house, which he quickly left. The hand's work is an ambiguous quantity: manual is not menial, and no craftsman or son of craftsman ever wants to be a drudge. Rousseau stressed his right to be respected from the time in early boyhood when he thought his Bernard aunt was implicitly demoting him in social terms because he lived in artisanal Saint-Gervais rather than the 'haute ville' like his cousin Abraham: whatever the geographical location, he was still by birth a 'citoyen de Genève' and thus a member of the highest class the small republic knew, a member of the Souverain or Conseil général which passed the laws and elected magistrates.[16] Even as a boy, the fourth Promenade of the *Rêveries* recalls, he knew the dignity as well as the pure functionality of hands as tools in manufacture, a word proclaiming the ambiguity of what it named. In that world automata had not yet assumed every function once performed by human bodies.

MÉTIERS

The same Promenade reminds us indirectly, as the *Encyclopédie* entry 'Métier' also does, that the latter word designated both trade (craft) and machine (loom), and through them activities Rousseau jibbed at if they signalled social inferiority—rough trades, depersonalizing looms, things marking the degree to which a society had become or was becoming industrial in the eighteenth century. Any loom enabled its operative to do mechanically much that had formerly been done by skilled, practised hands, practised to the extent that what they did was virtually automatic. They were hardly craftsman's hands, admittedly, for they were trained at

---

[15] However, Rousseau, who was not always careful, was constantly erasing mistakes when copying music scores.

[16] See Launay, *Rousseau écrivain politique*, p. 34.

best to be efficient, not independently constructive; but their motions still betrayed much hidden knowledge. A case in point is the skill Rousseau describes in the fourth Promenade, a hand movement familiar to weavers that the ingenuity of Vaucanson would soon exclude altogether from the process of clothmaking: feeling fabric as it was being woven on the loom, to check the tension of the threads and thus the closeness of the weave.[17] In his cousin's Pâquis manufactory the young Jean-Jacques's hand was not so much inexpert as unlucky, caught within the mechanism and so badly crushed that two of his fingernails were torn off.[18] For the experienced weaver, the hand's memory—a phenomenon also discussed in Diderot's *Neveu de Rameau*, but from another angle[19]—would have prevented such an accident.

Yet the automation of the weaving process some years later, though considerable,[20] was still insufficient to satisfy everyone, including, perhaps, the critic whose approval mattered most: Louis XV, unhappy at the variable quality of French silk production, made it clear that he wanted the whole process regularised, which could be done only by excluding the already limited human factor described. Vaucanson therefore added a refinement to the loom's mechanism that enabled the threads to be mechanically maintained at a constant tension, and later on made the situation for human operatives even worse—or better, from another point of view—by designing looms (powered by donkeys) that were capable of weaving, automatically, complex patterns of flowers and birds.[21] Machines, of course, remain indifferent to those tactile aspects of creation through which the maker's individuality is expressed. It is a principle that mattered to Rousseau.

His image of handwork as the activity above all others that would have brought him real fulfilment is both homespun and romanticised, a combination mirrored in the various arts and crafts movements since his day. For the teenage boy just escaped from labour in Ducommun's workshop, unsure of what lay ahead, work did not immediately present itself as a need of any kind; support was what he wanted when his life took a turn he disliked (being sent by Mme de Warens later on to the seminary in Turin, for example), and jobs never seemed a priority if subsistence could

---

[17] Textiles were Switzerland's first important manufacturing industry, going back to the Middle Ages: silk was processed in Zurich and the cloth made in Fribourg, while the linen and cotton industries were focused on Saint Gallen.

[18] *Rêveries du promeneur solitaire*, I.1036.

[19] Diderot, *Le Neveu de Rameau*, *O.C.*, III.9.

[20] See Diderot's entry 'Bas'; also A. Labour and A. Weber, *Le Bas*, CIBA, 56 (November 1964), p. 1962 (on Hindret).

[21] See Sennett, *Craftsman*, p. 87.

be assured by some other means. Forced to leave the Basile household, he
allowed his protectress to find him paid employment elsewhere, with the
one implied condition that it should not be servile.[22] The lackey's position
he obtained in the household of the Comtesse de Vercellis was lightened
in his eyes only by the fact that he was not obliged to wear a livery there,
his uniform being 'à peu près un habit bourgeois'. Together with his work
as the Comtesse's scribe (which he put himself up for by showing her letters he had written to Mme de Warens), this was reassuring to his sense of
self-worth. While on the one hand her lack of human sympathy for Rousseau prevented the countess, as he writes, from seeing him as anything
more than a menial, on the other he made it plain to her household that
'je n'étais pas à ma place'.

Was he really so misplaced, though? In terms of his bourgeois Genevan
birth, yes, but no in that he had left Geneva far behind, and the evidence
of his status and accomplishments since then did not promote his claim
very effectively. When the Comtesse died of cancer, all the carefully accu-
mulated evidence of his superiority was washed away by the painful and
much discussed circumstance of the stolen ribbon.[23] Whether or not his lie
was the product of earlier mistreatment (the brutality of Ducommun, to
which he ascribed his new tendency to be devious) cannot now be settled;
perhaps his subsequent contrition shows that the episode was essentially
foreign to his moral nature, perhaps not. In any case, he still felt humiliated at having to accept a position in the house of the Comte de Gouvon
immediately after, even though the falsely incriminated Marion may never
have found a decent situation again, her sex in every sense less protected
than his. Rousseau's flagging sense of self-worth was boosted, all the same,
by the occasion[24] on which, at a Gouvon family dinner, he—again spared
the ignominy of wearing livery—proved better able to translate their Latin
motto for the assembled company than a family member was himself.[25]
Did his involuntarily spilling water on the lap of the young daughter of the
house on the same occasion simply underline the disparity between mind
and hand? He might have argued so.

An ambiguous episode, then; but the *Confessions*, and Rousseau's life in
general, describe the hurt, misdirected, or deceiving hand at least as much
as the hand triumphant and felicitous. The crushed fingers of the fourth
Promenade measure the extent and limitation of human dexterity, manual 'feel', in a world where machinery has begun the irreversible shift from
domestic to industrial economy, while the erotic hand that seals a boy's

---

[22] *Confessions*, I.80.   [23] *Confessions*, I.84–7.
[24] See also Jean Starobinski, *La Relation critique* (Paris: Gallimard, 1970), pp. 98–154.
[25] *Confessions*, I.95.

passive sexual identity (Mlle Lambercier spankâs him, thrillingly)[26] later defines an old man's sensitive caressing, a gentleness that made him, as Thérèse Le Vasseur insisted, a much better lover than the young Boswell.[27] The errant hand that stole a ribbon in the Vercellis house, or took apples from Ducommun's store, became the artist's hand that copied (letters, music) or originated literature, though some might argue that it never really proved a craftsman's hand except in mastering penmanship, hence manuscript. Later that same hand loved drawing flowers, however unskilfully, picking, pressing, and dissecting them for herbaria or a young girl's botanical education, while the hand that wove ribbons for young mothers also played the keyboard, expressing the passionate love of music which Rousseau says he owed to the aunt who brought him up. The hand both real and metaphorical marks every stage of his life, sometimes gloriously, often not.

All the senses bar one have their specific organ—smell has the nose, sound the ear, sight the eye, and taste the tongue; but our whole body registers the tactile. If this makes touch our most universal sense, it may also weaken our awareness of its particularity. It has been endowed with magical properties over the ages (the king's touch one such instance, the laying on of hands to cure scrofula mirroring Christ's miraculous interventions), although the old guild master's assaying of metals by the hands-on method of squeezing and rolling them in order to test their purity and power of resistance was clearly more pragmatic. By Rousseau's day belief in the magic hand was regarded, at least among the educated, as mere superstition, a mark of credulousness rather than of scientific faith in material sensory power.[28]

Touch is unquestionably the craftsman's primary sense; sight, hearing, smell, and taste are subordinate to it. Kant thought touch to be the window to the mind, and it provides a ready metaphor for abstract actions—*shaping* language, *feeling* rhythm, *handling* arguments, *moulding* attitudes, operations that Rousseau, significantly but unpersuasively, often claimed to find supremely difficult. Machines remain unmoved by those tactile aspects of creation, the feel of wood or marble, for example, through which the maker's individuality is expressed. Or, in a different craft, this: the centring of clay on the potter's wheel, bringing the small ball to the right state for throwing, the ripple of movements from hand and wrist

---

[26] *Confessions*, I.15: 'Qui croiroit que ce châtiment d'enfant receu à huit ans de la main d'une fille de trente a décidé de mes gouts, de mes desirs, de mes passions, de moi pour le reste de ma vie…?'.

[27] See Chapter 6, and *C.C.*, XXVIII.347–8.

[28] On this theme more generally, see Constance Classen (ed.), *The Book of Touch* (Oxford and New York: Berg, 2005).

accompanied by an inclination of the head and neck, with a slight tautening of the shoulders: these are effects whose cause and purpose are less easy to describe than to feel, but where the sense of touch is more closely involved than that of sight, even than the workings of the brain. The hands acquire a voice for what may otherwise remain both inarticulate and unarticulated.

There is a more everyday illustration of this manual poetry, if one that we can only imagine a Rousseau *de nos jours* practising. The variable point of the lead pencil, an instrument invented in the nineteenth century, offers endless calligraphic possibilities: sharp and hard, soft and yielding, clear in outline, shaded and feathered, fine with upstroke, broad with downstroke, all these effects and many more; but the basic act of sharpening the lead may bring its user sensuous fulfilment to match any of these operations. The set of movements it requires has long been familiar to writers, draughtsmen, and artists, and affords both tactile pleasure and aesthetic satisfaction: angling the penknife's blade with exquisite skill, cutting wood and lead cleanly and at a perfectly judged angle, testing the fineness of the point against the fingertip, giving an effortlessly elegant trajectory to the shavings as they fall into a basket—there is a simplicity and perfection in this little arc of exactitude connected with something craftsmanlike that Rousseau would have recognized, the use of a simple tool to repair and refine another in an operation correlating functional and sensory response in a small but vital ritual. Cutting the quill, with the significantly named penknife, was perhaps the nearest eighteenth-century equivalent.

The extended *Encyclopédie* entry 'Plume à écrire' reminds its reader of the central part the latter has played in Western culture since the Middle Ages, and tells the novice who does not prefer the steel-nibbed pen (as Rousseau, to judge by his manuscripts, usually did) how to customize it. Information of this kind was also contained in the printed guides on writing and lettering available in his day, and as an apprentice engraver he would have been familiar with them: they provided samples of script to be imitated and instructions on how to space and join letters, execute up- and downstrokes, make ink channels in nibs with a slitter—various sizes of which are also illustrated in the plates accompanying the *Encyclopédie* entry 'Ecriture (art méchanique)'—, cut oblique, pointed, and round nibs or quill ends for different hands, sit for writing (similarly in both sexes), position arms and legs, grip writing instrument, and so on. The plate of a young man writing that illustrates the entry 'Ecriture' incidentally places Paillasson's *Art d'écrire* within easy reach of his desk, though no such aid is shown in the companion plate of a young woman. The omission may or may not be significant: had the engravings been designed to illustrate the markedly anti-feminist *Emile*, it surely would have been.

WORK AND LEISURE

After he returned from the Turin catechumens' seminary he had been
sent to by Mme de Warens in order to convert to Catholicism, Rousseau
would resume the type of clerk's work he had so ignominiously done
for Masseron, though in different circumstances and to different ends.
Having settled with Maman outside Chambéry in Les Charmettes, he
began a job with the Chambéry Surveyor's Office, which had been
charged by Victor Amédée II of Savoy with recording landowners' properties for tax purposes. Rousseau did not dislike this employment,
though he exaggerates its duration—two years, he claims, but in fact he
left after eight months to start teaching music. There is some evidence
that his father was concerned enough about his son's lack of profession
at this time to write him an admonitory letter about it, for Jean-Jacques
drafted a reply which pointed out with some sharpness that becoming a
craftsman depended on completing an apprenticeship, that apprenticeships cost money—Isaac had illicitly spent the interest on all the money
his wife had left her two sons before their majority—,and that the
apprenticeship he had in fact started in Geneva had not been to his
taste.[29] So he continued living the contented life he had fallen into on
returning from Turin, and once he and his protectress Maman had made
Les Charmettes, their permanent summer home he devoted himself to
various 'petites occupations'[30] that filled the day without upsetting his
tranquillity, describing their various exertions simply as amusements—
essentially, gardening[31] (the survey he worked for in Chambéry records
the garden's exact measurements), reading, and sometimes harvesting
produce. In the second *Dialogue* he observes that he cannot 'rester oisif
sans souffrir', and 'passerait volontiers toute sa vie à bêcher dans un
jardin' provided he could daydream to his heart's content and never be
made to think rationally.[32] He undertook relatively little hard physical
exertion in the course of his life because of various undiagnosed and
probably psychosomatic conditions;[33] the real digging he would do,
down and down through the living roots of human growth and habit,
was with the pen.

No paid work at this earlier stage, then, but a stretch of apparent economic and emotional sufficiency. The *Confessions* contrasts their 'petite
maison' and 'petit ménage champêtre' with the 'prison' of the Chambéry

---

[29] *C.C.*, I.29–33 (end Autumn 1735).   [30] *Confessions*, I.231.
[31] *Confessions*, I.231, 233, 237, 239. He may also have gardened at the Hermitage, a
property of Mme d'Epinay's at which he later lodged.
[32] *Dialogues*, I.845.   [33] *Confessions*, I.227–8, 248.

apartment, which Maman kept on to ensure the continuance of her landlord the Comte de Laurentis' goodwill: her 'petite pension' from the Crown apparently depended on it. For Mme de Warens, of course, no more did any paid work than her protégé. What would worry Rousseau increasingly as their life together continued were her ruinous attempts to earn money by setting up manufactories and becoming a 'grosse fermière', schemes that met an inevitable doom. At heart it hardly seemed to matter, though: as the stirring opening to Book 6 of the *Confessions* reveals, Rousseau spent most of his time simply being happy.

If part of the pleasure was that of frank inactivity, a bliss that became the template for other forms of absolute contentment, it seemed to run counter to the ethos he implicitly proposed elsewhere and for others, as when, for example, in a letter to Malesherbes of 28 January 1762 he launched his familiar attack on 'tous ces tas de désœuvrés payés de la graisse du people pour aller six fois la semaine bavarder dans une academie'[34]—those same academicians who would later (negatively) decide the fate of his revolutionary scheme for musical notation.[35] Yet though exploiting no peasant, he had nonetheless lived with and off a woman whose own wealth had been acquired, not by labour, but in the form of a royal pension that could only by stretching definitions be described as earned, since she had simply been charged to make converts to the Roman Catholic faith of King Victor Amédée II. Conversely, Rousseau's later professions of personal 'oisiveté' fail to account for the fact that he produced an enormous body of work over a relatively short writing career.

As he makes clear elsewhere, his idleness at Les Charmettes was anyway relative. He undertook a serious programme of self-education, working with an intensity sharpened by the hypochondriacal conviction that he had not long to live, though the deeper implications of the following admission seem not to have struck him: 'réellement il est singulier que je n'ai jamais fait de grandes maladies à la campagne'. He compares the comparative leisure he enjoyed there with the fitful but nagging round of duties in Annecy, where Maman had previously lived. While claiming that 'Je passois mon tems le plus agréablement du monde', he had in fact constantly been involved in business he found disagreeable: 'C'étoient des projets à rédiger, des mémoires à mettre au net, des recettes à transcrire; c'étoient des herbes à trier, des drogues à piler, des alambics à gouverner',[36] in the intervals of fielding hangers-on, charlatans, and other importunates.

---

[34] *O.C.*, I.1143 (to Malesherbes, 28 January 1762).   [35] *Confessions*, I.285.
[36] *Confessions*, I.109. For more details on her financial and other enterprises see Albert de Montet, 'Mme de Warens et le pays de Vaud', Mélanges, Société d'histoire de la Suisse romande, seconde série, vol. III (Lausanne: Georges Bridel, 1891), pp. 1–254.

This aggrieved playing along with the fantasies of a woman constantly engaged in empty business may have lessened by the time they began to spend time at Les Charmettes, but the folk remedies and what Rousseau otherwise regarded as useless fabrications continued occupying their time.

For, somehow, against his better judgement, he was drawn into Maman's world of potions and nostrums, as he attempted to make invisible ink. Why this project? He never explains; but his efforts ended with an explosion that temporarily blinded him, if not for as long as the six weeks the *Confessions* suggests. His interest in such processes remains mysterious. It might perhaps have fitted in with the concept of an acceptable brand of semi-science corresponding with the mood of the times, one connected with invisible powers, mystical energies, fluid growth and change, everything, in short, that the 'hard', disenchanting, real universe abhorred. Was unreadable writing also linked subliminally with the world of as yet unavowed or invisible fantasy, the world of wonder he later explored as a writer? Had he simply become infected by Mme de Warens's fascination with futile recipes? Was he anticipating his future diplomatic career, where hidden deals and half avowed enterprise would be the order of the day? Was making invisible ink simply a way of obscurely denying the humble secretarial jobs he had just done? All are just about possible; none seems at all probable. The *Encyclopédie* entry preceding that for 'Encre sympathique', on 'Encre noir à l'usage de l'imprimerie', may alert its reader to what would later be Rousseau's obsession with the blackness of type in his published works, but it would be highly provocative, to say the least, to link the contrasting idea of invisible ink with the authoritarian attempts to censor certain types of writing made in Rousseau's own day, as his own would be suppressed. More poetically, we might contrast their often very public nature, Rousseau's defiant refusal to deny authorship of anything he wrote, with the comparative invisibility achieved by other writers, including Diderot and, with qualifications, Voltaire. Rousseau was the least invisible writer of his times, no matter what efforts were made to silence (blind) him or wipe out the evidence of his writing.

REPRODUCTIONS

He had already made his first paid attempt at the particular kind of inscription that would be his permanent adult profession: not the copying of documents, extracts, and letters such as he did in Turin and would later do in Venice and France, but the copying of music. The *Confessions* places this momentous occurrence in Lyon, where the adolescent Rousseau, blithely singing a cantata as he walked along, had caught the ear of a cleric: 'Il me demande si je n'ai jamais copié de la musique? Souvent, lui dis-je, et cela étoit vrai; ma meilleure maniére de l'apprendre étoit d'en copier. Eh bien, me dit-il; je pourrai vous occuper quelques jours durant lesquels rien ne vous manquera pourvu que vous consentiez à ne pas sortir de la chambre. J'acquiesçai très volontiers, et je le suivis'.[37] Yet 'il faut avouer que j'ai choisi là dans la suite le métier du monde auquel j'étois le moins propre', since his inattentiveness led to countless omissions, duplications, transpositions, and deletions—'non que ma note ne fut belle et que je ne copiasse forte nettement', but the errors and lacunae made the pieces he transcribed impossible to perform. The real craftsman is absorbed by his occupation, an absorption that is a single-minded attentiveness to what he does. Remembering his uncraftsmanlike early failings, Rousseau later remarks in the entry 'Copiste' of his *Dictionnaire de musique*:

> Il est plus important que la Musique soit nettement et correctement copiée que la simple écriture: parce que celui qui lit et médite dans son cabinet, apperçoit, corrige aisément les fautes qui sont dans son livre, et que rien ne l'empêche de suspendre sa lecture ou de la recommencer: mais dans un Concert où chacun ne voit que sa Partie, et où la rapidité et la continuité de l'exécution ne laissent le tems de revenir sur aucune faute, elles sont toutes irréparables[38]

The year was 1731; another two decades would pass before he began to earn a real living copying music. Given that the first *Discours* had by that later date won the Dijon academy prize, his unambitious choice of profession may seem surprising, though it filled a social need (as some of the copying done in his dotage—notably his handwritten version of Mézeray's history of France—did not): for much of the music composed in Rousseau's day remained unprinted and unpublished. Whether his transcription was a craft in precisely the sense implied by the *Encyclopédie*'s subtitle is perhaps unimportant; it was a safe, unprovocative, and reasonably remunerative manual activity. And, vitally, it satisfied Rousseau's artistic soul: he 'understood', felt, lived what he copied. From that first job in Lyon onwards, it was a paradigm example of the kind of pleasure that most fulfilled him, one built on the paradox of simultaneous absence and presence. Just as he felt that he would experience a sense of perfect freedom incarcerated in a prison cell, or imagine summer most vividly and completely in the depths of winter,[39] so here he stood absent from the artwork in the sense both that he copied what was not actually being

---

[37] *Confessions*, I.169. See also *Dialogues*, I.831.
[38] *O.C.*, V.735.   [39] *Confessions*, I.171–2.

performed, and also that, as its copyist, he did not generate it at first hand, but was present in the manifest particularity of any score he copied, marked with his personal touches and, occasionally, through his independent intervention, as he supplied on the copied sheets what the originator had intended to set down, but omitted or got wrong. In other words, work like this both sounded and refrained from sounding the note of originality, or any (metaphorical) note at all.

As time passed, too, this sort of occupation let him live what he called an almost automatic life, preferable by far to the upsets and sufferings of his past literary calling. 'Plus j'éxamine cet homme dans le détail de l'emploi de ses journées, dans l'uniformité de cette vie machinale, dans le goût qu'il paroit y prendre, dans le contentement qu'il y trouve, dans l'avantage qu'il en tire pour son humeur et pour sa santé; plus je vois que cette maniére de vivre étoit celle pour laquelle il étoit né.'[40] While the world takes him for a genius, a charlatan, a miracle of virtue, or a monster, 'la nature n'en a fait qu'un bon artisan [...] dont l'état habituel est et sera toujours l'inertie d'esprit et l'activité machinale [...]. Une des choses dont il se félicite est de se retrouver dans sa vieillesse à peu près au même rang où il est né, sans avoir jamais beaucoup ni monté ni descendu dans le cours de sa vie.'

When Rousseau wrote these words from the *Dialogues*, his own life had, of course, itself been copied, though in a distinctive sense: the *Confessions* presents itself as a reflective image, not a work of imagination or literariness. In that sense, obviously, all writing based on what has been experienced is a version of mimesis, working like the retina to capture (temporarily or not) and reflect back what it has perceived. Yet it interprets at the same time as reflecting, just as vision itself does. To move beyond this notion to the proposition that life itself, with all that it contains, offers only an image of something ultimate, half-intuited at best, is to embrace the metaphysical philosophy of Platonism, which Rousseau never consistently did. His religious faith, indeed, seemed to preclude it, as well as his practical need to inhabit a 'terra firma' (at least if that phrase be expanded to include water) in inhabiting the world.

It was while living at Les Charmettes that he drafted the cautionary playlet *Narcisse*, which examines the questions of copying and adapting, of truth and representation, in art as well as in life, that would preoccupy him much later on—in the first *Discours* and the *Lettre à d'Alembert sur les spectacles*, and also in the preface to *Narcisse* written over twenty years after his first conception of the play itself. In all these works there is a marked hostility towards culture and the arts, but *Narcisse* is distinctive in first

---

[40] *Dialogues*, I.849–50.

exploring issues of gender and human vanity that would concern Rousseau later, and which are here related to the matter of self-representation and presentation of the other. They are themes that would be raised again, if with a slightly altered emphasis, in *La Nouvelle Héloïse*, where Julie commissions for Saint-Preux a miniature of herself which he has an artist alter to make it less idealized, truer to life. *Narcisse* too describes the retouching of a portrait of the central character, but from the opposite point of view: here the image is beautified, made feminine so that Narcisse/Valère may legitimately fall in love with himself—a rather Marivaudian scenario in its focus on rites of testing and deceiving. (Rousseau indeed showed the sketch to an apparently approving Marivaux in 1742, when he first arrived in Paris.) The copy's link with vanity is at its essence: a portrait both gives back, like a mirror, and presents a foreign object, here the emptiness of self-regard. It makes us think of artifice contrasted with truth, of vanity not *vanitas* (the painted still-life image of perishable objects), and cautions against imitation that attempts to stabilize the transient. Yet art itself embodies this resistance, however much enactment seems to challenge it. So, fleeting music is made permanent, first in writing, then through copying: before the age of sound recording, lastingness depended on transcription. Rousseau's copies made the once heard re-presentable.

His other duplications must be considered later on—books on botany, for instance, which the seventh *Rêverie* shows him transcribing as the craze for flowers and plants repossesses him in old age,[41] and which he must copy out because he cannot now afford to buy back volumes he once owned: practical transcription, then, unlike that of Mézeray's *Histoire*,[42] copying become a *vade mecum*, an essential adjunct to his life experience. Yet Rousseau calls his new-found passion for plants and flowers an 'étude de pure curiosité'.[43] *Pure* or empty, 'pur de', voided or devoid of: emptied so that something (more essential) fills it? Needless or essential? Voiding may be vital psychologically, like the clarifying of catharsis, and fulfilling in aesthetic terms. It gives Rousseau agency in nothingness, action seeming functionless, as a child's play may seem, but necessary at some deeper level. Books, once thought dispensable, no longer are: they now serve a purpose that may lack significance for others, but for Rousseau meets a basic need. Music that has not been learnt, laid up in the heart (re*cor*ded), needs its copyist too, giving him fulfilment that is literally vital, though for others it is not: letting playful man and craftsman harmonize. Music copying as Rousseau did it was an art, and a contemporary described his

[41] *Rêveries*, I.161.
[42] See in this connection Pierre Prévost, *Lettre sur Jean-Jacques Rousseau*, in *C.C.*, XL.268.
[43] *Lettres sur la botanique*, *O.C.*, IV.1188.

transcripts thus in terms that recall first of all the unfinished apprenticeship
with an engraver, then his fondness for drawing:

> Elles ne laissaient absolument rien à désirer. Notes, paroles et signes, tout
> semblait être moins l'ouvrage de la plume que du burin [...]. Il se piquait
> même d'y mettre du luxe et de la prodigalité, s'il est permis de nommer ainsi
> l'élégance la plus recherchée. Chaque première page, après le titre, était ornée
> d'une vignette ou d'un fleuron; une belle encre rouge marquait le genre du
> morceau et faisait ressortir à l'œil les piano et les forté; les paroles étaient
> alignées sous le chant avec un réglet; un tiret proprement façonné servait à
> réunir les parties qui devaient aller ensemble. Enfin, au bout de la dernière
> page, le nombre total des mesures était rapporté, et le tout se terminait par
> un chiffre ou une signature en lettres initiales à peu près de cette manière,
> *J.R. cop.*; telle était la copie de Rousseau.[44]

No printer, it appeared, was equal to this task, perhaps unexpectedly: print,
after all, had long since freed men from the grinding labour of reproducing
manuscript.[45] But copying music was for Rousseau like a kind of play, of
literal recreation, that which restores and refreshes, *recruits* quite as much
as recreates, gives back to the subject what has been spent or lost. If *Homo
faber* makes, *homo ludens* may remake. While copying Mézeray, rewriting
him in a specific sense, re-presenting him, would occupy Rousseau's hand
pleasurably, copying music answered a more intense need: it exercised the
mind's ear and the scribe's hand at the same time, body and spirit in syn-
chrony. When Rousseau handwrote the *Histoire*, he was living far from
Paris, hence far from work; music copying meant living in or near the capital. Nowhere else, not even Lyon, let that living be made dependably. Paris
let him both copy music and botanise (he walked from city to countryside
in a matter of minutes until old age); so Paris re-awoke the need to copy
flower books. He could stay alive by copying music, and feel alive by seeing
and studying plants. Music passes, but the scribe lays hold of it; the plant
dies, but book and press preserve it.

In his 1765 *Salon*, Diderot remarks of Chardin's still lifes that they
display 'nulle verve' and 'peu de génie', but 'beaucoup de technique et de
vérité'.[46] Chardin's limitations were those of the everyday, the world of
functional painters who belonged to the Académie de Saint-Luc rather
than (or, as in Chardin's case, as well as) the Académie royale: the guild
painters, the trade painters, the sign painters, those whom a later age
might call commercial or graphic artists. Their work would have struck
Rousseau by its practicality. Engraving was another practical business, or

---

[44] Claude Eymar, quoted in *C.C.*, XXXIX.315 (on visiting Rousseau in 1774).
[45] Eisenstein, *Printing Press*, II.661.   [46] Diderot, *Salons*, XIV.118.

might be so: not when it simply re-presented pictures, but when its purpose was to mark numbers and letters, or designate ownership. Engravers in the 'higher' mode may well have feared, as Blake did, that to be a copyist was simply to be part of a mechanical process; but it was a matter of angle as well as of technique, of point of view as well as of straight mimesis (if such a thing existed), from trompe-l'œil upwards. Representationalism always meant translation, and translation never was the thing itself. The art lay in establishing a vantage point, seeking ways to represent realities as well as fantasies: the copyist must find acceptable divergences, not, as his Lyon patron told the young Rousseau, hopelessly failing to re-render the object of imitation, but making presentation personal as well as faithful, within appropriate limits.

As a writer Rousseau often emphasises inspiration, a sense of propulsion that seems to put him outside himself, driven to write and to compose; but there are other kinds of composition. A printer's compositor, for instance, set up type exactly corresponding to an author's text; his work called for simple manual translation, not intervention by the intellect, still less manual invention; for the hand, in such work, should not 'think' adaptively. Clarity and fidelity were paramount: the printer's compositor worked, as the phrase has it, at second hand, not first.

Rousseau's work as music copyist is remarkable, not merely for its beauty and (eventual) reliability, but also for the simple fact that he stuck at it. He had given up engraving and would, from the early 1760s, give up most kinds of writing, or the writing he regarded as important, but copying earned him his bread. While his *Dictionnaire de musique* calls the best copyist the most transparent one, the one who puts the minimum of self between page (score) and reader, its practitioner still had his own fingerprint, though the scribe's differed from the famous writer's. He was in fact not a scribe, but a transcriber, enhancing within acceptable boundaries the 'reality' he was re-presenting. Part of his pride as copyist was that of an artist, but part was simply that of the good workman or artisan. When Bernardin de Saint-Pierre asked him if he could not have taken on a different profession Rousseau replied very specifically:

Il n'y a point d'emploi qui n'ait ses charges. Il faut une occupation. J'aurais 100,000 livres de rente que je copierais de la musique: c'est à la fois un travail et un plaisir. D'ailleurs je ne me suis ni élevé au-dessus ni abaissé au-dessous de l'état où la fortune m'a fait naître: je suis fils d'un ouvrier et ouvrier moi-même; je fais ce que j'ai fait dès l'âge de quatorze ans.[47]

---

[47] Bernardin de Saint-Pierre, Jacques-Henri, *La Vie et les ouvrages de Jean-Jacques Rousseau*, ed. M. Souriau (Paris: Cornélie & Cⁱᵉ, 1907), p. 65.

And the second *Dialogue* confirms the sincerity of this statement: 'Travailler de la main et laisser ma tête en repos me recrée et m'amuse.'[48] The Prince de Ligne would mockingly compare this pride in doing a humble job well with that of Molière's Sganarelle (in *Le Médecin malgré lui*) making bundles of firewood,[49] but the craftsman copyist knew otherwise. Copying became the image of the moderation he wished to live his life by, a mark of his refusal to accumulate riches simply for the sake of having more (and more than other people), evidence that he was living by the principles, lay as well as religious, of Geneva and its Calvinist heritage. He copied through the days of literary fame and worldly fortune, because to do so showed commitment to a moral way of making things—not extravagantly, but with quiet method. Crafting copies, slowly, with a calligraphic art and typographic measure, let him strike the balance between work and life that would carry him through years of difficulty, proclaiming a deliberate choice of what to do and how to live. Decoration might be functionally redundant, yet its beauty counted. Ligne had seen it as a trifling matter, useless like engraving (as Emile declares that trade to be); but Rousseau found in it both pleasure and a discipline, as he did in faith itself—fruitful orthopraxis[50] that declared the soundness of useful jobs well done.

His age would come to seem the very age of duplication, of machinery that let his novels sweep through Europe and engravings of his characters proliferate beyond imagination, but with this came a loss of individuality Rousseau regretted: hence his copying by hand of fiction, letters, even life, for others and himself. Re-presenting music seemed to fit within the same tradition, though the means to print it had existed for three centuries before Rousseau became a copyist. Cochin's *Encyclopédie* entry 'Gravure', it is true, dates this innovation only to the seventeenth century, and the first example of line-engraved scores specifically to 1675, further commenting on the sheer perfection of such work in a process that is 'd'autant plus utile aujourd'hui, qu'il sert à conserver et à transmettre à la postérité les plus excellents morceaux de musique'. Yet print had never made the manual copyist redundant. The cost of engraving or otherwise mechanically producing sheet music could be prohibitive, and the human cost as well: a note possibly attributable to Dr Charles Burney in Rees's *Cyclopaedia* accounts for a decline in machine-engraved

---

[48] *Dialogues*, I.839.

[49] Prince de Ligne, *Lettres et pensées*, ed. Mme la baronne de Staël-Holstein, 2 vols. (London: B. Dulau & Co., 1809), quoted in *C.C.*, XXXVIII.323.

[50] On orthopraxis as an element in religious practice, see Mary Carruthers, *The Craft of Thought: Meditation, Rhetoric, and the Making of Images* (Cambridge: Cambridge University Press, 1998).

music in the eighteenth century in terms of humane reflection, the reluctance of clients to cause unemployment among copyists. But the entry 'Copiste' in the *Dictionnaire de musique* more pertinently comments on the disadvantages of printing what may not be sufficiently in demand to be financially worthwhile, further observing that in Italy, 'le pays de la terre où l'on fait le plus de Musique', reproducing scores mechanically had failed: 'd'où je conclus qu'au jugement des Experts celui de la simple Copie est le plus commode'. The lesson Rousseau learned in Lyon is rehearsed, emphatically and with feeling: the best copyist is simply the one whose work is the most accurate, who never sets appearance above clarity.

Rousseau certainly felt slighted by those, like Rameau, who in denying his competence as a composer[51] implicitly also denied his ability to supply missing copy in the works he transcribed: for '[le Copiste] doit [...] être exercé dans les diverses styles, reconnaître un Auteur par sa manière, et sçavoir bien distinguer ce qu'il a fait de ce qu'il n'a pas fait'. At the same time, he knew that to exercise his profession appropriately he must forget whatever creative, and sometimes even corrective, ambitions he might possess:

> Les paroles doivent être écrites bien exactement sous les Notes, et correctes quand aux accens et à l'autographe: mais on n'y doit mettre ni point ni virgule, les répétitions fréquentes et irrégulières rendant la ponctuation grammaticale impossible; c'est à la Musique à ponctuer les paroles; le Copiste ne doit pas s'en mêler.

As this self-denying ordinance shows, the machine-like regularity offered by the *Dictionnaire de musique*'s account is a virtue: creative copying is debarred for the simple reason that the copyist is subservient to the creation, required simply to transmit a work not his own.

This obviously marks a significant similarity with the world of the machine as Rousseau's society began to know it, and its converse in that of the craftsman. Mass duplication is alien to the world of craft, though broad likeness—external similarity and functional equivalence between different craftings of a given model—is assumed. Yet the evidence of Rousseau's copying underlines the fact that individuality is, in the appropriate circumstances, a selling point, not uniformity; that what we may have taken to be a modernist, post-industrial dissent from the canon of exact parity has a long history. (The ethos of Romanticism is of course discernible here.) We need, additionally, to distinguish between one

---

[51] On this, see Rousseau's letter to J.-B. Bouchard du Plessis, *C.C.*, II.87 and 88, n. E and n. e (14 September 1745).

craftsman's generic product and another's. To buy a Rousseau version of someone else's score is to buy his personal marks, the flourishes, the contrasting inks, the carefully chosen paper, and so on. As the handwritten copies of *La Nouvelle Héloïse* indicate, there is a premium attached to the author's manuscript version of a text that has also been printed and circulated, particularly in an age of duplication.

Would Rousseau have been intrigued to know, impossibly, that in the very year of his death Erasmus Darwin, whom he seems to have met in England in the mid-1760s, would send the first duplicated handwritten letter, prepared on his mechanical copying machine or 'bigrapher'?[52] (Slightly earlier, James Watt had devised a roller press that could also copy letters.) Interested, perhaps, but probably not moved. No duplicate, and certainly no eighteenth-century forebear of the carbon copy, could match his originals, the distinctive colours, the subtle gradations in the inking, the precisely angled upstrokes and downstrokes, the finely individuated calligraphic symbols.

AT SECOND HAND

The ethics and aesthetics of copying were discussed by Diderot in a dialogue Rousseau probably never read (he had fallen out with its author by the time it was drafted), but which sheds some light on the issues of sameness and difference, obedience to model and the artistic value of inspiration, that surround his career. The *Paradoxe sur le comédien* of 1769 weighs up the merits in dramatic performance of absolute identity or consistency on the actor's part against inspired variability. Uniformity wins the argument, though readers may wonder if it should: they might, for instance, insist on the potential superiority of the one-off, the stage performance that can be sublime one evening, if indifferent the next, because the price of possible indifference is worth paying when it permits occasional sublimity. Diderot's argument may loosely be described as Classical, its converse as Romantic; but the opposition might also be seen as that between automatism and habit on the one hand and, on the other, individual craftsmanship whose variability can be both a positive and a negative quantity. Louis XV wanted machine-contrived regularity from Vaucanson's constructions; others might prefer the roughness and unpredictability of the human factor. Is the latter response more or less likely in an age of highly developed technology? It all depends. Rousseau

---

[52] See Jenny Uglow, *The Lunar Men* (London: Faber, 2002), p. 306.

might have taken neither side in the *Paradoxe*'s debate, his professed view of actors as it emerges from the *Lettre à d'Alembert* of 1758 being the Plato-inspired one that all their kind, along with their audience, are hypocrites.

Other aspects of artistic realization continued to preoccupy him, some of long standing. One was the system of musical notation he brought with him to Paris in 1742, a fraught matter for Rousseau because he believed so passionately in its merits, at least until Rameau pointed out its besetting elementary weakness. Yet had it been adopted, it would surely have left him a much poorer man as a copyist than he in fact became, even, indeed, ended his preferred career altogether, forcing him to live off his own writing. The *Confessions* makes much of his numerical scheme for designating musical notes to replace the conventional symbolic one,[53] without willingly admitting to its essential disadvantage: the inferiority of numbers to pictographic symbols in vertical as well as horizontal relation to one another (having, that is, both paradigmatic and syntagmatic force). Yet according to the *Confessions* this drawback was no more evident to other members of the Académie des sciences to whom he presented his scheme than it had been to himself. Despite the setback, in any case, he first had the memorandum printed, then, he claims, successfully taught a young woman to sight-read by his method over a three-month period. 'Ce succès fut frappant, mais ignoré. Un autre en auroit rempli les journaux, mais avec quelque talent pour retrouver les choses utiles, je n'en eus jamais pour les faire valoir.'[54]

These thwarted hopes perhaps represent the second 'Heron's fountain' episode in his life, the second failure of an innovation or device to win him fortune and glory—this time, at least allegedly, a project designed for the purpose of supporting Mme de Warens.[55] The first was a failure with a mechanical contraption, the second with a theory; the first involving something given to Rousseau, the second his invention; but both alike in mystifying him, if not others. Whether or not fate or experience had been tugging him in a new direction, from apparatus to concept, from copy to idea, he apparently learned little from it. Having arrived in Paris with a musical scheme, a playlet, and a few coins, he would stay despite the insufficiency of all three as life supports. That he had earlier given up the office job in Chambéry for the sake of music—music teaching and music making[56]—seemed not much to concern him either. It was the professional rejection that stung. During his early years in

---

[53] *Confessions*, I.284. [54] *Confessions*, I.287.
[55] *Confessions*, I.271–2. [56] *Confessions*, I.189.

Paris, when he was himself establishing a reputation as a composer as well as writer, he would meet Rameau again; but a radical scepticism as well as a more straightforward sense of enquiry would alter Rousseau's attitude to music and writing. Why words? Why sounds? Practical engagement seemed simpler to maintain.

3
Art or Craft?

It was not simply Calvinists in Rousseau's day who claimed that art was dangerous: many others said (and seemingly believed) that plays should preach, pictures lecture, and novels tell a moral tale. Had these been mere theories, Rousseau would have suffered less for what he wrote. But it was a sermonizing age in which authority was quick to judge the work of art as somehow 'wrong', or not 'right' in approved ways, hence not really useful, consequently 'bad', and therefore rightly censored—bitter truths that Rousseau would discover when condemned to exile and disfavour for the irregular doctrines of both *Emile* and *Du contrat social*.

Yet art had seemed to fill his early Paris days with simple and straightforward pleasures. He wrote some brief dramatic works, went often to the theatre (if 'only' twice a week when funds were low), and played chess with Diderot and other friends. In more serious mood he and Mme Dupin's stepson Dupin de Francueil did one of Rouelle's chemistry course (Rouelle had also been Diderot's instructor in the subject). In mid-century the seriousness refocused and became more settled. Rousseau's two discourses dating from that time, the first on science and the arts (or *knowledge* and the arts), the second on inequality, read like clear correctives to his earlier optimistic view of social life. They culminated in his moving outside Paris in 1756 to work on other serious things.

Rousseau had by then begun to think of writing as more problematic than he earlier assumed, for reasons that the first *Discours* explains. His chosen theme was hardly novel: views on how man's artfulness and artistry relate to living the good life have been expressed throughout the history of culture, and Rousseau, drawn to both the invented and the natural, felt them urgently from 1749. Although his call to a new kind of Puritanism seemed fresh enough, the influence of old Calvinism lingered, and must be weighed against his evident and frank enjoyment of the arts from earlier days (pleasures he did not immediately renounce after the fateful walk to Vincennes). He wrote the operetta *Le Devin du village* in 1752, and as late as 7 September 1755 declared to Voltaire that 'si les lettres étaient maintenant anéanties, je serais privé de l'unique plaisir qui me reste', even though 'si j'avais suivi ma première vocation [in craft] et que je n'eusse lu ni écrit, j'en aurais sans doute été plus heureux'.[1] Given these uncertainties, we have to ask how seriously he meant the cautions of the *Discours sur les sciences et les arts*.

A reconsideration of *Narcisse* may help to clarify these matters. The play shows Valère's error as a sensual and aesthetic one, with strongly moral overtones: the retouched portrait, unlike Julie's 'moral' miniature in *La Nouvelle Héloïse*, will change the subject's sex but not its beauty, an ambiguity that is a part of mimesis itself. Most copies are not meant to be deceptive, obviously, though trompe-l'œil painting and 'real' counterfeits (rather than the ones Ducommun accused the young Rousseau of making) unquestionably are. The kind we see in *Narcisse*, also meant to trick, is what Barthes calls a decoy, a word that bears a heavy moral charge. The decoy's purpose is to fool and then reveal, unveil the nature of the trickery and show the person tricked, that is, the subject (Valère) who is also the object—of mockery, of art, art as a game as well as moral quantity, as skill (in artistry) but also as a blind (through artifice). The plot can be resolved only when artifice becomes an open form of art, a 'pure' mimesis.

Rousseau, however, may already be doubting whether art can ever be 'purely' anything. If he only hints at this in *Narcisse*, hesitancy will become assertion later on. Had the artwork—here the portrait—been admired disinterestedly,[2] without cupidity or sensuality, admired aesthetically, in other words, Valère's response to it might have been called objective. But is this the right, the best, or even a possible, response when we look at pictures of ourselves? Only, surely, if we do not realize who it is we contemplate. Valère does not know that he is looking at himself, yet his interest is no more objective. Perhaps, as an unwitting self-admirer, he innocently seeks a form of identification rather than, or before, painterly qualities, likeness of image before application of pigment, distinction of light and shade, conveying of perspective, and so on: the latter was what Diderot called the long view, whereas contemporaries of the sitter, like the sitter him- or herself, seek resemblance above all else.[3] Valère has only seen (and been) a decoy in this complicated business, only a disguised version of mimesis. Or perhaps, the victim of a double bluff, he has simply focused, though unconsciously, on what makes the similarity to self persuasive, since this is

---

[1] *C.C.*, III.165.   [2] Compare Scruton, *Beauty*.
[3] Diderot, *Salon* of 1763, *O.C.*, XIII.354.

what counts most for the self-lover. Surely, though, such a self-lover should know this image 'is not' him? The individual, after all (or so Rousseau claims in his *Confessions*),[4] is best suited to discerning what and who he is, since he alone has access to his inner self; painters, in contrast, are confined to the external, and even there, in Rousseau's view, they fail to really see. This explains why he disliked the portrait Allan Ramsay painted of him later on, as we shall discover.

Valère-Narcissus thinks he knows himself, but is in truth fixated on the outside view. Rousseau's play says no more about the higher demands of art and morality in this connection, which is both natural (the comedy did not seek any such depth) and provoking (because it might have let him put a subtler argument about the cultural effects of art than any offered by the *Discours sur les sciences et les arts*). Not even the late preface to *Narcisse*, the addendum he wrote to accompany its eventual premiere in 1753, chooses to develop this line of thought, despite dealing throughout with the *Discours* rather than the play itself.

He made as though to address these issues in the *Lettre à d'Alembert*, although in fact he still neglected most of them. For the moment we may simply note that in constructing drama from a renovated myth he both declared the relevance of metaphor to modern moral life and announced the place of fun, of playfulness, in culture: the play as 'jeu', a more or less straightforward game of make-believe. Or was it something much more serious after all? Rousseau's misgivings about drama developed throughout the 1750s, but in this early work he sees corrective moral action as compatible with a good joke, at least as far as Valère's sister and fiancée, the perpetrators, are concerned, an amusing hoax with serious intent, a useful action as well as a diverting one. The first goal of the plot the sister devises is to make her foolish brother quite disenchanted with himself, as the women closest to him are, make him learn to see behind his altered but bewitching image, force him to experience the unmagicking essential, in this case, to right perception: art's illusions may be pleasant, but they still require a critical assessment.

There is a moral version of this view in the *Lettre à d'Alembert*, a work whose main concern is disenchantment of the audience, not the character, and which describes a disillusion that sets in when the play is finished and the theatre left behind; 'bad' disenchantment, then, because the play itself had won the public over, made them accept moral principles they afterwards forgot. In *Narcisse*, conversely, the mistake is internal: to cure Valère of his delusion, to free him from erroneous belief, the disenchantment has to work

---

[4] *Confessions*, I.5; also p. 1149 (introduction to the Neuchâtel manuscript).

on stage. It is a different way of making drama useful (as the artwork seldom is, in Rousseau's view); but it brings no vindication of imagination, since Valère's false belief is caused by blinkered, superficial vision. Later Rousseau feels more negatively still about the power to make things up, or the inability not to succumb to imagination; he develops the intensified mistrust of art that helps explain why he returned to craft.

A fragment of another drama, *Pygmalion* (1762), presents confusion similar to *Narcisse*'s, but repositioned for a different moral and aesthetic effect. Here the artist, not his subject, is deceived by beauty, falling so in love with his marble Galathea as to think her a real woman; no deliberate trickery, then, but still a fatal self-obsession (seduction by his own mimetic powers), the same flaw, in essence, as had prompted Valère's aberration. Ten years before that, however, *Le Devin* had seemed to query art itself, or artistry with all of its deceptiveness, presenting a 'divine', a 'cunning-man',[5] whose magic spells in fact involve no more than simple common sense. This charming and successful piece thus paradoxically displays that scepticism towards art the first *Discours* had proclaimed, while handling it quite differently.

Let us return to the *Discours sur les sciences et les arts*. Perhaps our understanding of it will be helped if we take the point of view ascribed to Diderot, that Rousseau's argument against the benefits associated with the arts and sciences was the product of deliberate provocativeness, simply meant to make his contribution stand out against the more conventional views of others.[6] Diderot claims that it was he who encouraged Rousseau to adopt the dissenting course, knowing him to be a lover of paradox, but comments in his *Essai sur les règnes de Claude et de Néron* that it had also been a familiar topic in classical antiquity.[7] It was one, besides, that Rousseau could have met with in the course of his self-education programme as a young man at Les Charmettes, however far those principles seemed from the Paris life he later led. Whatever the case, its appeal for him was surely enhanced by the sumptuary prohibitions, the emphasis on self-denial and the dangers of luxury, of his Genevese upbringing. Yet, as is often said, neither the first *Discours* nor the *Discours sur l'origine de l'inégalité* five years later in fact argues the need for mankind to revert to the primitive state, even if that were possible, merely proposing that some of the benefits of

---

[5] As Dr Charles Burney's English translation of Rousseau's work calls him.
[6] On this matter, see Felicity Baker, 'La Route contraire', in *Reappraisals of Rousseau*, ed. Simon Harvey et al. (Manchester: Manchester University Press, 1980), pp. 132–62, at pp. 132–5.
[7] See also Robert Wokler, 'The *Discours sur les sciences et les arts* and Its Offspring: Rousseau in Reply to His Critics', in Harvey et al., *Reappraisals*, pp. 250–77, on its derivativeness.

civilization had been too uncritically promoted by, among others, the *philosophes*. Yet it is equally hard to deny the link between Rousseau's illumination on the way to Vincennes, his craft background, and the sense of utility and purpose that infused his writing after 1749. The same purposefulness also underlay the *Encyclopédie* project headed by Diderot, but it was the Vincennes experience that let Rousseau see, with a clarity he had not experienced before, the link between writing as pleasure and writing as human need. It did not, however, let him foresee all the force of circumstances that would tip him from art to craft in later years.

RHETORIC, TRUTH, AND WORLDLINESS

Whatever its weaknesses—and Rousseau himself was critical of the raw, unsystematic nature of its argument[8]—, the *Discours sur les sciences et les arts* displays a powerful eloquence whose origin is quite different from the college-taught linguistic skills of *philosophes* like Diderot and Voltaire,[9] past masters of the theory behind such figures as *enargeia* (visualization) and *passio* (a transport whose negative extremes Diderot depicts in Rameau's nephew and one of the Mother Superiors in *La Religieuse*). Rousseau looks more radical than Diderot, perhaps, in the way he sets about moving his reader, but uses radical intention to the conservative end of maintaining traditionalist values—values that rampant industrialism would soon call into question, and which acquire an odd elitist tinge from their counter-progressive nature. If he wanted reform, and the first and second *Discours* showed he did, it was not to be at the price of crude materialist principles. He loathed the dehumanizing machine-mindedness of modernity that many of his fellow *Encyclopédistes* supported.

In other words, in combatting the kinds of human progress that imperilled the simple man's subsistence Rousseau was proposing a democratic politics, despite the fact that this opposition might maintain a status quo that served the interests of the dominant class. His inclinations were, in fact, both revolutionary and anti-radical, a conflict that helps explain why he would often be misunderstood. He wanted a world that favoured *hoi polloi*, not capitalists, as a footnote he added to the 'Dernière réponse à Bordes' (relating to the first *Discours*) makes clear: 'l'argent qui circule entre les mains des riches et des Artistes pour fournir à leurs superfluités, est perdu pour la subsistance du Laboureur; et celui-ci n'a point d'habit

---

[8] *Confessions*, I.35–2.
[9] See John Spink, 'Rousseau and the Problems of Composition', in Harvey et al., *Reappraisals*, pp. 163–77, for a related observation.

précisément parce qu'il faut du galon aux autres'.[10] The desirable new order sometimes seemed to him identical, though it was not, to the order of nature against that of artificial aristocratic privilege. The difference lay in the divergent attitude to conservatism of these separate orders.

His uncertain allegiance leads to some logical deficiencies in the first *Discours*; yet the combination of an urgent but unschooled rhetorical intent and an as yet unrealized attraction to writing creative and imaginative literature, literature of his own, still makes it a powerful piece of writing. The error in conception, as his opponents thought, and as he himself would occasionally think, lay in his decision to make inner conflict a public matter; to move from being merely a thinker, with a thought-in-progress that he might continue probing in the interests of objective truth, to appearing, nakedly, a rhetorician with an audience, a set of readers to persuade; hence to make an entry into public space[11] for this most individual of men. The readership was one his radicalism refused to appease.

The potential gap between inner feeling and outer conviction would be further explored in the second preface to *Julie ou la Nouvelle Héloïse* of 1761 and the *Essai sur l'origine des langues* he also published that year, but it had emerged a decade earlier. May words properly obscure the very clarity they ought to seek, like a portrait that improves its sitter? Are they, in such cases, any different from the specious words of sophists, the crafty (hence dishonest) wordsmiths Rousseau kept his distance from throughout his life? The *Idée de la méthode dans la composition d'un livre* that he apparently wrote around 1745 had discussed the rhetorician whose seductive tricks of language eclipse the truth he ought to be conveying, to an end whose wider application he may never have intended to maintain.[12] (The 'real' truths perhaps resembled those Rousseau was transcribing around that time for his then employer Mme Dupin, who planned a vast work on women, though more general observations such as those found in the seventeenth-century moralists may also have contributed to the argument.) Favouring eloquence over truth is a rhetorical move that he had never meant to sanction, and his critique of what the first *Discours*

---

[10] *Discours sur les sciences et les arts*, O.C., III.79. As Mandeville and others had suggested, useless luxury may keep the poor man gainfully employed. The end of the seventh *Rêverie du promeneur solitaire* evokes the miserable condition of workers in the mining and metallurgical industries at the very time Adam Smith, Voltaire, Diderot, and others were celebrating the productivity associated with industry as part of a move towards greater liberty. See Deneys-Tunney, *Un Autre Jean-Jacques Rousseau*, p. 68.

[11] On this general concept, see Jürgen Habermas, *The Structural Transformation of the Public Sphere*, trans. Thomas Burger (Cambridge: Polity Press, 1989).

[12] *O.C.*, II.1242–7.

calls 'arguments spécieux' remained as absolute throughout his life as its expression in 1750.

What, though, of the words of Socrates in the first *Discours*, or the impassioned oratory of Fabricius that follows them? They vindicate Rousseau's attacks on rhetoricians dressed as thinkers whose false eloquence gets the better of the earnest and sincere philosopher: 'Les Poëtes, les Artistes, les Fanatiques, les Rheteurs triomphèrent; et Socrates périt'.[13] (The classical source, Plato's *Apology of Socrates*, names 'artisans', not 'artists', but it hardly suited Rousseau, constructing myths of pre-artistic folk integrity, to denigrate the humble, honest maker together with those others he accuses.) Not that Socrates and Fabricius bear any superficial resemblance to one another: the first is a philosopher whose discourse seems a model of honesty, with its sober setting-out of due procedure ('J'ai examiné', 'je me suis apperçu', 'j'ai répondu'),[14] the second a fighter-orator whose words are meant to move his audience openly, and whose address is filled with repetition, accumulation, and other such devices, figures that anticipate the *Dialogues* two decades later with their 'Jean-Jacques' inflamed by the 'vive effervescence' of the ideas which he hopes to impress upon his reader, 'etincelles de génie qu'on a vu briller dans ses écrits durant 10 ans de délire et de fiévre'.[15] Whether deceptive in its seeming absence, then, or urgent and direct in its appeals, eloquence operates by using powerful images and personal address, always driven by the search for language worthy of its author's truth-telling enterprise.

Thus the prosopopoeia of Fabricius, Rousseau will remark in a letter to Malesherbes in January 1762, came ready formed to his mind and was set down as a factual yet pious act of mortal record: 'Voilà comment lorsque j'y pensois le moins je devins auteur presque malgré moi', fatally propelled into the career of author for better or (as Rousseau inevitably concludes) for worse, when 'l'attrait d'un premier succés et les critiques des barbouilleurs me jetterent tout de bon dans la carriére'.[16] 'Une vive persuasion,' he writes, 'm'a tenu lieu d'eloquence'—this rhetoric-slamming proviso stands, ironically, as the perfect example of an artful or rhetorical preterition, the *captatio benevolentiae* through which the speaker tries to win the listener's sympathy by pointedly disclaiming all ability to do what he is clearly doing very well. Lack of fluency, Rousseau goes on, made it impossible for him to express the 'foule de grandes verités' he sensed as he sat, stunned by supreme enlightenment, under the spreading oak. In

---

[13] 'Dernière réponse à Bordes', *Discours sur les sciences et les arts*, III.73, Rousseau's footnote.

[14] *Discours sur les sciences et les arts*, III.13.

[15] *Dialogues*, I.829.   [16] *O.C.*, I.1136 (12 January 1762).

roughly similar fashion, the *Discours sur l'origine de l'inégalité* of 1755 will reach back to the very genesis of language, a communicative means that is perversely forced to deny itself ('l'impossibilité presque demontrée que les Langues ayent pû naître, et s'établir par des moyens purement humains'),[17] overwhelmed by the effort to describe the 'espace immense' of silence. Why, indeed, should we suppose words adequate to express our incomprehension of whatever man has at least partially generated, language along with other things?

But of course Rousseau found the words, and went on doing so throughout his writing career; we may assume he was aware of what he did, and would continue thus at least until stopped by force. This is consonant with what we know about his inveterate practice of saying he could not do what he could and did do, or did not enjoy advantages he actually possessed, such as the robust good health that let him walk and botanise almost to the end of his life despite his certainty from adolescence onwards that he was either close to death or at least a chronic sufferer from a variety of ailments. It might be wise, in light of this, to doubt his total disaffection with a culture, a form of civilization, that let him on the one hand write and, when he was allowed to, sell his work with great success, and on the other earn a humbler living copying music. Catching him at this is never difficult; all it takes is weighing the sheer volume of his œuvre against his claims to dislike writing and prefer 'oisiveté', though we might qualify this last by noting that for him true leisure often meant a laying up of matter, mental and emotional, best experienced in fortifying retrospect, through reverie. The literary translation of this state occurs with his last, unfinished, work.

The fact that such daydreaming generates great literature is partly what distinguishes the vacuous-seeming state described in the fifth Promenade of the *Rêveries* from other sorts of timeless indolence—that of the savage life he occasionally imagines, for example, a condition seemingly devoid of past or future, or the karma-like detachment from the world of time described in Diderot's *Encyclopédie* entry 'Délicieux'.[18] But there is another contrast to be drawn, a stronger one this time, with the immoral indolence he detects in the pampered band of Academicians, men who talk and prosper while the peasants starve, men as vain and thoughtless, Rousseau thinks, as Nero fiddling while his city burned. Was this the tacit force that led him to distinguish in his own case a 'loisir' that was not quite 'oisiveté',[19]

---

[17] *Discours sur l'inégalité*, III.151.

[18] See Roland Mortier, 'A propos du sentiment de l'existence chez Diderot et Rousseau. Notes sur un article de l'*Encyclopédie*', *Diderot Studies*, 6 (1964), pp. 183–95.

[19] See also *Confessions*, I.641, and *Dialogues*, I.824.

the former a time for reflection both empty and valuable, as the first *Discours* conceives it? If he knew himself to be a great writer, then yes. He certainly felt such emptiness to be materially distinct—a benign unclutteredness—from the 'oisiveté' of the uselessly idle,[20] members of what we call the chattering classes, or, more sympathetically, the community of intellectuals.

If Diderot called the thesis of the first *Discours* an old argument warmed up, he surely also felt himself directly implicated in it for having been the involuntary cause of Rousseau's life-changing walk, a walk to see his friend in Vincennes jail (where Diderot had been committed for the alleged heresy of his *Lettre sur les aveugles*). Others were, perhaps surprisingly, more openly receptive; for if d'Alembert's comment in the *Discours préliminaire* to the *Encyclopédie* was that 'Il nous siérait mal d'être de son sentiment à la tête d'un ouvrage tel que celui-ci', his implication was that the *Encyclopédistes* none the less *were* of that opinion, a fact Grimm confirmed:[21] Rousseau had 'oddly' converted nearly all the *philosophes* to the arguments of his first *Discours* (though Grimm actually names 'entre autres' only himself and Diderot). It was, of course, impossible for Rousseau to remain unmoved in practical terms by the beliefs he now proclaimed. They meant, for instance, that he could no longer consistently profess his real adoration of Molière, still less openly go to any performance of his plays—a genuine deprivation in comparison with the discarding of fine linen, expensive wig, and other superficial trappings of a civilized life that he gave up in his reform. But it is unclear that Rousseau, as a moralist, followed a consistent code of hostility towards the arts. If he had done so, it is not music copying he would have embraced as a career.

He knew, uncomfortably, how vulnerable such inconsistencies made him to the attacks of enemies; it is why he devotes most of *Narcisse*'s preface to defending a position they saw as indefensible, a defence that highlights all his pride in being a craftsman along with his professed incomprehension of vulgar materialist obsessions. The weakness of their understanding is the scandal, he declares, together with their mistaken belief that he cares for social prestige. Such errors made them draw the wrong conclusions about his sincerity, to believe

que cessant de vouloir vivre du travail de mes mains je tienne à l'ignominie le métier que je me suis choisi et fasse des pas vers la fortune, s'ils remarquent en un mot que l'amour de la réputation me fasse oublier celui de la vertu, je les prie de m'en avertir, et même publiquement, et je leur promets de jeter à l'instant au feu mes Ecrits et mes Livres, et de convenir de toutes les erreurs qu'il leur plaira de me reprocher.[22]

The fact that *Narcisse* had been written over a decade before its public performance at least clears Rousseau of a major inconsistency, but the logic of what follows is less easy to see: 'En attendant, j'écrirai des Livres, je ferais des Vers et de la Musique, si j'en ai le talent, le tems, la force et la volonté: je continuerais à dire, très franchement tout le mal que je pense des Lettres et de ceux qui les cultivent'.[23] Why, then, did he try as hard as he did to have the play publicly performed, or compose *Le Devin du village* between the writing of the two *Discours*?

At least some aspects of the public response to the *Devin*'s success embarrassed him, and the *Confessions* describes how he avoided the royal patronage it earned on its first Court performance,[24] self-conscious as he felt about his unkempt appearance and embarrassed by the effects of the urinary complaint that made public appearance a torture. He did, however, accept a hundred louis from the King, fifty from Mme de Pompadour, fifty from the Opéra, and five hundred francs for selling the rights over the engravings prepared for the printed edition to Pissot, 'en sorte que cet Interméde, qui ne me coûta jamais que cinq ou six semaines de travail, me rapporta presque autant d'argent, malgré mon malheur et ma balourdise, que m'en a depuis rapporté *l'Emile*, qui m'avoit coûté vingt ans de méditation et trois ans de travail'.[25] The conclusion to the work, though entirely conventional in terms of pastoral tradition, may carry an added charge in light of Rousseau's subsequent departure from Paris for the provinces, where he could both write more concentratedly and live more freely:

> L'Art à l'Amour est favorable,
> Et sans art l'Amour sait charmer;
> A la ville on est plus aimable,
> Au village on sait mieux aimer.

These words are almost like echoes of Marivaux's comedies, while the reference to art may make us think of *Narcisse* and an entire pastoral tradition.

Avoiding royalty, Rousseau also felt that he had kept his principles intact. This let him stick to his self-denying ordinance of relying on no one but himself, and particularly no outside circumstance, for his subsistence, and additionally enabled him to preserve a freedom that his Paris

---

[22] *O.C.*, II.974.   [23] *O.C.*, II.974.
[24] *Confessions*, I.377–87.   [25] *Confessions*, I.386.

life had already begun to compromise. The distractions of the city, he reasoned, would stop him working in the regular fashion his tastes and needs required. So it was wholly natural that 'je m'en revins copier' once the initial interest in the piece had passed, particularly as the Opéra had succeeded in depriving him of the fee it owed him for public performance of his other works. Even reduced to less than a quarter of what it should have earned him, all the same, the income for *Le Devin* allowed him to live in comfort for several years and 'suppléer à la copie, qui alloit toujours assez mal'.[26]

It was appropriate that a work of such bucolic simplicity should have won him public acclaim; but it was also ironic. For the copying, however badly it was going, still had to be done at the hub of things, in or near Paris,[27] though he regularly left the city to walk alone in the Bois de Bou-logne, 'méditant des sujets d'ouvrages, et je ne revenois qu'à la nuit'— more or less as happened in the last decade of his life when he escaped Paris to botanize in the company of Bernardin de Saint-Pierre, though then without consciously having any future writing to think about. He would, all the same, almost inadvertently compose one of his greatest works at that time.

Back in the 1750s the country, specifically the forest of Saint-Germain, provided both a point of reference for his next composition and a back-ground of peace and solitude (apart, Rousseau says, from the presence of Thérèse Le Vasseur and two other women who made the necessary domes-tic arrangements without ever disturbing his thoughts): only thus could it be 'mentally' written as he believed his best works were. Nothing in that description, clearly, recalls the remarkable conditions under which the first *Discours* had been conceived; what occupied him now was something quite different, his proposed entry for the Dijon academy's new essay prize on the origin and nature of human inequality. Planning it took four peaceful days, which Rousseau spent plunged in an archetypal *locus amœ-nus*[28] in the forest 'sans souci de rien'. The sweeping ambitions of what became the *Discours sur l'origine de l'inégalité entre les hommes* of 1755 were traced 'fiérement' in the *Confessions*, the adverb conveying less the confidence that stemmed from his having won the academy's earlier prize with what he knew to be an inferior piece of writing than from the sense of grandeur he derived from first envisaging a topic of such vast scope and then assessing his chances of rising to its challenge. His words underline this complexity: 'je faisois main basse sur les petits mensonges des hommes',

---

[26] *Confessions*, I.386.   [27] *Confessions*, I.390.
[28] On the *locus amœnus*, see E. R. Curtius, *European Literature and the Latin Middle Ages*, trans. Willard R. Trask (Princeton: Princeton University Press, 1973), pp. 192–4.

while 'Mon âme exaltée par ces contemplations sublimes [of "l'homme de la nature" as opposed to "l'homme de l'homme'"] s'élevoit auprès de la divinité'.[29] This, he implies, will be the discourse of his regenerative art, art not as degraded copy of an already degraded model, but as original interpretation: for Rousseau is already writing with the God's-eye view, the supernatural perspective he occasionally adopts over ten years later in the *Rêveries*. But it is also art in the sense that it is composed of, and with, artistry: no *divertissement* (signifying originally a turning aside, only later an amusement) to deflect attention from existential misery, but a prophetic discourse that proclaims itself fittingly and honourably as truth with precisely the words required, and no others.

The idea that imaginative writing is fuelled by leisure or rest is one we often encounter in Rousseau, though usually with the proviso that leisure itself provides space less for writing than for meditating or clearing the mind completely: he more than once regretfully mentions not having written down the thoughts he played with on a walk or turned over in his mind in bed. But that is how it has to be: inspiration, he believed, requires uncluttered freedom from most practical engagement, its flow inevitably stemmed by any process as businesslike as notetaking. There is, in writing words, something inherently distracting from the experience of 'oisiveté', an ideal blankness radically compromised by the operations of the intellect. The ostensibly more intrusive motions of physical activity restore it, by contrast, the feet that are paralysed when the hand transcribes the notions thought presents now becoming free to work independently of the thinking process. For, while verbal language is conventional, an unnatural mode of communication, the images that flood his mind when he is disengaged are beyond normal expression, seeming spontaneous. Since speech is a tool of human rationalism, it can of its nature be triggered only by thought; and since thought, he insists, is a process of unnatural and enormous difficulty to him, articulating it must also be a matter of great complexity. Few writers in the history of literature, it must be said, have given the impression of using words more naturally than Rousseau.

Tracing man's development from primitivism might be a concern of the second *Discours*, but the first had already made him dwell on the development of literary language, if not on its transcription. Rhetoric, the science of eloquence, came with man's ease in handling an ever-increasing stock of locutions, and rhetoric made possible a science of sophistry, of 'sophismes agréables qui ont encore plus d'éclat que de subtilité, [...] séduisant par un certain coloris de stile et par les ruses d'une logique adroite'.[30] It is the

---

[29] *Confessions*, I.388.   [30] 'Préface d'une seconde letter à Bordes', *O.C.*, III.107.

insubstantial art that Plato's *Gorgias* opposes negatively to the technical skills which let man understand the true nature of things.[31] Those who deal in such artifice make truth and falsehood indistinguishable to themselves and others, supporting what they say 'par des arguments spécieux'. From this it is a short step to pronouncing that 'toutes nos sciences ne sont qu'abus, et tous nos savants que de vrais sophistes'. But what can a 'vrai sophiste' 'truly' (as opposed to logically) be? Like a Cretan liar?

By sleight of hand, as it were, Rousseau's very different rhetoric will defend the thinker (himself) by the simple expedient of antiphrasis: the 'mensonges des hommes' are countered by the truthtelling 'apologiste de la nature aujourdui si défigurée et calumniée' of the later *Dialogues*,[32] given the attributes of perverse, mendacious man simply in order to demonstrate his difference. Here supposition, on which the *Discours sur l'inégalité* rests (just as the *Discours sur les sciences et les arts* had done), slips smoothly into certitude, as though a week of country air and healthy food let Rousseau see the pre-history as well as history of man, an altogether higher demand than that made of the 'devin du village'. For nature's apologist could have found the model he needed only in his own heart. Such flagrant subjectivism cannot be further compromised by fresh revelation masquerading as objectivity ('En le considerant, en un mot, tel qu'il a dû sortir des mains de la Nature'),[33] since man is, apparently, 'conforme de tous temps, comme je le vois aujourd'hui'. And the most telling insight into truth is provided by the same image of sturdy dependability as had guaranteed the truths Rousseau perceived on the way to Vincennes: 'Je le vois se rassasiant *sous un chesne*, se désalterant au premier Ruisseau'.[34] Security once provided, there can be nothing to fear from the freely admitted fact of the second *Discours*'s 'story', its hypothetical nature ('Commençons donc par écarter tous les faits');[35] for as *Du contrat social* will later claim, everything issuing from nature is good, and the insights afforded to Rousseau the writer are bathed in a virtuous natural light. Thus things that have been 'conjectures' become 'raison', and the latter's 'conséquences' form themselves into a 'systeme' yielding first 'resultats' and then 'conclusions': preliminary deference almost becomes defiance.

Both *Discours* are preoccupied by the matter of origins, if not by specific chronology; for them, the 'better' time there once was is a matter of ethos, not of date, a fact that gives Rousseau's argument richness as well as flexibility, if not absolute conviction. Both offer hope in tracing a process of gradual degradation that may be repaired, though they offer no prospect of

[31] *Gorgias*, 465a.   [32] *Dialogues*, I.936.   [33] *Discours sur l'inégalité*, III.134.
[34] *Discours sur l'inégalité*, III.135 (emphasis added).
[35] Preface to *Discours sur l'inégalité*, III.132.

total retrieval, only of improvement. The *Inégalité* sets the improvement in a context of praxis, almost a gymnastics of progress: the human body declines avoidably as well as inevitably, the avoidability a function of reliance on body substitutes otherwise called tools. Yet Rousseau makes clear at the start of this *Discours* that he is not concerned with detailing (imagining with clarity) the precise functional means that insidiously suppresses man's bodily resource or potential. 'Le corps de l'homme sauvage étant le seul instrument qu'il connoisse, il l'employe à divers usages, dont, par le défaut d'exercice, les nôtres sont incapables.' But then there is precision: having an axe weakens the wrist; having a sling, the arm; a ladder or a horse, the legs. Man's life is thus complicated at the same time as simplified by tools that, enabling him to do more, also, and concurrently, permit him to do less. Rousseau is uninterested in attempting to recreate the body of primeval man, disdaining to ask, for instance, if his long fingernails and toenails were primitive claws or not;[36] he takes the body as an object of philosophy, which entails admitting that there is no scientific basis for the comparisons he draws (thus his supposing man to have been always as he is at present). The lesson of the second *Discours*, however, like that of the first, necessarily involves making assumptions: that the modern body is an inferior version of a primitive model, say, even though the earlier one is inaccessible. The reason for this is to be sought in the evident fact of social disempowerment polemically articulated by *Du contrat social*: 'L'homme est né libre, et par-tout il est dans les fers',[37] a state with physiological as well as moral consequences.

TOOLS AND PROGRESS

As Robinson Crusoe will later teach Emile, self-sufficiency may be achieved when the individual confines his wants to basic needs, provided that a minimum kit of natural resources exists for him to convert into vital aids or supplements. An abundance of such devices, on the other hand, progressively dis-arms him, as the substitute functional means insidiously suppresses bodily resource or potential. But there are ways of resolving this difficulty. Craft keeps us in touch with our body, although using ever more craft tools may separate us from it. The tool agglomerate that is an automatic machine increases this distance, so that the development from a craft economy to a manufacturing or industrial one always

---

[36] Preface to *Discours sur l'inégalité*, III.135.   [37] *Du contrat social*, III.351.

means lessening our capacity for unaided independent praxis. Making more tools or tool agglomerates for ever more purposes brings with it, not just an ever-increasing power of individuals over their environment, but also its converse, reducing them to a state of dependency that compromises the most basic as well as the most complex actions. What the history of humanity reveals, says Rousseau, is the unequal distribution of tools and the tool surrogate, money (to buy machines as/and servants with), enabling some but not all of us to equip ourselves with the means to do those things we cannot or do not wish to perform unaided. In other words, we form a hierarchical society, one of unequals.

The *Discours sur l'inégalité* argues that social hierarchies are at present and historically real, though when there were no institutions they were of course, unlike natural inequality, non-existent. Moreover, the corruption of social values means that it is not only the impoverished who want, or will generally want, to improve their position in the composite whole, but also their superiors. Without a moral transformation of human character it is impossible to imagine the more privileged, the tool- or machine-rich, ceding their advantage to let the tool-poor rise to their level. Rousseau's social contract will later set out ways in which subordination and injustice of this kind may be repaired, ways entailing strengthening the arms of the disadvantaged in whatever way this can best be done (fiscally, materially, morally, or otherwise). But what if we take as our analogy of society the machine components that are separately inactive and disempowered, but collectively operational? This presupposes that no individual part is 'naturally' more important or able than any other: only collectively can they function, empowerment achieved on the shop floor or in the assembly room. Such an image suits Rousseau's illustrative purposes, as suggested by the old analogy of the watchmaker God, the knowing power that puts the parts together and is in that sense their master. The case of the craftsman is more complex. He has a working body (his own) he may train, but knows that only tools make him a maker; the more tools and materials (usually), the more complex the product he can make.

This may in turn remind us that division of labour is both a benign and a malignant force, as a comparison with the human organism suggests. When all the parts work adequately the 'machine'—as the eighteenth century often called the human body—may function, but not, or not fully, when only parts of it are operational. The difference with non-animate machines may be that human parts, unlike (some) machine parts, lose their flexibility and ability to respond when unused over time: lacking praxis, they simply wither. But is it crucial that everything remain in perfect working order? An acceptable product can often be made by partly functional machines, if not, as Diderot's *Encyclopédie* entry 'Bas' makes clear, in the case of complex ones such as looms, just as partly functional humans can do certain things adequately—when, say, the hands and arms are active, though the legs refuse to work. As society develops, social ruses and scientific discoveries multiply to let us feel the benefit of partial functionality, a process that gratifyingly enhances our sense of involvement in an otherwise mechanical procedure by cutting short the work of machine manufacture and letting the human factor play its part: in making houses, furniture, or clothes from kits, for example, or making cake from ready prepared ingredients. In some cases (the house kit), becoming involved in manufacture may be prompted by the desire to save money, in other cases (the cake mix) to save trouble or demonstrate, whether truthfully or not, one's caring nature.

It may be vital to the maker that the tools involved retain a certain simplicity; if not, they risk collectively weakening the instrument that is truly at the heart of the production process, the maker himself. Machinery that both enhances and replaces human craft eventually de-skills us out of sheer complexity. Rousseau's society was one far less disempowered by industrial machinery than our own is, and our own doubtless far less so than a future one will be—unless, at least, the doctrine of staying in touch be commercially and industrially developed, and in more sophisticated ways than with the cake or bread mix. But all progress or advance is a matter of differing degrees, just as alienation, the process of distancing us from some vital source or resort in a hostile world, is always relative. Its forms stem to a greater or lesser extent from the loss of a sense of stewardship, social, religious, ecological, or other. We mould our societies, Rousseau argues, by devising various and contrasting ways to delegate or arrogate responsibility. Tools are just one part of the picture.

We may, of course, deny all responsibility for stewardship, particularly that of global governance, a process that can simply seem too vast to be conducted or actively cared about by individuals and small societies. Rousseau's 1756 exchange with Voltaire on the Lisbon earthquake pinpoints possible types of human response (or impotence) in the face of suffering caused by natural disaster, calamities so vast as to appear beyond our capacity to help. In this connection we might consider the lengthy ninth footnote to the *Discours sur l'origine de l'inégalité*, where a picture of wilful disempowerment—of man by man or other forces—is presented.[38] The issue, explicitly evoked or not, is that of perfectibility, a quality or property apparently distinguishing man from other living creatures. Do humans, blessed with insights that other species lack, possess the means to make of life something better than it appears under 'natural' conditions?

---

[38] *Discours sur l'inégalité*, III.202 (note to p. 142).

Rousseau's note rehearses the range of human achievements that should conduce to our contentment, operations that have tamed the universe: marshes drained, mountains climbed, rivers dammed, seas sailed, countries discovered. It concludes negatively, however, suggesting that man's entire achievement is reducible to the enslavement, persecution, or comprehensive disadvantaging of some by others, a process that culminates in suffering on an almost unimaginable scale.

Voltaire's *Poème sur le désastre de Lisbonne* had taken the destructiveness of the Lisbon earthquake as illustrating a form of evil that inexplicably exists on earth, which cannot be accounted for by human action and must therefore be attributed to some force beyond our own capacities. Diderot, a materialist, drew a similar conclusion non-metaphysically and non-morally, describing earthly events as simply produced, without intention, by faulty geological structures. Rousseau blamed the number of deaths caused by the earthquake, though not the seismic shock itself, on social developments, notably the 'civilized' human practice of building dwellings upwards as well as outwards and thereby creating far more densely populated areas than before: a Lisbon made of single-storey buildings would have suffered far fewer fatalities than actually occurred. (When he returned to Paris, none the less, Rousseau would himself live in a tenement, perhaps assuming that the French capital's earth would never quake.) Voltaire's reply to Rousseau was *Candide*.

The central observation of Rousseau's letter on providence of 18 August 1756 is not original. He could, for example, have found it in Seneca, the 90th of whose *Epistolae morales* comments that Posidonius was wrong to think mechanical tools the invention of the wise: tools prove our ingenuity, not our wisdom, for bountiful nature enables us as well as the rest of creation to live without artifice. We have already encountered this view of Seneca's. But he also remarks that philosophy did not devise 'shrewdly contrived' buildings rising storey above storey from the ground, and claims that builders had been happy in the days before architects; evil and hence unhappiness were ushered in with the advent of luxury. This was clearly an observation after Rousseau's heart. Voltaire's barbed comment that reading the second *Discours* made him feel like walking on all fours[39] does not disguise the philosophically problematic as well as morally abhorrent fact of natural disaster, but suggests the moral abhorrence without drawing from it a lesson fatal to religious belief. Anticipating the conclusion drawn in *Candide*, that man must simply accept a benign

---

[39] 'Il prend envie de marcher à quatre pattes quand on lit votre ouvrage' (which Voltaire has just described as 'votre nouveau livre contre le genre humain'), Voltaire, *Correspondance complète*, XXVII.230 (30 August 1755).

providence whose rationale he cannot account for, is scarcely new; but should we assume from it that a vegetative existence in which one neither tempts nor challenges providence is preferable to an active one? The injunction to cultivate one's garden, with or without a range of appropriate tools, leaves the matter open.

Touch, for Rousseau, was meant for constructive things, things created over time rather than the quick fix of an uncraftsmanlike instant: like Midas, he preferred real food to the food of solid gold created by a hand's glancing and unwitting contact. Praxis governs his philosophy of life, in this as in other respects. No craftsman, of his very nature, really wants the one complete and wish-fulfilling answer to the practical problems he engages with; he has too great a respect for the orderly process of hand-work, of product creation that is neither industrial in scope nor buried deep in impenetrable mystery. Although craft rests on continuity, it is not the soulless continuity of the conveyor belt; rather, it is cumulative or holistic, its processes necessarily involving tactile skills, and bound by time. Dominating matter offers no route to such an end; what the crafts-man seeks is an even-handed sustainability, or what might nowadays be called a constructive environmentalism, a fruitful way of living in and at peace with the world, however randomly terrible some worldly occur-rences appear. It is an attitude all Rousseau's ecological principles might endorse.

This urge for productive usefulness is constant in him, however great the pull towards pleasure of his early writings. That is why discourse attracted him as an intermediate vehicle for advancing doctrine (if not orthodoxy), the first *Discours* a passionate essay, the second a more closely reasoned exposition, both of them statements of intent. His early years had not forewarned of such uncompromising purpose, yet none of his intermittent playfulness, in operetta or dramatic sketch, could really call it into question. His works to come continue this pursuit of social renova-tion without denying the pleasures of invention. The personal reform of his early forties sets up an attitude his future work will reinforce; his dif-ferences with Voltaire as with Diderot announce a non-conformity that is to be made a way of life.

Both *Discours* work pragmatically. Each uses polemic as a tool—not always delicate or sensitive—to cut into public consciousness and explore its unseen aspects, forcing thought out of readers, proposing new inter-pretations. They take a stand against convention, suggesting ways of building a new structure, one of them favouring individual asceticism, the other various types of social integration. The works of fancy Rous-seau wrote before them or alongside them conflict with neither; all lay bare the fallacies of art. Good art, they say, requires perspective; stand too close and you miss the bigger picture, too far away, the detailed one.[40] These writings in conjunction show the power of rhetoric while refuting its real temptations: the first *Discours* unveils the untrustworthiness of knowledge and illusion, the second other forces, mental as well as physical, that mould our lives. In a different presentational mode and style, *Le Devin* makes clear that what might seem beyond practical control in fact responds to human effort and the power of suggestion, as the Cunning-man enables the lovers to perceive. These works all argue for pragmatic principles, principles that Rousseau's later writings further clarify. His open letter to d'Alembert in 1758, responding to the latter's *Encyclopédie* article 'Genève', then a couple of best-selling novels published in the early 1760s, were forces powerful enough to keep tugging him to and fro, from praxis to invention, from copy to creation, from craft to art and back again.

[40] This is essentially what the phrase 'ut pictura poesis' means in Horace's *Ars poetica*.

4

Drama and Life

HISTRIONICS AND INTEGRITY

The circumstances that produced the *Lettre à d'Alembert sur les spectacles* are well known, and Rousseau retraces them in book 10 of the *Confessions*. He had passionately disagreed with the observation of d'Alembert's *Encyclopédie* entry 'Genève' that a theatre should be established in the city, objecting that dramatic performance expresses all the artificiality of man's relations with other men, cheapens the real virtues of pragmatic interaction on which society should rest, mocks morality, and exalts the show of doing—the central aspect of any actor's performance—rather than the truth of being.[1] That these issues are interconnected is immediately clear. Whether other sorts of antagonism informed Rousseau's writing is probably unimportant, though a general antipathy towards the idea of changing Geneva's cultural life radically may have been accentuated by his (moderate) antagonism towards Voltaire, whom he suspected of influencing d'Alembert's article in spirit if not in letter.[2] Rousseau was, however, consistently more generous towards Voltaire[3] than the latter towards him, and the former's paranoid suspicion that the *philosophes* and their associates were plotting against him was still embryonic in the 1750s. Crucially, Voltaire had not yet publicized Rousseau's abandonment of his children by Thérèse, and when he did Rousseau did not suspect him of being the report's author. The betrayal would none the less fuel his general sense of insecurity and guilt, and therefore his preoccupation with the matters of personal integrity already detectable in the *Lettre*'s argument.

---

[1] John S. Spink, *Rousseau et Genève* (Paris: Boivin, 1934), p. 153, notes that the article was written when d'Alembert was staying with Voltaire in August 1756; its sections on religion could only have been based on d'Alembert's conversations with the latter and four ministers whom d'Alembert had come to know. The digs at Calvin were obviously influenced by Voltaire, and in a letter to Vernes of 22 October 1758 d'Alembert says that the article was indeed partly by him (Rousseau, *C.C.*, V.183).
[2] On Voltaire's own theatre at Ferney, just outside Geneva, see ibid., VII.371; Voltaire attacks Rousseau, ibid., VIII.287, 322.
[3] On Rousseau's generosity in this respect, see *Rousseau et Genève*, IX.69, XXXVIII.26–42, 50, 58, 59.

A work attacking drama was unlikely to convince those friends and enemies Rousseau had left behind in Paris at the time of his reform. He could hardly deny his addiction to the theatre and to writing playlets for performance there; nor had *Le Devin*'s spectacular success served its author's new-found principles well. As long as he remained associated with the theatre, his stated disaffection with it and its products must seem suspect. The first *Discours* had, reasonably enough, implanted in the public mind the paradox that its author, though a writer, mistrusted authorship, or at least saw writing as a dubious enterprise. It might therefore quite reasonably be asked whether the author of the *Lettre à d'Alembert* could possibly be writing—again—sincerely, from the heart, or pleading hypocritically (like actors) and for perverse celebrity. For as his one-time friend Diderot suggested in connection with the *Discours sur les sciences et les arts*, Rousseau was fond of biting hands that fed him.

Any sense, besides, that the *Lettre* had been drawn from him despite himself seemed contradicted by its rhetorical finesse, unless, of course, that finesse was regarded as the 'natural' accompaniment to the Vincennes epiphany. But then perhaps, rather aptly, it resembled the eloquence of actors, the words of men without responsibility for *what* they said, but shading its expression, *how* what they said was articulated, as they thought best: each a 'pantin merveilleux', Diderot's *Paradoxe* would say, rather like the scribe Rousseau had been in earlier life, mediating prose but not composing it. Few, after all, could understand inflection as Rousseau did, knew how language gets its shape from its enunciation, and hence depends on context for its harmony to flow. What else, after all, can individual performers bring to parts they play and words they say? Yet the analogy breaks down in the end. It was hard to see the author of the *Lettre* as simply 'speaking' words that came from outside him, even though his topic was not unfamiliar: hostility towards play-acting had its place not just in Christian orthodoxy, but also in established philosophical and lay tradition dating back at least to the ancient Greeks. The intensity of Rousseau's rhetoric might be seen as simply expressing the energy that came naturally to him, however fearful of the power of language he elsewhere appeared.

The disadvantages he saw in setting up a playhouse in Geneva are clearly, if tendentiously, expressed. Going to the theatre intrudes on family time, breaks up societal assemblies on which the health of state and people rests, promotes vice by showing virtue mocked on stage, compromises truth by furthering the taste for mimicry, yet fosters man's belief in what is not the case, as all other art forms do, so encouraging unfettered flights of fancy (a notion Rousseau got from Plato's Idealism). Whether he suspected someone else of having helped d'Alembert or not, Rousseau did consider that Voltaire's own interests would be well served by the building of a theatre in Geneva, given the proximity of his fiefdom Ferney and the fact that some Genevese already attended dramatic performances in the playhouse he had had constructed there. They were surely unlikely to agree that theatregoing was a bad idea.

Yet many saw Rousseau's objections to the d'Alembert proposal as a rallying of the righteous, a call to arms of citizens whose tastes were still undamaged by societal corruption:[4] whether fervent Calvinists or not, they must see the force of reasoned argument and Rousseau's brand of 'feeling', impassioned rhetoric. True, his image of the native Swiss, endowed with sturdy homespun virtues, might antagonize some readers, harking back unhelpfully to an earlier age, an age, perhaps, that never was; but who would not emerge enlightened from the opposition of corrupted urban living and lives shaped by the rhythms of nature and community? The contrast between Parisian vice and Genevese integrity could hardly be more pointed. On the other hand, the integrity relies on an acceptance of surveillance that might seem distasteful to some, though it is one that would underpin the operation of the virtuous community at Clarens in *La Nouvelle Héloïse*, and so, apparently, commands Rousseau's assent; it qualifies some basic freedoms that he praises elsewhere, formulating as it does a range of civic or domestic duties that might seem unpleasantly restrictive. Given this, should it not have made Rousseau himself uneasy? Perhaps not, as *Du contrat social* will later indicate: compensations in the form of general liberties may make the loss worthwhile. Yet his personal writings reveal how greatly he disliked curtailment of any kind, however given to prescribing social duty to others.

What are the real alternatives to the enjoyment playgoing affords, he asks, answering that the basic principle is to make the daily lives of citizens so rich they do not seek escapist pleasure.[5] He thinks a small or medium town a community of the right size for this cleansing enterprise: there what might elsewhere seem to be a stupefied, anonymous assiduousness is instead a proud and energetic fervour, where the citizen, 'vous montrant des prodiges de travail, de patience, et d'industrie, croira ne vous montrer que des choses communes à Paris'.[6] The *singeries* of high society, reflected in theatricals where all are simply copying someone

---

[4] Linda Kirk, '"Going Soft": Genevan Decadence in the Eighteenth Century', in Roney and Klauber, *Identity of Geneva*, pp. 143–54, observes that many Genevese of the lower rank seemed to side with Rousseau (p. 146).
[5] *Lettre à d'Alembert*, V.54.   [6] *Lettre à d'Alembert*, V.55.

else, give way to real creativeness, with 'plus d'esprits originaux, plus d'industrie inventive, plus de choses vraiment neuves; parce qu'on y est moins imitateur, qu'ayant peu de modéles, chacun tire plus de lui-même, et met plus du sien dans tout ce qu'il fait'.

The following presents a scene from Rousseau's childhood that has become celebrated, recalling the industrious free men of the Neuchâtel region who, while cultivating their own land, spent whatever time they had left over indoors (in wooden houses they had built themselves) on 'mille ouvrages [de leurs] mains', especially when the season stopped them farming.

> Jamais Menuisier, Serrurier, Vitrier, Tourneur de profession n'entra dans le pays; tous le sont pour eux-mêmes aucun ne l'est pour autrui; dans la multitude de meubles comodes et mêmes élégans qui composent leur ménage et parent leur logement, on n'en voit pas un qui n'ait été fait de la main du maitre. Il leur reste encore du loisir pour inventer et faire mille instrumens divers, d'acier, de bois, de carton, qu'ils vendent aux étrangers, dont plusieurs même parviennent jusqu'à Paris, entre autres ces petites horloges de bois qu'on y voit depuis quelques années. Ils en font aussi de fer; ils font même des montres, et ce qui paroît incroyable, chacun réunit à lui seul toutes les professions diverses dans lesquelles se subdivise l'horlogerie, et fait tous ses outils lui-même.[7]

When Rousseau was living in rural Neuchâtel, he commented on the typically Swiss spirit of industry, which led to the establishment of 'des manufactures dans des précipices, des ateliers sur des torrents'.[8] The Montagnons of years gone by had possessed a practical and scientific genius anticipating 18th-century industrial and mechanical developments, making among other things a range of pumps and siphons that recall the Heron's fountain Rousseau had been given in Turin. None of this resourcefulness, he writes, would have existed had a theatre been established in their midst. Yet even without one these communities became corrupted, such that 'cet heureux pays [...] est sur la route du mien': revisiting the area later on as he sought refuge from his persecutors, he found 'un autre paysage un autre air un autre ciel d'autres hommes, et ne voyant plus mes Montagnons avec les yeux de vingt ans, je les trouve beaucoup vieillis'.[9] This of course severely damages the

---

[7] *Lettre à d'Alembert*, V.56. See also Marius Fallet-Scheurer, *Le Travail à domicile dans l'horlogerie Suisse et les industries annexes* (Berne: Imprimerie de l'Union, 1909), which makes clear that this was an idealized vision. I am grateful for further information to M. Jean Piquet, Conservateur adjoint, Musée international d'horlogerie, La Chaux-de-Fonds.

[8] *C.C.*, XV.49–50 (to duc de Luxembourg, 20 January 1763).

[9] *Lettre à d'Alembert*, V.57.

case against the theatre he has been advancing in the *Lettre*, though he does not point it out.

Instead, he carries on contrasting all the benefits of craft and craft mentalities in simple, uncorrupted worlds with the rotten products of an urban lifestyle, seeing how the canker he associates with staging plays has spread into the wider world,[10] but still focused on the wealth and health of one place in particular. New money brought by foreigners and strangers to Geneva, drawn by plays performed there, will destroy the appetite for civic and domestic life, give citizens a ruinous taste for leisure, sap familial commitment, and infallibly corrupt the natives' manners. (Perhaps he has forgotten that Calvin permitted dancing in the city on the grounds that visitors from outside liked it;[11] perhaps, too, that at one point in his life Isaac Rousseau himself taught dance for a living.) According to Rousseau, this general decadence stretched to actors and actresses too, dissolute by nature and associated, as their Greek name of *hupokritēs* suggests, with inauthenticity, since their art of speaking words put in their mouths by others ends all sense of personal responsibility. (Diderot reconsiders this age-old opinion in his *Entretiens sur 'Le Fils naturel'*, published within a few months of the *Lettre à d'Alembert*, as well as in the later *Paradoxe sur le comédien*.) As the hedonistic Rousseau of the 1740s became, with qualifications, the stern moralist of the following decade, so the nostalgia he felt for the city of his birth, which was soon to turn so radically against him, found more powerful expression. After all, his decision to leave Paris in 1756 had been fuelled in part by a growing distaste for the godless matter-mindedness of his acquaintances there, men and women leading lives he saw as false and empty. By the time he conceived the *Lettre*, Mme d'Epinay's Hermitage, where he had been living, had also become tainted by his mistrust for urban sophistry, hers and other people's. The riposte to d'Alembert, accordingly, would be composed in the nearby refuge of the Maréchal de Luxembourg at Montlouis, which for a time became his home; for Rousseau, though a Swiss, was never such a democrat as to abhor all representatives of the ancient aristocracy and their properties.

It hardly seems material to his general discussion in the *Lettre* to be troubled by the morality of actors in d'Alembert's Geneva playhouse, but he is concerned about it none the less. Why? Presumably because he fears that their alleged depravity may somehow be translated to the audience. Yet if it be accepted that they are just copyists, this claimed depravity

[10] *Lettre à d'Alembert*, V.59.
[11] For a different emphasis see John Witte and Robert M. Kingdon, *Sex, Family and Marriage in John Calvin's Geneva* (Cambridge: Eerdmans, 2005), pp. 454–5.

should surely be seen as subordinate to the nature of the characters they are playing, unless they are bad at acting. Rousseau's conviction that dramas tend towards immorality means, of course, that he expects bad characters to dominate, or good qualities in the characters to yield to bad ones: his interpretation of *Le Misanthrope*, indeed, depends on this assumption. It is a questionable view, however, whose proper consequence should surely be, not that actors be discouraged from pursuing their profession, but that drama not offer them one; the fault is not with players but with what they play. Plays therefore should be pulped if already printed, forbidden if not. Yet Rousseau refrains from drawing so extreme a conclusion. His more practical concern with the question of the actor's and audience's absorption in performance was not new: it had been constantly debated since classical antiquity. Horace's 'si vis me flere/dolendum est ipsi tibi'[12] presents one side of the argument, Rousseau's *Lettre*, at least to some extent, the other. In discussing the performer whose ambition (and perhaps duty) is 'de se passionner de sang-froid, de dire autre chose que ce qu'on pense aussi naturellement que si l'on le pensoit réellement',[13] Rousseau takes it as axiomatic that the actor, displaying emotions he is mimicking, none the less obtains the audience's sympathy. This is straightforward enough, though 'interest' might be a more accurate term than 'sympathy'; but he sees it negatively, simply, it appears, because of his belief that drama, like the art of rhetoric generally, favours vice rather than virtue. Were that true, however, the audience at a performance of *Le Misanthrope* might still desirably approve of Alceste's worsting by Célimène because he is a moralizing fool rather than regret it because Célimène is shallow and flirtatious. Can we in fact be sure which character (if either) we are meant to be supporting? Did Molière resolve the issue? Rousseau thinks he did but that he got it wrong. A straightforward reading of the play might seem to confirm this assumption, but there is no reason to assume that *Le Misanthrope* should be interpreted straightforwardly.

Rousseau's objections seem to rest on the belief that (Célimène's) fickleness is worse than (Alceste's) hypocrisy; but if that is what he thinks, he does not say so openly. Instead he shifts the focus back to the acting of plays, not the writing of them, now contending that since 'la tentation de mal faire augmente avec la facilité […], il faut que les Comediens soient plus vertueux que les autres hommes, s'ils ne sont pas plus corrompus'. This puts a new slant on the matter by making rhetorical conviction, and possibly also the actor's self-conviction (if they are separate from one

---

'If you wish me to weep/you too must be grieved', Horace, *Ars poetica*.
Lettre à d'Alembert, *O.C.*,V.73. Diderot's *Paradoxe* would take the same view.

another), a moral rather than artistic issue: plausible actors may self-servingly mimic virtue offstage as well as on, perhaps because they are good actors and see the advantage to be derived from using their mimetic skills exploitatively, or because they are such good copyists, or act in such persuasive dramas, that they deceive themselves as well as their audience. In the latter instance, seemingly an entirely benign one, they are less hypocritical than credulous or otherwise susceptible, a possibility that Rotrou's drama *Le Véritable Saint Genest* had examined a century earlier. It is because of his assumption that drama is dangerous, particularly in its untold mimetic power—dangerous as spectacle and dangerous as morality piece—that Rousseau worries about the theatregoer being led astray by watching people act as other people. Given the negative view of art in all its complex forms and influences he has espoused, he can hardly avoid tarring actors with the same brush as dramatists and even audiences.

His overall conclusion, if perhaps a disappointing one, cannot surprise the reader, given that both *Narcisse* and the first *Discours* had made apparent how Rousseau, like Plato, associates art with deception, occasionally salutary, as with Narcisse/Valère, but usually not. Although a different kind of consequence would later lead to his punishment in the early 1760s for writing works whose rhetoric the authorities associated with the wrong kind of effect, the sort that led to unrest, we might prefer to view imaginative writing of the kind he did at the start and end of his creative life in terms of Freud's belief that literature enacts the hedonistic urge to swap reality for the pleasant world of daydreams (which is, of course, how reading books had worked for Rousseau in his boyhood). In no sense in the early part of his career did he intend to give up practising the arts because of the cautionary tale told in the first *Discours* and later continued in the *Lettre à d'Alembert*, though he would unquestionably suffer on account of the ideas literature permitted him to develop.

THE TASKS OF LEISURE

The preface to *Narcisse* had said that man should cherish, not destroy, the arts; yet Rousseau as an adult saw all their power to quash our sense of what is real, divorcing us from our collective selves through the double counterfeit of performed drama. Far better, thinks the *Lettre*, for citizens to make their own artistic spectacle by joining in a fête, a communal activity whose virtue is its very generality. But what exactly should its nature be? Rousseau does not say. It seems improbable that gatherings of this kind could celebrate such art as issues from great insights like that of 1749, which split Rousseau from his old self and replaced it with a new one; for who should create such art if not Rousseau himself? Involving citizens en masse could hardly lead to radical and positive experience unless the fête were governed by a knowing 'œil vivant', similar, perhaps, to the legislator-figure of *Du contrat social*, one who infuses hearts and minds with a dim awareness of what laws they should enact, then leaves them to work the details out themselves. (Fêtes, of course, should be more joyous than legislative gatherings; the civic ceremonies Rousseau seems to have in mind may loosely anticipate those arranged during the French Revolution by the painter and pageant master David.)[14] Community performances of this kind, while not particularly artistic, may be contrasted in their honest moral essence with the 'arts' of civilization and urbanity: 'les bras, l'emploi du tems, la vigilance, l'austére parcimonie; voila les trésors du Genevois; voila avec quoi nous attendons un amusement des gens oisifs, qui, nous ôtant à la fois le tems et l'argent, doublera reellement nôtre perte'.[15] Surely these home-grown affairs would be craft-focused in the way village fêtes are, with their weaving, knitting, bric-à-brac, corn dollies, and the like. We might almost be back in the world of Rousseau's Montagnons.

A pressing danger in modern society, he has already told his reader, is the creation of leisure, a seemingly natural consequence of the production of works of art that require free time on the part of the consumer to be enjoyed. Or is it that leisure needs pleasant pastimes, such as those involved in the contemplation of art, in order to be filled agreeably? Rousseau sees the potential conflict between these alternatives, and knows that each may lessen culture's value by making it the handmaid of society. Yet to bring about the reverse process—putting society in thrall to culture—is equally dangerous, if in different ways. His theory and practice of leisure cannot be fully explored ahead of the circumstances that brought them to their most open and frank expression with the condemnation of his books in the early 1760s and his expulsion from those places he most wanted to live in, condemned to (comparative) leisure as a refugee, in short; for the present, we need note only that what concerns him as he writes the *Lettre* is the kind of idleness associated specifically with cultures that support dramatic performance. A central reason for his condemnation of the latter is the first of those we have considered: that enjoying culture's products requires time to be made, demands a kind of theft,

[14] See David L. Dowd, *Pageant-Master to the Republic: Jacques-Louis David and the French Revolution* (Nebraska: University of Nebraska Press, 1948); Mona Ozouf, *La Fête révolutionnaire, 1789–1799* (Paris: Gallimard, 1976); Paule-Monique Vernes, *La Vie, la fête, la démocratie* (Paris: Payot, 1978).
[15] *Lettre à d'Alembert*, V.85.

stealing time from occupations that might use it more constructively. To make this killjoy verdict seem compelling, Rousseau needs us to agree that the amusements of leisure are acceptable only when they are also necessary or useful;[16] but this appears inherently implausible. And should we, in any case, continue to accept a claim that has merely been stated, not argued, however widely canvassed in his own day and however familiar the association between leisure, art, and purposiveness? Has the association been proposed simply because moralists, conscious of art's straightforward seductions, want people to be reasonable about, and through, consuming it? If they had thought art depended on utility they might have found it unappealing, at least until they actually encountered it.

Another of Rousseau's assumptions in the *Lettre* also needs scrutinizing. Is it good for fathers to spend all their free time with their families rather than elsewhere? Rousseau may have self-mortifying reasons for wanting us to think so, but self-exonerating ones for arguing the reverse: he knows, uncomfortably, the answer to the more elemental question whether it had been a natural or unnatural act to discard his children in their infancy. He states, vaguely, that 'L'état d'homme a ses plaisirs, qui dérivent de sa nature, et naissent de ses travaux, de ses rapports, de ses besoins',[17] but without drawing from it the comforting conclusion that a man might find vital sustenance in the precious moments of disengagement from his duties as head of the family, whether or not he chose to spend some of those moments at the theatre. Surely Rousseau is the last person entitled to settle this matter; nor could he look to his immediate family for a model in this respect, given that his own father Isaac, the 'meilleur des pères', was a man of pleasure who does not seem to have pressed his young son to join him in Nyon after leaving Geneva. In the *Lettre* Rousseau chooses to focus on a more austere conception of paternity than that presented by his closest relatives and himself.

Perhaps we should approach the matter from another angle. Rousseau's desire to show that a man working productively and regularly at his job would be unable to enjoy moments of relaxation away from it, whether or not he was distant from wife and child, may be less a reaction to his personal experience of family life than to the Protestant milieu in which he had grown up and to which he returned in later life. Its essence consisted in the ascetic Christian belief, which Calvin had established as a matter of principle, that a man lacking duties gives way to unnatural passions, particularly vice. It was a notion Calvin developed into a veritable

---

[16] *Lettre à d'Alembert*, V.15.   [17] *Lettre à d'Alembert*, V.15.

theology of praxis, a physical state of being productively busy that required supervision to be consistently maintained.[18] The example of Rousseau's relatives, and still more so of Rousseau himself, suggests that it is a distinctly idealistic view, and it is certainly one that derives from early Calvinism rather than its more pragmatic later developments. His conviction of social corruption was insistent enough to inform what he attempted to make into a coherent and all-embracing theory of human interaction, which meant attempting to persuade his reader that it is desirable to exercise caution in enjoying whatever is non-essential but undeniably pleasurable— an entirely familiar injunction in traditional Christian doctrine that was easy enough to incorporate within such restrictive patterns of existence as the Calvinist. That of Sparta, which Rousseau had idealized since childhood, may underpin the theory too, and adapting it to the different case and purposes of the modern world seemed straightforward.

Yet if it appears equally natural to associate art with this non-essential pleasure (and craft with need), Rousseau's works in one sense make the association problematic. Quite apart from the didactic burden of much that he wrote (material intended to correct mankind rather than divert it), literary creation for him itself spelt labour, not ease: there are too many declarations throughout his personal writings of the pain involved in shaping a single sentence to his satisfaction for the reader to ignore. When he says that he could remember almost nothing of the detail of the Vincennes experience to develop in later works apart from the *Discours sur les sciences et les arts*, we may infer that his most memorable works of public doctrine no less than his openly fictional writing involved an exercise of the imagination. But imagination is a double-edged quantity, undeniably welcomed as a power facilitating literary composition (composition that would otherwise be slow and arduous), but mistrusted for its very fertility. From the 1760s on Rousseau pointedly and pertinently blamed this faculty for the various 'disasters' of his life, whatever delightful experiences it had given him in childhood and early adulthood. For his reader, of course, the case is very different.

UTILITARIANISM AND SENSIBILITY

The association of craft with utility is more straightforward, and the horologist's trade his family practised epitomizes it. Rousseau himself was less a maker than his forebears, less obviously useful in everyday material terms (his unfinished apprenticeship made that more or less inevitable),

---

[18] Compare Foucault, *Surveiller et punir*.

his trade of music copyist closer to the arts than crafts, though in comparison with, say, Diderot's or d'Alembert's principal activities it certainly
relied on manual skills. Calvinism always predicated honest work, ways of
doing that went hand in hand with faith. Whatever hedonistic pleasures
he enjoyed in Paris, neither they nor all the years spent living with the
whimsical and pietistic Mme de Warens could gainsay the lasting influence on Rousseau of sturdy Protestant morality, its pragmatism, its urg-
ings of a frugal practicality. That is why his condemnation by Geneva for
the doctrinal aberrations of his published work so greatly shocked him,
making him break his ties with the city—ironically, given the influence of
his birthplace on *Du contrat social* and the more self-denying of *Emile*'s
doctrines, not to mention the moral protestations paraded in *La Nouvelle
Héloïse* and its prefaces. In other writers such professions might have been
mere words, things conceived and said out of expediency, but in Rousseau
they were of the essence. This does not, of course, gainsay the moral ambi-
guities of some of his works, particularly *La Nouvelle Héloïse*.

The *Lettre à d'Alembert*, which predates the latter, also anticipates some
of its concerns. It identifies key factors that have, in Rousseau's view,
denatured modern man, alienation through art foremost among them,
and suggests some remedies, including the community-building brotherhood of craft. The presentation is not simply based on the opposition
between imaginative joy (art) and practical sustenance (craft), although
that contrast is given its due weight; Rousseau explains why Geneva in
particular relies on an ethic of communal hard work to prosper, why
industriousness contributes more to social harmony than it might elsewhere.[19] The issue is one of subsistence. If a few are very prosperous, many
live in comparative poverty because their land lacks richness and fertility.
'Il y a bien des Villes plus pauvres que la nôtre où le bourgeois peut donner beaucoup plus à ses plaisirs, parce que le territoire qui le nourrit ne
s'épuise pas, et que son tems n'étant d'aucun prix, il peut le perdre sans
préjudice.' The Genevese have to be time-rich (with that time not devoted
to, or stolen by, leisure activities) to be prosperous, and time-richness
comes from habits of application and frugality. Industry, for them,
depends not on possessing abundant natural resources, but on devising
complex, time-consuming ways to use their few raw materials profitably,
which means that they have scant leisure to devote to profitless pleasure.
What for Calvin was a set of moral injunctions or commandments is for
them a commercial necessity.

---

[19] *Lettre à d'Alembert, O.C.*, V.85.

Le people genevois ne se soutient qu'à force de travail, et n'a le necessaire
qu'autant qu'il se refuse tout superflu [...]. Il me semble que ce qui doit
d'abord frapper tout étranger entrant dans Genève, c'est l'air de vie et
d'activité qu'il y voit régner. Tout s'occupe; tout est en mouvement; tout
s'empresse à son travail et à ses affaires. Je ne crois pas que nulle aussi petite
Ville au monde offre un pareil spectacle. Visitez le quartier St-Gervais; toute
l'horlogerie de l'Europe y paroît rassemblée. Parcourez le Molard et les rües
basses, un appareil de commerce en grand, des monceaux de ballots, de
tonneaux confusément jettés, une Odeur d'Inde et de droguerie vous font
imaginer un port de mer. Aux pâquis, aux eaux-vives, le bruit et l'aspect des
fabriques d'indienne et de toile peinte semblent vous transporter à Zurich.
[...] Les bras, l'emploi du tems, la vigilance, l'austére parcimonie; voila les
trésors du Genevois; voila avec quoi nous attendons un amusement de gens
oisifs, qui, nous ôtant à la fois le tems et l'argent, doublera reellement notre
perte.[20]

D'Alembert's article had mentioned much of this, though matters then
were changing. The first *Discours* had been unwilling to concede that certain political states might cultivate the arts with impunity, but its focus
was morality, not economics. In any case, the *Lettre* does not revise the
earlier view of art's inherent dangers; it merely associates a double jeop-
ardy with cultivating art in barren regions, a lesser one in fertile lands.
Must we redefine the 'proper' reach of art, then, in cultures that are comparatively undamaged by it, or at least are not damaged twice over? Insist
that it be useful in the sense that craft is, though not in the same way? If
we succeed in this, then surely Geneva may build its playhouse.

There is, of course, a way of saving art we have not yet considered, one
only implicit in the *Lettre* because its opposite is powerfully argued; a
route acknowledged by theoreticians and even by some dramatists in
Rousseau's day. The rise of sensibility, so closely linked with his name,
spawned literary works in which what mattered was the arousal and
expression of deep feelings, happily resolved or not. Perhaps we should
attempt to adapt our concept of culture's reach and purpose to accom-
modate these extremes—allow, for example, that a work of art may just as
properly discomfit as conduce to pleasure (a theory whose latitude enabled Sade to call his *œuvre* moral), because humans are predisposed to
enjoy having their emotions aroused, and drama does this more effectively than other art forms by the plurality of its appeal in performance,
addressing both the eyes and the ears of spectators. Might the vividness of
dramatic performance not be usefully harnessed to the promotion of
moral actions? Diderot's new genre of *drame*, for instance, conceived and

---

[20] *Lettre à d'Alembert, O.C.,* V.85.

written at precisely this time, was meant to be useful in just such a way, as were the plays on republican themes (Voltaire's *Brutus*, for example) staged gratis for the populace during the French Revolution. But will such dramas be as popular, and thus potentially as effective, as Molière's *Misanthrope* (leaving aside the vexed question of whether the latter, on which Rousseau spills so much ink, contains a moral doctrine or not)? Rousseau thinks that they will not—and the fortunes of the *drame* genre, which audiences refused to love, mostly bore him out—, perhaps because he assumes that playgoers find the spectacle of human irregularity more alluring than that of virtue, or passionate excess more exciting than unsullied goodness, whether or not that is because humans belong to a fallen species.

This is what makes Rousseau's view of culture apparently so different from that of others in his time, and so much closer to the analyses of dispassionate commentators in the previous century. The *Lettre* takes it as axiomatic that playgoers will be changed by the dramas they see, but only temporarily; that they will pay homage to moral rectitude by feeling solidarity with virtuous characters and (possibly) repulsion towards their antagonists on stage, but will leave such fine feelings behind them in the theatre once the performance is over, so demonstrating the truth of La Rochefoucauld's maxim that hypocrisy is simply the homage vice pays to virtue. Consumers of art, in other words, are not lastingly changed by experiencing it, however passionately the effects of sensibility (or any emotion-arousing state) may be felt by them at the time. This conclusion might seem to have the comforting corollary that negative as well as positive effects are merely fleeting; but if this is what Rousseau thought, he was unable to persuade the public authorities of it, those who banned the circulation of *Du contrat social* and *Emile* for their ungodliness. So we are not, on this interpretation, inspired to imitate the 'good' Alceste or the 'bad' Célimène: Rousseau implies the former but neglects to consider the latter, whether because in the spirit of Plato (and Calvin) he imputes overriding negative power to art, or for some other reason. This moral negativity, as well as its reverse, is discussed in Diderot's *Le Neveu de Rameau*, probably conceived at the beginning of the 1760s, but was curiously ignored in the *Fils naturel* (1757) and the *drame* theory that accompanied it. Perhaps this simply shows that Diderot, despite appearances, was as ambivalent about moral indoctrination through art as Rousseau appeared to be; but only in Rousseau's case does the overwhelming potential power of literature to harm—author rather than consumer—seem to have resulted in its abandonment, largely because he openly published his writings, and suffered for it, while Diderot mostly refrained from doing so.

Thus it is, Rousseau concludes, that the worldly-wise Molière wrote *Le Misanthrope* in order to show the man of principle undone in the face of social corruption, and thus it is that popular art is never moral, and why Geneva must stand firm against those who propose to establish a theatre within its walls. The modern world rates superficiality above profundity, sets appearance and reality against each other (though the state of Geneva may be an exception), and lets appearance win. Thus, furthermore, are artificial needs generated at the cost of real ones, and goods that flatter pride and vanity produced in developed societies. As luxury and idleness proliferate, so wickedness takes root and basic human relationships degenerate, with disproportionate wealth in the hands of the few and boundless suffering afflicting the many. The Golden Age was that stage in the history of man when the brutish struggle to stay alive gave way to peaceful coexistence and mutual supportiveness, but decline set in with the arrival of over-refinement and the assertion of material and moral inequalities (an argument that the second *Discours* had already advanced).

The *Lettre à d'Alembert* marks Rousseau's third major effort, in a period of great literary fruitfulness, to save society from itself by developing a theory of leisure that tied it productively with the world of work, and thereby to re-establish a new form of mutuality. The Golden Age provided a model for developing the 'arts' of agriculture and metallurgy to the benefit of all, so enabling craft to flourish as a cohesive and constructive force, before a negative materialism—the desire for more goods than were needful, often for the purpose of asserting superiority over those possessing fewer—led to general social corruption. Rousseau's Geneva myth provides a parallel to this picture, enabling him to express an old theory with fresh urgency. The past pattern, he argues, predicts the future decline, one that will see Geneva fall as other societies have already fallen. Individual and collective alienation must inevitably ensue.

The moral focus of Rousseau's argument, then, has shifted. The first *Discours* saw morality as adversely affected by the development of the arts and sciences, while the preface to *Narcisse* traced a more complex relationship between them.[21] The *Lettre*, finally, relates the pleasure principle (which, it realistically assumes, will generally be set above that of utility) to the performance of drama, whose effect it sees as directly linked to a compromising conformity between plot and public taste.[22] Is the same type of pattern found in practical life? Rousseau says that it is, but with a qualitative distinction between types of human response sought in the real world and in the theatre. Real objects, he implies, answer, or are made

---

[21] Preface to *Narcisse*, II.972–3.   [22] *Lettre à d'Alembert*, V.16–17.

to answer, physical requirements, calls for sustenance in the widest sense; imagined ones, characteristically having no practical purpose in view, simply mirror society's mores and flatter human passions, however depraved. It is in this sense that art objects differ from craft products, for craft aims to make a positive practical difference to human states, not merely reflect types of similarity (a distinction that rests on the assumption of art's mimetic essence). Craft's purpose is not to be mimetic or cautionary, or abstract in any sense; rather than re-present, it *adds on* in the service of practicality. In that respect there may be no need for its benefits to be 'sold' to the potential consumer; it answers preexisting needs, rather than creating desires of which the subject was unaware.

Rousseau's verdict on the human search for diversion rather than correction, in the theatre or elsewhere, may remind his reader of Pascal's theory of 'divertissement', the pastime sought by the idle to mask what is truly lacking in their lives. The goal of both writers is to reach the 'gens oisifs'[23] (a type radically distinct from Rousseau the 'oisif') who seek only the flattery of their passions, and whose amusement wastes both time and money. It is, one might think, the polar opposite of the only type of responsible theatregoer Rousseau could have envisaged, the one whom Diderot's *drame* genre is intended to address. Yet Rousseau appears to take no account of the latter possibility, perversely (or self-servingly) focusing on the 'degrading' genre of comedy and the alleged lampooning of *Le Misanthrope*'s Alceste. Why? In large part, probably, because he had fallen out of sympathy with Diderot, the 'former' friend and critic so pointedly invoked in the prefatory notice to the *Lettre*.[24] If Rousseau ignores the radically corrective intention of *drame*, the insidious attack he assumed Diderot had launched against him in *Le Fils naturel* proper may be sufficient explanation. This was the Rousseau who, both despite and because of the Vincennes experience, would vow to give up writing literature and turn instead to craft after the public authorities had censored the 'useful' *Emile* and *Du contrat social*. The fact is deeply ironic. If he had been prepared to promote the claims of *drame*, he might have saved himself the trouble of writing the *Lettre*.

Diderot's play is famous for the line Rousseau took to be a dig at him, Constance's statement that 'Il n'y a que le méchant qui soit seul.'[25] The notion of being alone *and yet* doing good to one's fellows became inextricably associated with its antithesis in Rousseau's mind and life, and is given poignant expression in one of his 1762 letters to Malesherbes.[26] It is a hypothesis that

---

[23] *Lettre à d'Alembert*, V.85.   [24] *Lettre à d'Alembert*, V.7.
[25] Act IV, scene 3.   [26] *O.C.*, I.1143 (28 January 1762).

Diderot had considered only to reject it in *Le Fils naturel*, where the apparent misfit Dorval is cured by a good woman's love of the belief that the best thing he can do for society is withdraw from it, so ceasing to contaminate the lives of others through the apparently (but altogether unexplained) fatal consequences of his living as an illegitimate son in their midst. Doing the right thing by men in absentia and in apparent inactivity was a tricky notion to convey persuasively, but Rousseau believed that he was doing it in his country seclusion by reflecting on and drafting the moral works published in the early 1760s. He may have appeared idle to his former friends and associates, in other words, but knew himself how mentally and socially engaged he was: he had consecrated himself to the planning and writing of texts that would attempt to resurrect and then express the vital doctrines glimpsed en route to Vincennes.

Let us return, finally, to Rousseau's theory of imagination and audience response. It is one thing, we may consider, for the naïve consumer (such as the child Jean-Jacques) to become every character he reads about, but quite another for the mature adult to do so; and Rousseau provides no illustration of the latter type. The discerning adult does not require an uncritical imaginative identification in order to be absorbed by literature, since reading has become for him a more strongly intellectual process than it can be for the child, one that permits—and perhaps even demands—a degree of distance from the subject at hand. Rousseau, however, denies this distance, resting his case on the 'contagious' *and essentially negative* effect of art on its consumer. It is the quintessential, but oddly despairing, view of the 'homme sensible'. Hence the embargo on art already implied in the *Discours sur les sciences et les arts* and later suffered with the public burning of his books. The *Lettre* both reflects the former and anticipates the latter.

NATURE AND ART

Yet for as long as the need to write obsessed him—for as long, that is, as he possessed insights related to the inspiration of 1749—, Rousseau carried on writing. The account the *Confessions* gives of the process that led him to start what became *La Nouvelle Héloïse*[27] makes it sound like the 'sensible' (feeling) product of febrile exaltation, best resolved through the imaginative resources literature put at his disposal: he declaredly wrote the first few letters with no plan and no sense of the plot a novel would require. As has

[27] *Confessions*, I.427–36.

often been remarked, his infatuation for the aristocratic Sophie d'Houdetot, Saint-Lambert's lover, was not the catalyst for the writing but the focus for its continuation. Yet the passionate explosion this implies, and which indeed characterizes the opening section, found its corrective in the later one describing Julie's 'mariage de raison' to the arch-rationalist Wolmar. Every principle of this dry, methodical man stands counter to the once rampant forces of Julie and her lover Saint-Preux's sensibility, at least until Julie's sudden conversion on her wedding day: if love for both of them was mirrored in great works of literature they read together, living, for the Wolmars, is a matter of practicality, not poetry. This contrast is figured in the polarity of country and town, moderation and excess, necessity and luxury, authenticity and falseness, collectedness and alienation, and other antitheses familiar in Rousseau. All, to a degree, exemplify the opposition of craft and art. Yet the contrasts are not straightforward.

We know that Rousseau was powerfully drawn towards Paris,[28] more strongly than he shows Saint-Preux to be, and that some of his later discomfiture there stemmed more from the embarrassment his health caused him than from a radical dislike of urban life. (His letters to Malesherbes of January 1762 contain a degree of special pleading in this respect.) We know, equally, that the country as well as the city became home to the mechanical arts that both brutalized man and saved him from physical exhaustion. Nothing is simple in this regard, though the *Encyclopédistes'* aim to unify brain skills and hand skills was an attempt to defuse old arguments and assumptions about social and intellectual hierarchies. Rationalism, which created machines, did not simply denature; it might as easily help humans to flourish. The rural economy of the Wolmar estate is a rationalist one, a colony run along frugal lines and according to (bourgeois) principles of thrift, eschewing luxury and waste and promoting the contrasting qualities of sobriety and proportion as though it were a latter-day offshoot of Calvin's Geneva.[29] Clarens advertises the wisdom of living according to the means available, where the economy of simple exchange makes money almost redundant (Rousseau has already described such an economy in Swiss mountain communities). The estate produces goods that, in combination with those grown by Julie's father the baron d'Etange, cover all the homestead's basic needs in food, drink, textiles, and other commodities, and where whatever is surplus to requirement can be ploughed back into the 'business' or sold outside by hiring extra journeymen's labour.[30]

---

[28] See Jean-Louis Lecerc, 'Rousseau critique littéraire. "Le cœur" et "la plume"', in Harvey et al., *Reappraisals*, pp. 215–31, at p. 225.
[29] Compare Sewell, *Work*, p. 70.   [30] *La Nouvelle Héloïse, O.C.*, II.442–8.

Clarens has, so to speak, its own sumptuary laws, and easily respects the unwritten prohibition on showy wealth and vainglorious display.[31] Julie epitomizes this spirit, blending the homespun with the elegant, her whole person an example to be imitated by those around her, a model of restraint for men as well as women to observe. In their persons she and Wolmar embody all the virtues of good husbandry: that the estate is run on paternalistic, sometimes positively repressive lines seems to offend no one, partly, no doubt, because the workers' lives simply mirror the pattern of continence preached and practised by master and mistress, whose union is one of prudent respect, not rampant sexuality. Despite appearances, Wolmar represents Everyman, as Emile will later do; he is a man who has, with one important proviso, tried all the professions 'dont jamais homme de [ma condition] ne s'étoit avisé',[32] even lived as a peasant, anticipating Rousseau's claim in the first preamble to the *Confessions* that 'sans avoir aucun état moi-même, j'ai connu tous les états; j'ai vécu dans tous, depuis les plus bas jusqu'aux plus elevés, excepté le trone'.[33]

Julie's prudent and restrained creativity is symbolic as well as practical. What in a different milieu seemed doctrinaire here becomes practical, rational moderateness, all reinforced by an ethos that makes the contrived appear natural. Julie is a worker, not a thinker, artisan as well as mistress, her wisdom practical, born of experience, entailing bodily engagement with the physical world, a decent feminine activeness of the sort society has consecrated: a woman who sews, clothes, and organizes the domestic interior. Her gynaseum is a centre of textile production, mirroring *in petto* that of Switzerland itself, where spinning and weaving were initially cottage industries developed as adjuncts to agriculture. The textiles made at Clarens are almost all home-produced, with only wool sent away to be made into cloth[34]—to Geneva, perhaps, where its manufacture dated from the mid-sixteenth century. Since the estate's products are meant above all to be useful, only secondarily attractive, it disdains the silk that must be processed in Zurich and Geneva,[35] because silk is a luxury. The median type of cloth manufacture, blending beauty with practicality, was that of 'toile peinte' such as Rousseau's relative Antoine Fazy produced in

---

[31] *La Nouvelle Héloïse, O.C.*, II.550–1.
[32] *La Nouvelle Héloïse, O.C.*, II.492.   [33] *Confessions*, I.150.
[34] See Ulrich Pfister, 'Craft Guilds, the Theory of the Firm, and Early Modern Proto-Industry', in S. R. Epstein and Martin Prak (eds.), *Innovation and the European Economy, 1400–1800* (Cambridge: Cambridge University Press, 2008), pp. 25–51, p. 49.
[35] Pfister in Epstein and Prak, pp. 25–51, p. 49.

the factories at Eaux-Vives and then Pâquis, based on the model imported from Holland.

The Elysée, the garden Julie makes to mark her reform from lover to wife, displays only art that conceals itself, the natural-artificial garden that marked a final synthesizing stage in horticultural style, the composite type described in Watelet's *Essai sur les jardins* of 1774.[36] The Elysée eschews everything that is outlandish (Rousseau hated exotic plants), letting the everyday show to advantage, with wild flowers thriving and dominating the cultivated ones amongst which they are scattered,[37] the whole an antithesis of the seventeenth-century 'geometrical' or 'rational' French garden associated with Le Nôtre, and instead promoting the horticultural landscape inspired by eighteenth-century England.[38] If Saint-Preux slams Stowe for its purpose-built artifice and manufactured ruins, things that flout all claims to naturalism, others saw it as a blessedly idealized landscape, one even including its own Elysian Fields, a miniature world abhorring rectilinearity and manifest order, disguising man-made inventions in favour of successive vistas that proclaimed the virtue of formlessness. This quality of naturalness is of course somewhat compromised by the means through which it is sustained and flourishes, as Saint-Preux claims is also true at Stowe;[39] the water running through the Elysée has been diverted from elsewhere, as it was in the Bossey garden where Rousseau and his cousin built their aqueduct, its source undeniably the work of humans, and only apparently resembling the spontaneous and energetic love of Julie and Saint-Preux. It is, in fact, controlled by the rational mind, just like Julie's marriage, like Clarens itself. And at the end, like Rousseau's aqueduct, it is broken up, destroyed.

Does this end the tension between what is natural and what has been crafted in order to deny its source in art? Among the various answers provided by Rousseau's writings, *La Nouvelle Héloïse* reveals with particular clarity the difficulty of preserving the balance between nature in art and art in nature. As the Elysée flourishes only through calculation, so too do the Wolmar marriage and the entire estate of Clarens subsist according to a rigid interpretation of dutiful work and performance. Husbandry,

---

[36] See William Howard Adams, *The French Garden 1500–1800* (London: Scholar Press, 1979), p. 115; Dora Wiebenson, *The Picturesque Garden in France* (Princeton: Princeton University Press, 1978), p. 65.

[37] *La Nouvelle Héloïse*, II.471–9.

[38] See, *inter alia*, Sophie Le Ménahèze, *L'Invention du jardin romantique en France, 1761–1808* (Neuilly-sur-Seine: Editions Spiralinthe, 2002).

[39] *La Nouvelle Héloïse*, II.484.

sexual as well as economic, requires respect for norms and limitations, as all human creation does: fertilizing ground that would otherwise be barren belongs to agriculture, which *Emile* will call the highest of the various estates developed by man.[40] Re-naturing, as the Wolmars attempt it, involves repeatedly feeding the soil so that it produces more than it would do uncultivated; left untended, it is simply lazy, as 'désœuvré' as we may imagine the restless, rootless, futile city-dweller chasing life's diversions to be.

Perhaps what the agricultural artist does, though, is make the body's real engagement with the world of nature count:[41] only then may his knowledge be called truly grounded, like the artisan's. This view, that art and practical experience belong together, informs the *Encyclopédistes'* desire to re-route human understanding so that the practicality associated with the world of craft became as highly valued as the products of the arts and sciences. This in turn matched Rousseau's faith in 'sensible' (felt) experience in the *Confessions*, that knowledge we possess because we have felt it in and with our bodies rather than intellectually learnt it: the 'matérialisme du sage', the craftsman's knowledge in essence, a matter of touching, feeling, seeing, even smelling and tasting, whatever is material. And 'de toutes les occupations qui peuvent fournir la subsistence à l'homme', *Emile* will announce, 'celle qui le rapproche le plus à l'état de Nature est le travail des mains'.[42]

According to the *Confessions*, Rousseau did a fair copy of parts I and II of *Julie* in the winter of 1757–8 'avec un plaisir inexprimable, employant pour cela le plus beau papier doré, de la poudre d'azur et d'argent pour sécher l'écriture, de la nom pareille bleue pour coudre mes cahiers, enfin ne trouvant rien d'assez gallant, rien d'assez mignon pour les charmantes filles dont je raffolais comme un autre Pigmalion'.[43] (Gilt-edged paper had been prohibited even for the pages of the Bible by the Calvinist city fathers of Geneva, but the bible of sensibility *La Nouvelle Héloïse* became another matter.) Why copy in the age of print? Rousseau knew that such an undertaking was the most flattering he could contrive for two favoured readers. When the Maréchale de Luxembourg heard that the novel was in press, and made clear her interest in it,[44] Rousseau first read sections to her and her husband and then promised to transcribe it for her by hand, as he was already doing for Sophie d'Houdetot, at an agreed rate. A letter he wrote Sophie on 23 November 1757 reported that he was about to begin this task, starting with part II;[45] he continued with part I,

---

[40] *Emile*, IV.460, 470.   [41] See Smith, *Body*, p. 19.
[42] *Emile*, IV.470.   [43] *Confessions*, I.436.
[44] *Confessions*, I.522.   [45] *C.C.*, IV.374.

and was paid two louis for the 351 pages completed. In late October 1758 he briefly halted work on her copy, offended by the insult he had received from Saint-Lambert in response to the attack on Diderot contained in the preface to the *Lettre à d'Alembert*,[46] though there was, according to the *Confessions*, a swift reconciliation and hence resumption of work. 'Les copies de Mad^e d'Houdetot qu'elle m'engagea de reprendre, mes ouvrages que je continuai de lui envoyer quand ils paroissoient, m'attirérent encore de sa part de tems à autre quelques messages et billets indifférens mais obligeans'.[47] The fifth volume was finished in October 1759, with the entire manuscript eventually filling six small volumes of 2,000 pages. The Maréchale's version was complete by the end of 1760.

For a man who had copied thousands of pages of notes as amanuensis to Mme Dupin, this was evidently not a troublesome process; it became a powerfully sensuous one, indeed, when the aesthetic pleasure of calligraphy was complemented by the use of fine paper, and when the powder horn was filled, not with the usual ground-up chalk or pumice stone, but with the dust of precious metals. But was what motivated Rousseau a sense of responsibility towards his clients, towards his novel, or towards himself? Probably all three. Making the duplicate manuscripts certainly met the essential requirement of keeping his hands occupied when reflection had become intense and even burdensome. Above all, it fulfilled his need for a specific kind of leisure: 'C'est d'ailleurs une occupation oiseuse qui laissera à mon esprit [then meditating the project that became *Emile*] le temps de se remettre et aux idées effarouchées le temps de revenir s'il y a moyen'.[48] These reflections relate to his apparent betrayal by Diderot, Mme d'Epinay, and other erstwhile supporters, and combine in an image that makes copying seem almost a kind of moral blotting-paper, able to absorb, neutralize, or amortize the bitter gall of experience. (Ox or oak gall, incidentally, was the main constituent of eighteenth-century ink, mixed with gum Arabic for smoothness of flow.)

As for the Maréchale de Luxembourg, Rousseau seems to have misinterpreted a letter she sent him in response to one of his dated 29 October 1759 in which he makes the following remark: 'Quoique vous soyez surement une très bonne pratique, je me fais quelque peine de prendre de votre argent: regulierement ce seroit à moi de payer le plaisir que j'aurois de travailler pour vous'.[49] Her reply, Rousseau notes in the *Confessions*, 'me fit tomber des nues'; but her simple response to his claim, 'Je ne vous en dis pas davantage', surely expresses respect rather than irritation.

[46] *C.C.*, V.170 (11 October 1758).   [47] *Confessions*, I.501.
[48] *C.C.*, V.378 (30 November 1758).   [49] *Confessions*, I.523.

Rousseau's state of mind as he continued with these copies was certainly complex enough to make misunderstanding a constant danger. His feelings for Mme de Luxembourg are described in the *Confessions* as uneasy: 'Je n'ai [...] jamais été très à mon aise avec Mad^e la Maréchale. Quoique je ne fusse pas parfaitement rassuré sur son caractére je le redoutois moins que son esprit. C'étoit par là surtout qu'elle m'en imposoit',[50] although he became more relaxed as her respect and liking for him grew. Relations with Sophie d'Houdetot were another matter, and it is hard not to feel that doing this kind of handwork for her filled an erotic need of Rousseau's. The banished Saint-Preux, after all, copying Julie's letters to him into a bound volume, explains that they compensate for the physical presence now denied him; until then he has reread them obsessively, 'ne fut-ce que pour revoir les traits de cette main cherie qui seule peut faire mon bonheur',[51] such that the sheets have become creased and fragile. Writing freshly transcribed versions (where 'j'avancerai lentement' to prolong the pleasure) generates a store which 'ne me quitera de mes jours; il sera mon manuel dans le monde où je vais entrer'. Here the copying amounts to a form of possession of the other, through possession of her words—a kind of narcissism, perhaps, in conjunction with the copying of his own.

For just as Rousseau himself, like many of his contemporaries, made copies of the letters he sent, during his stay in Môtiers he also transcribed several of those he received into a blank volume as preparation for the memoirs he was then, at Rey's request, planning to write.[52] When Sophie d'Houdetot asked him to destroy those she had sent him he complied, but was greatly upset when he discovered that she had done the same with his. Saint-Preux's fondness for copying extends beyond this, however, as the episode of the corrected miniature portrait of Julie illustrates.

Rousseau's concern for the look of his manuscripts was not mere coquettishness. Although his drafts are sometimes over-written and otherwise revised,[53] they are seldom hard to read, even where the script becomes diminutive. If the version meant for Rey none the less came to seem too untidy for that purpose to Rousseau, it remained in his own hands. He made alterations to it as he wrote the later sections of the novel and while he was doing Sophie d'Houdetot's copy; the final version he sent his publisher between April 1759 and 18 January 1760 was, he wrote, therefore to be followed precisely, the text printed on good paper and with 'le plus grand soin, caractére et format dont nous conviendrons [...].

[50] *Confessions*, I.p. 522.   [51] *La Nouvelle Héloïse*, II.229.
[52] *Confessions*, I.607.   [53] See *O.C.*, II.lxxiv–lxxv.

On suivra exactement mon manuscrit, l'orthographe, la ponctuation, même les fautes, sans se mêler d'y rien corriger'.[54] This last instruction reminds us of his stated preference for euphony over grammatical correctness in cases where their respective requirements clashed: as he told Rey, who had on one occasion made the word 'femme' plural against Rousseau's desire, 'l'harmonie me paraît d'une si grande importance en fait de style que je la mets immédiatement après la clarté, meme avant la correction'.[55] He makes Julie his exemplar in this respect: 'elle avait l'oreille trop delicate pour s'asservir toujours aux règles, même qu'elle savait. On peut employer un style plus pur, mais non pas plus doux ni plus harmonieux que le sien.'[56]

The evidence suggests that Rousseau spent less time than the dates of his various submissions to Rey implied on the recopying his authorial fastidiousness required, refusing to post him the successive parts of the novel until he had been paid for the previous ones (Rey was sometimes dilatory). Sophie d'Houdetot's version took him over two years to complete, but the Luxembourg copy much less. To ring the changes he chose to customize the latter version by adding to it a digest of the Milord Edouard/Lauretta Pisani imbroglio[57] which he had earlier rejected partly because of a vague and unflattering similarity between Lauretta and Mme de Luxembourg, but which fatally returned to his mind as he cast around for further ways in which to tailor the Maréchale's copy to its recipient: 'J'eus la stupidité de faire cet extrait avec bien du soin, bien du travail et de lui envoyer ce morceau comme la plus belle chose du monde; en la prévenant toutefois, comme il étoit vrai, que j'avois brûlé l'original, que l'extrait étoit pour elle seule et ne seroit jamais vu de personne à moins qu'elle ne le montrât elle-même'[58]—which, he ruefully reflected, was precisely calculated to make her see disobliging resemblances between herself and Bomston's lover. He remained in ignorance of her feelings about this backhanded compliment until some time later; for the present, 'à ma très grande surprise, elle ne me parla pas du cahier que je lui avois envoyé'. Although he based the Luxembourg version not on the Rey manuscript, but on an earlier one that he then modified, her copy, like Mme d'Houdetot's, is of exquisite clarity and neatness. Doing a scribe's work, evidently, was for Rousseau anything but a mechanical process; it told a parable of personalization in an increasingly machine-driven world.

[54] *C.C.*, VI.44 (14 March 1759) and *O.C.*, II.1335.
[55] *C.C.*, V.111 (8 July 1758).   [56] *O.C.*, II.693, n.
[57] *O.C.*, II.524–5.   [58] *O.C.*, II.525.

His alertness to orthographical as well as typographical beauty was matched by his keen monitoring of the proposed illustrations. Gravelot's original drawings would eventually be bound into the Luxembourg copy of *La Nouvelle Héloïse*, with the engravings done after them inserted into the regular printed text. But according to Rousseau, his middleman Coindet, guessing that he planned to present the drawings to the Maréchale, played him false by making the gift himself, allegedly in order to curry favour with her husband, even though, Rousseau remarks, they 'm'appartenoient à toutes sortes de titres, et d'autant plus que je lui avois abandonné le produit des planches, lesquelles eurent un grand débit'.

Rousseau had originally thought of commissioning Boucher for the illustrations,[59] before reflecting that he was too mannered and possibly too self-important for the task, while Cochin was too busy. (Mme d'Houdetot, who in a letter to Rousseau of 1 December 1757 expressed interest in seeing the pictures, suggested Carle Van Loo,[60] but this notion seems not to have been taken further.)[61] Depicting Rousseau's detailed scenes sometimes required a degree of resourcefulness and particularity no artist could supply, though their intention was less to encourage an impossible and comprehensive accuracy than to suggest a mood: 'car pour rendre heureusement un dessin', Rousseau vaguely observes, 'l'Artiste ne doit pas le voir tel qu'il sera sur son papier, mais tel qu'il est dans la nature'.[62] The essential difference between visual and verbal art, the former spatial but static and the latter temporal but non-depictive, were widely discussed at about this time. In the first scene to be illustrated, for example, Rousseau seeks a complexity that seems beyond the scope of any artist: 'Julie doit se pâmer et non s'évanouir',[63] and Saint-Preux's face must express both pleasure and alarm. The second is equally impressionistic: the kneeling figure of Edouard 'imprime du respect aux autres, et [...] ils semblent tous à genoux devant lui'. In the third, writes Rousseau, a gesture of cold disdain should be mitigated by an air of compassion for Saint-Preux, whose attitude is meant to suggest that his friend's gaze is discountenancing him. In the fifth Saint-Preux kisses Julie's hand with a mixture of love and grief that conveys his desire to catch smallpox from her. In the tenth, having thrown himself out of bed and grabbed a dressing-gown, he wanders about the room groping after objects and feeling his way to the door. Other prescriptions are similarly and impossibly demanding. Gravelot did his best, all the same.

[59] *C.C.*, IV.384 (5 December 1757).   [60] *C.C.*, IV.382.
[61] *C.C.*, IV.390 (14 December 1757).   [62] *O.C.*, II.761.
[63] *O.C.*, II.763.

Some of Rousseau's objections to the illustrations were easier to address than others, admittedly: in a letter to Coindet of 12 November 1760, for example, he protested that the artist was making Julie and Claire too flat-chested. Other criticisms simply seem unimaginative ('le crayon ne distingue pas une blonde d'une brune') or unhelpful in other ways ('Le burin marque mal les clairs et les ombres, si le Graveur n'imagine aussi les couleurs').[64] While acknowledging that the static nature of visual images is provoking, he thinks it can be overcome to a degree: 'il faut voir ce qui precede et ce qui suit, et donner au tems de l'action une certaine latitude; sans quoi l'on ne saisira jamais bien l'unité du moment qu'il faut exprimer',[65] an observation that seems of little practical use. The essential principle remains this: 'L'habileté de l'Artiste consiste à faire imaginer au Spectateur beaucoup de choses qui ne sont pas sur la planche', though it is surely a matter of opinion how this can best be done. No illustrator, he knows, can succeed without the reader's imaginative sympathy, the same projection, concessive or not, as all reading requires. A letter from Rousseau to Rey of 17 April 1760 hints at a more prosaic theory of graphic representation in literature that makes clear Rousseau's concern with the overall look of his novel. Hence his vetoing Rey's proposal of small vignettes at the beginning of each book:

il faudroit trouver des sujets rélatifs au caractère de l'ouvrage, et c'est ce qui n'est pas aisé. Il faudroit que les figures fussent élégantes et légères; et c'est ce que la vignette du discours sur l'inégalité ne me laisse espérer ni de vos dessinateurs ni de vos graveurs. En général les figures, et surtout celles qui demandent de l'expression, sont très difficiles à rendre dans les vignettes parce que l'espace est trop petite. Dans un recueil tel que le nôtre des vignettes maussades gâteroient tout. C'étoient des estampes qu'il nous faloit; tous les sujets en étoient piquans, elles auroient été charmantes; c'eût été peut être le plus agréable recueil d'estampes qu'on eût fait en ce siécle, et je suis très sûr qu'elles seules eussent fait la fortune du livre.[66]

Are these imagined decorations like the 'indifferent' ornaments the *Confessions* proposes (the substitution of imagined truths for facts he has forgotten), that is, not really indifferent at all?[67] A strict Calvinist interpretation would have deprecated both, but strict Calvinism no longer quite obtained in the city of his birth, and which he had anyway left far behind. The useful bit of writing, such as the first *Discours*, was not rendered less so by the supplement of vignette or other type of decoration, the intellect not clouded or disturbed by aesthetic beauty any more than the serviceable qualities of the craft object are compromised by some beautifying addition. Printer's lace may coexist with other types of graphic enhancement both to elevate a publication that proclaims the interplay of line and light, of graphics and typography, and to bring about that sympathy Foucault discerned between container and contained. The 'feeling' fabrication of a book, that is, may be as much a part of its identity as what its printed words proclaim, craftsmanship and art enhancing verbal meaning in a mutually supportive act of declaration. Each supplements the other, helps complete it, if we take the verb 'suppléer' in its newer sense (one with which the 'supplément' of Rousseau's guilty sexual pleasure contrasts) as designating not that which can *replace* but that which *complements*. There is no projection into pure aesthetic space or its semantic counterpart, even if that were possible, but a constant and enriching move from form to thought and back again.

The success of *La Nouvelle Héloïse* was independent of its illustrations, however; the text alone created a sensation. What followed it, ironically, earned Rousseau a different notoriety, one he bitterly regretted. At its heart were the abstract precepts, the allegedly unChristian doctrines, of *Emile* and *Du contrat social*. Yet abstraction contradicted all the lessons *Emile* aimed to teach—lessons on craft consciousness and handwork that Rousseau's childhood days in his father's workshop had first given him. They seemed to capture the essence of a manual age.

5

Emile, Wealth and Wellbeing

BODILY RESOURCE

The letter Rousseau wrote Malesherbes on 12 January 1762 mentions *Emile*—'le traité de l'éducation'—as one of the three works he had conceived en route for Vincennes in 1749,[1] when a sudden vision showed him how man's natural goodness had been warped by social institutions. The insights *Emile* relays were radical in its time, and remain so. Yet its response to the Enlightenment project of improvement, or 'perfectionnement', still seemed to some readers retrograde, particularly in its attitude towards the intellectual development of man (and woman). Rousseau's purpose, however, had simply been to balance the claims of mind against those of the body, in which respect *Emile* owed much to predecessors such as Locke's *Some Thoughts Concerning Education*. Its focus on the need to banish physical restriction and so promote free bodily expression was less innovative than its treatment of some other eighteenth-century themes.

The anti-bookishness the work parades looks odd in light of Rousseau's own activities, especially from the late 1750s to the early 1760s, a time when he was much busier writing than working as a music copyist. Given what he had to say, this seems reasonable. Books, we know, and Rousseau knew, for good and ill are adjuncts to the job of living, extending us in thought as practical tools extend our limbs and faculties: the lens gives our eyes greater reach (such metaphors often borrow from the language of touch), the telephone our ears and voice, wheels our legs and entire body. But the volumes Rousseau borrowed as a boy from La Tribu's lending library, along with those, like Plutarch's *Famous Lives*, belonging to his father, and the novels he inherited from his mother, awakened him to possibilities beyond the usual data of sensory experience, enhanced or otherwise. Equally clearly, as Julie and Saint-Preux discovered, their doctrine might be dangerous if taken as a guide for life. Hence the warnings *Emile* will articulate.

[1] *O.C.*, I.1136.

Perhaps this means no more than that books which stretch the mind should be approached with caution, just like other mind- and body-stretching tools the mentor reserves until Emile has become acquainted with more fundamental life supports. The first step in his elementary education is to insist that Emile make the basic implements and instruments he needs to live, since to receive them ready made will narrow the range of practical possibilities he should be exploring. Toolmaking lets him stay in touch with ordinary substances, making certain (reasonable) demands on practical intelligence and bodily adaptability, and significantly extends his power over the phenomenal world. Even so, his teacher counsels moderation, thinking it an evil of advanced society to have so many tools that individuals never test their own physical resources:

> Que pensera-t-il en voyant que les arts ne se perfectionnent qu'en se subdivisant, en multipliant à l'infini les instrumens des uns et des autres? [Emile] se dira: tous ces gens-là sont sotement ingénieux. On croiroit qu'ils ont peur que leurs bras et leurs doigts ne leur servent à quelque chose, tant ils inventent d'instrumens pour s'en passer. Pour exercer un seul art ils sont asservis à mille autres, il faut une ville à chaque ouvrier. Pour mon camarade et moi nous mettons nôtre génie dans nôtre addresse; nous nous faisons des outils que nous puissions porter par tout avec nous.[2]

Parisians who pride themselves on all their talents would know nothing on Emile's island, and so be forced to become apprentices; for it is better to exercise a rough justice in which the haves are made have-nots than to leave the status quo unchanged. All unnatural inequality is reprehensible, Rousseau thinks, but the socialised type particularly so; 'proper' victims may therefore be targeted while the overall process of social levelling works itself out. As the *Discours sur l'origine de l'inégalité* makes clear, however, rough justice is never preferable to real even-handedness.

Machines, even though they may be merely tool agglomerates, must be handled cautiously. Rousseau does not mention them in describing the development of Emile's practical intelligence, knowing that they can alienate the user by distancing him from direct engagement with the world around him. Individual tools, by contrast, visibly extend the human reach, with the visibility enhanced by the user's practical understanding: by making tools we become an active part of all the processes they facilitate, processes that might otherwise be depersonalized. 'S'il travaille lui-même, à chaque outil dont il se sert il ne manquera pas de se dire: si je n'avois pas cet outil comment m'y prendrois-je pour en faire un semblable ou pour m'en passer?'[3] This is part of the deconstruction of the 'managed'

---

[2] *Emile*, IV.460.   [3] *Emile*, IV.460.

world that forms part of Emile's practical education. From childish curiosity about his environment, he advances to complex understanding, with complexity broken down into discrete perceptions: 'd'instrument en instrument il voudra toujours remonter au prémier',[4] never content with mere supposition about how metal is obtained or where the fabric of a wooden chest comes from. The role of tools is to do what human limbs and organs cannot, to mine metal or chop down trees as much as to gaze at stars or inspect the microscopic forms of living things.

Emile is concerned with curiosity and curiosity's creative realization, invention; with anchoring the mind while using the body's resourcefulness. Staying in Paris hemmed Rousseau in, as he explained to Malesherbes; he needed seclusion to nurture thought and give it practical expression. So does Emile, at least to a degree. But whereas Rousseau wanted solitude in order to develop specific ideas, Emile needs country living to develop physical freedom and its extension into moral space, the room required for learning lessons about life. This openness is vital for the active education planned for him, the process of learning through doing. Living apart from the crowdedness of cities lets the boy experience extent, the sense of which promotes his bodily awareness and sharpens his ability to focus on a range of different physical perceptions. Cumulatively, they help Emile to understand the world. Keeping bodies supple, Rousseau thinks, alone permits the mental flexibility humans need ('mens sana in corpore sano'): it will make Emile conscious of possibilities the untrained self is ignorant of simply because it relies on settled sensory and mental aids. And 'plus nos outils sont ingénieux plus nos organes deviennent grossiers et maladroits; à force de rassembler des machines autour de nous, nous n'en trouvons plus en nous-mêmes'.[5] Tools empower the self at the price of weakening it.

We cannot escape this paradox: machines are made by man, yet they outstrip him. Diderot's *Encyclopédie* entry 'Bas' quotes Charles Perrault's comment that complex mechanisms exceed the range of even the most cultivated minds, that 'Ceux qui ont assez de génie, non pas pour inventer de semblables choses, mais pour les comprendre, tombent dans un profond étonnement à la vue des ressorts dont la machine à bas est composée, et du grand nombre des divers et extraordinaires mouvemens'. The point of the detailed *Encyclopédie* descriptions and illustrations of different machines is not to enable readers to use them—the 'heure de travail qui lui [Emile] apprendra plus de choses qu'il n'en retiendrait d'un jour d'explications' states the obvious fact that what is learnt with the head

---

[4] *Emile*, IV.460.   [5] *Emile*, IV.443.

inevitably fails to yield what direct practical engagement does—but to give them the maximum degree of practical understanding. By the time the *Encyclopédie* entries such as 'Bas' were published, the borrowed seventeenth-century plates drawn to illustrate what became Réaumur and Duhamel de Monceau's *Description des arts et métiers*, widely used by Diderot, were out of date.[6] It is likely, furthermore, that his acquaintance with the engineering and other manufacturing processes described in many *Encyclopédie* entries was based on material borrowed from the Bibliothèque du Roi rather than hands-on experience in the workshop.[7] In its referential or virtual nature, besides, language can only attempt to copy a non-identical medium, not *be* that medium, which clearly qualifies its usefulness as a tool for re-presenting implements and processes. What compendia such as the *Encyclopédie* do best is to teach their users how and why to wonder, make them read for knowledge of the universe's laws and their practical application by man, who since he cannot overcome them has to bend them to his purpose. In the process he reveals the extent to which the human race, thinking to dominate nature, in fact remains subordinate to it. If the villagers Rousseau attempted to dazzle as a boy had seen the real beauty of the natural laws harnessed by his Heron's fountain, they might have paid him for the sight; for machines express the universe's laws in ways that, whether understood or not, can astonish. Equally, they may leave us comparatively indifferent.

So man, whom Rousseau saw as God's creation, but whom contemporaries such as La Mettrie and Diderot regarded as a strictly materialist entity, was an infinitely complex machine, albeit one performing actions he could not account for and subject to forces greater than himself. As Perrault remarks, it is man in whom 'mille operations differentes se font pour le nourrir et pour le conserver sans qu'il les comprenne, sans qu'il les connaisse et meme sans qu'il y songe';[8] not even a Vaucanson could penetrate and imitate them all. Human perfectibility expresses a constant striving towards the state of completeness the natural world embodies; it is not yet that state, the goal of that striving. The *Encyclopédie* project was conceived in order to help achieve it.

    [6] On accusations of plagiarism by the *Encyclopédie* editors, see Georges Huard, 'Les Planches de l'*Encyclopédie* et celles de la *Description des arts et métiers*', in Suzanne Delorme and René Tatou (eds.), *L' « Encyclopédie » et le progrès des sciences et des techniques* (Paris: Presses Universitaires de France, 1952), pp. 35–46, esp. p. 40.
    [7] See Jacques Proust, 'De l'*Encyclopédie* au *Neveu de Rameau*: l'objet et le texte', in Jacques Proust (ed.), *Recherches nouvelles sur quelques écrivains des Lumières* (Geneva: Droz, 1972), pp. 273–340, esp. p. 278.
    [8] Quoted in *Encyclopédie* entry 'Bas'.

The ideal, as craftsman and engineer both know, is to turn the resourcefulness that helped man dispense with certain tools to the making of instruments that significantly expand his creative potential, in ways that compensate for whatever loss of bodily skill tool-using may entail. 'Au lieu de coller un enfant sur des livres, si je l'occupe dans un Attelier ses mains travaillent au profit de son esprit, il devient philosophe et croit n'être qu'un ouvrier.'[9] Where the senses are dulled, praxis as well as mind is stunted. The productive combination of solitude and nature, then, produces a yield different in kind from the material plenty of industrialism, or what passed for it in Rousseau's age, but, so *Emile* suggests, brings a superior benefit. If this is a romantic interpretation, it is one that has been present in one form or another over the ages: the pragmatic resurrection later associated with the various arts and crafts movements is, with qualification, argued in one of the only two books his tutor recommends to Emile, *Robinson Crusoe*, a work of which Rousseau had once thought of publishing an adaptation.[10] Defoe depicts a world even more isolated than Emile's, and where the abundance of goods beyond individual need is shown to be by definition otiose, that is, non-functional, 'oiseux', just like the idle man. In the merchant traders' world Crusoe has left behind, matters are quite different: what it parades is capitalism in full flower, never satisfied, as Rousseau was, with merely enough, always wanting more. Solitary man, however, can neither barter nor exchange. The consequence, as Defoe shows, is to establish a new system of (Puritan) moral values, one that will strongly appeal to Rousseau's inbred Genevese austerity.

Robinson Crusoe can justify involuntary isolation[11] much as Rousseau's letter to Malesherbes of 12 January 1762 does his own deliberate retreat: it constitutes, *Emile* affirms, the kind of solitude that is most productive for man, producing benefits not merely preferable to those of communal life, but simply unthinkable within its confines. Is Rousseau's argument too absolute? The moral collapse that follows Emile and Sophie's move from (good) countryside to (bad) town in his unfinished sequel *Emile et Sophie*, or *Les Solitaires*, implies not, but readers may be unconvinced.

Before Man Friday's arrival, solitary work (integrity of labour, rather than its division) is a necessity for Crusoe, not a choice; his self-governance

---

[9] *Emile*, IV.443.

[10] See *C.C.*, XV.289–92 (from Jacques-François-Daniel Burnand to Rousseau, 18 March 1763) and n. b; XVI.354–6 (J. H. Füssli to L. Usteri, *c.* 28 June 281763) and n. b.

[11] See Ian Watt, '*Robinson Crusoe* as Myth', in *Essays in Criticism*, I (1951), pp. 95–119, esp. p. 99; Defoe, *Robinson Crusoe*, ed. J. Donald Crowley (Oxford: Oxford University Press, 1981), pp. 62–3.

has other roots than Emile's, a matter of need rather than principle. Educating the apparently wealthy Emile means teaching the virtue, not the fact, of self-reliance, extending mental reach in tandem with the body's limited but still considerable resources. Paradoxically, the mentor sees toolmaking as desirable precisely when the body can do without its products, for often what supports the self's sufficiency highlights a further purpose that external aids can independently achieve. Learning from such unsuspected purposes is the real discovery: not the new thing itself, but its actualization first in mental, then in practical terms.

Rousseau deplores the artificially generated needs of a materialistic world, things often desired more for their perceived prestige or rarity than for their true necessity: the former, he insists, can never be the concern of moral education. For what is the value, say, of a mechanical precision bought at the cost of something more profound, the fact of our simply losing touch? At a much lower level, the hand that lets scales weigh a quantity forgets how to judge what it amounts to by feeling it in the palm or on the arm, or even simply from looking at it.[12] Self-reliance becomes vital when letting the body lose its 'memory' brings other losses. The body has a clock no clockmaker can truly imitate; still less can he overcome its organic, not mechanical, power of telling the time. In the same way, the eye that trains itself to see unaided may lack range and minuteness, but not keeping it alert, habitually giving it crutches, eventually condemns its owner to reliance on external aids.

This creed of self-help is neither original nor unexpected, but Rousseau develops it here in ways that both illuminate the book's pedagogical themes and anticipate his own later autobiographical writings. The stress on autonomy again invites comparison with *Robinson Crusoe*, since both books deal with work that dignifies and cures the human sense of alienation: the man of action forges bonds with his environment that sustain him even when the world turns hostile, with shipwreck in the case of Crusoe, with capture and enslavement in Emile's. Or is it less that the world can be made fitter than that its threat can be addressed and thus potentially resolved? Should we simply avoid certain incautious actions, putting to sea like Crusoe, going to Paris like Emile (and Sophie)? Crusoe does not need to trade, as he does, in humans or exotic merchandise, nor Emile (or Sophie) to experience the febrile city life: they are, or so it seems, repaired when forced to live in nature's way, making objects at no cost to their environment, living ecologically, and learning patience in ways that are productive. Making bread takes Crusoe years, not hours or

---

[12] *Emile*, IV.442.

minutes, because he has to fence, dig, and till the soil, grow the grain, mill it into flour, sieve it, prepare yeast, salt the dough, and make receptacles in which to bake it.[13] Emile's moral and practical rebirth can occur only after his capture at sea, when he has patiently won the trust and respect of his new masters. These are all lessons in a different kind of time from that which ordinary clocks measure—the time of experience.

HUMAN RELATIONS

As Rousseau knew when he withdrew from Paris, and as he tried to explain to Malesherbes, deliberate isolation makes the world suspicious of the solitary individual, though there are exceptions: we may let the craftsman work in private because his skills need uninterrupted concentration to express themselves, just as the gardener's work needs time to reach fruition. Young Emile's act in laying waste Robert's kitchen garden is reprehensible on two counts, its inherent destructiveness and its failure to respect another person's labour over hours, days, months, and years. Where the purpose of work is fully understood, due respect for it will normally follow; but where the solitude ensuring its completion is attacked, the cause may be simple incomprehension rather than deliberate ill will. Rousseau suspected the latter, perhaps wrongly, in Constance's line about solitude and moral virtue in *Le Fils naturel*, because its expression coincided with his retreat from Paris; possibly, too, he was wrong in taking himself to be the type criticized in de Jaucourt's *Encyclopédie* entry 'Solitaire', which derides the blind insociability of hermits.

He still drew comfort from feeling that this retreat was socially useful, particularly as it let him use the pen, an instrument he knew, despite all his disclaimers, to be uniquely powerful in his hands. But time as well as solitude and skill were needed, the twenty years of thought he said he had devoted to reflecting on the subject that became *Emile*, followed by the three it took to write the book. By contrast, the letter to Malesherbes excoriates those[14] whose empty speechifying is paid for by the peasant's long toil, and whose own thoughts allegedly do nothing to sustain mankind. Why should the idle live at ease, though materially unproductive, while the dispossessed producers of wealth suffer? Given Rousseau's outrage, we may wonder why his reading of *Robinson Crusoe* denies all importance to the observations about exploiting the defenceless and deprived in Defoe's story, and why he said that everything not pertaining to the hero's life on

---

[13] *Robinson Crusoe*, p. 118.   [14] *O.C.*, I.1143.

the desert island was mere 'fatras'. There is surely great moral significance in the tale of Crusoe's ignoring his parents' words on moderation, and the course of his planter merchant's life thereafter.

The right relation between children and their parents naturally preoccupied Rousseau as he wrote the novel, though Emile's parents are absent, perhaps dead, and therefore as uninvolved in their son's upbringing as Rousseau was in his own children's. Emile's tutor is no parent substitute, and cannot be; instead he is a moral guide and practical adviser, an 'œil vivant' with charge of Emile's passage from the state of childhood through to adolescence and then adulthood, even overseeing his charge's sexual development in a slightly sinister way. Usually, though, his concerns are more narrowly pedagogic.

Emile is to be raised as though he were of the people, though everything suggests his gentle birth. His artisan education may possibly reflect what Rousseau hoped for his own sons (but not daughters) at the Enfants-trouvés: a letter of his to Mme Dupin sets his decision to abandon them in the context of the state care envisaged for children in Plato's Republic,[15] and it is certainly true that charitable institutions in Paris did sometimes offer craft education that might otherwise have been delegated to the family.[16] Emile's case had been anticipated by such earlier works of educational theory as Erasmus's *Institutio principis christianis* and Bacon's *Simones fideles*, as well as Locke's *Some Thoughts Concerning Education*, which all took as given that even princes should engage in some form of manual activity, however unlikely to need it in their future lives, on the principle that sound minds inhabit sound bodies; so Louis XV became a skilful turner, as did his grandson Louis XVI, along with the kings of Denmark and Sweden and the Tsar of Russia.[17] Louis XVI was a keen locksmith too, as well as a horologist for whose craft education model workshops rather like dollshouses were built after the pattern of the *Encyclopédie* plates. The theory behind such training was that future rulers, as enlightened monarchs, had to understand what constituted their country's economic and social state; but inevitably the whiff of dilettantism remained, as it would do with Emile.

Yet in *Les Solitaires*, where he has to labour for a living, Emile finds his craft training indispensable. As a boy his mentor had given him practical support, 'car je suis convaincu qu'il n'apprendra jamais bien que ce que nous apprendrons ensemble'; 'Nous nous mettrons donc tous deux en

---

[15] *C.C.*, II.143–4 (20 April 1751).   [16] See Epstein and Prak, *Guilds*, p. 10.
[17] See Klaus Maurice, *Der drechselnde Souverän* (Zurich: Verlag Ineichen, 1985), pp. 24–8, p. 99.

apprentissage, et nous ne prétendrons point être traittés en Messieurs, mais en vrais apprentifs qui ne le sont pas pour rire; pourquoi ne le serions-nous tout de bon?'[18] But it is clearly an atypical apprenticeship, especially as 'Nous ne sommes pas seulement apprentifs ouvriers, nous sommes apprentifs hommes, et l'apprentissage de ce dernier metier est plus pênible et plus long que l'autre'.[19] Who but the privileged, besides, could train in company with their personal tutor? These episodes adumbrate the mentor's distinction between achieving the rank of craftsman and actually learning a craft, a distinction that in turn rests on the perceived contrast between aspiring to experience humanity (the universal lot) and displaying professional mastery (theoretically unachievable in Emile's case, given the constraints of time and practice). It presupposes a pupil destined for something more than the common artisan's existence.

Is it good that the well-off should, though possibly incompetently, practise a trade? Only if others are happy with their relative incompetence, or do not require them to supply a practical need, or if the tradesman does not sell his product. The purpose of a part-apprenticeship served by someone who appears unlikely to have to do the work he has imperfectly learnt about seems purely private, unless the training has helped shape the general character of a person destined, like the king or tsar, for public life, when it may bring benefits of other kinds. Were such a person to market his product we might be happy to accept his lesser skills because of other qualities he had, especially, perhaps, if he possessed what Weber calls charisma, and which we might term celebrity or snob appeal—if it were a question of a cabinet made by a 'royal', for example, or music scores poorly copied by a famous writer. If, however, we want more than to condone an experiment in dilettantism, the botched job is an unsatisfactory outcome. Where does Emile fit within such a schema? Given his unfinished apprenticeship, he risks being a jack-of-all-trades and master of none, his engagement always temporary, his labour never suffused with the profound understanding of the genuine professional worker, whether craftsman or not, one committed to no other calling, and whose expertise is honed by constant engagement with his trade. Realistically, someone who does not need to work professionally as a carpenter, but who has to train (to a limited extent) to become one, will never be professionally adept at his craft. If the purpose goes beyond ensuring that a boy like Emile has a rounded character that will serve him well in almost any area of life, must his mentor not ensure that the boy has been trained sufficiently to be able to practise his craft *in extremis*? Since Rousseau's aim is

[18] *Emile*, IV.478.   [19] *Emile*, IV.478.

not to write realistically, but to tell a fable, he allows Emile to reach this 'true' professional level. In real life we should get the properly crafted product we need from an expert maker. For Emile's education is not our practical concern.

Man's rank (with attendant privileges, such as not having to work for a living) is generally separate from desert. There have been no levelling circumstances to suggest otherwise in Rousseau's novel, and the usual social inequities pervade the world within and beyond it. Emile drops in on workshops rather than sharing the work/life integration of professional craftsmen, particularly craftsmen working from home rather than on another man's premises, who live on the job, and whose activity embodies an integrity to which the casual, occasional maker cannot aspire. The fact that Emile may not leave a workshop without trying his hand at the craft or trade practised there means less than Rousseau wants to imply; the habit will simply be a constant reminder that lucky birth is merely that, good fortune conferring unmerited elevation through simple privilege. It demonstrates, in other words, a perpetuation of the status quo, not its reverse, whatever social principles Rousseau may have argued for elsewhere. Only an individual with outside funding like Emile's could afford the personal series of journeyman's enterprises we see him engaging in, and probably only one of Emile's social elevation could expect to find a temporary place in one workshop after another, practising so many different trades, without inspiring mistrust or resentment. His moving from place to place in search of an imagined total education serves more as a series of consciousness-raising exercises, then, than as a useful contribution to society, an eye-opener of limited practical value for the future, an involvement with the artisanal world tempered and diluted by its pluralism. Craft does not here stand as metaphor, powerful or otherwise, for the claims of social desert against social distribution, the former crystallizing pre-Revolutionary egalitarian theory, the latter its opposite. Yet it is clear why Rousseau, born a citizen of republican Geneva, should morally support the cause of meritocracy.

Emile's upbringing, it is plain, fits him uneasily for society, given all the preferential treatment he requires and enjoys. He cannot experience work in the same spirit as someone who does it professionally as a matter of need: his mentor may have taught him much about the false distinction between work and leisure, but it is unclear what purpose has been served by Rousseau's presentation of the 'totalizing' life in which work, necessary or otherwise, is not drudgery and leisure no longer the sole respite from it. Perhaps it merely fits the model of the copying he made his living by, a job he liked and did for just as long as was needful, but no more (thus anticipating Engels's picture of the work practices of happy pre-industrial man). It does not save other artisans from being drudges, nor elevate the crafts above the limited regard in which they have traditionally been held. In poetic, not realistic, terms it perhaps serves best to illustrate the state the craftsman seems to epitomise, that of the worker whose professional pride brings with it a profound concern with doing a given task as well as it can be done, for whom a merely passable product is not acceptable (whether or not it suffices for his client), who can always sense when something is shoddy or sham, whose deference towards the objective standards of a 'proper' job admirably exemplifies the disinterested idea of the Good,[20] and whose attitude thus differs from that of, say, the typical production line worker, or any other type of operative whose job is automated, hence depersonalized. (We may also think here of the closedness of modern machinery that not only is incomprehensible to its user but also denies him the opportunity for bricolage: the sealed-in automobile engine, for instance, whose development has simply ended what until recently was the standard male leisure activity of 'messing about' with the car at weekends.) The craftsman preserves the quality Rousseau rates so highly, 'amour de soi', self-respect.[21] But it is surely a quality to which no dilettante like Emile can lay claim.

PRAXIS AND PRAGMATISM

A notional advantage of giving the highly educated a craft training might be in bringing together the process of having ideas and making things to the benefit of both, and, conceivably, to the benefit of society at large. Its reverse is perhaps implied by Rousseau's formulation in book III that 'Celui qui mange dans l'oisiveté ce qu'il n'a pas gagné lui-même le vole',[22] though we might prefer to see the issues which this statement polarizes in less oppositional terms. The seemingly 'oisif' may be exonerated, for instance, by being mentally active in some socially advantageous way, whether craftsmanlike or not, so earning moral as well as material capital; or his 'oisiveté' may be as blameless as the respite fairly earned by any worker. Some at least of the academicians Rousseau castigates for idling unproductively in their academies presumably became academicians for some positive reason, having invented useful things, for instance, like Vaucanson, or composed exquisite music, like Rameau. If they are indeed

[20] See Crawford, p. 19.
[21] See *Emile*, IV.491–2, 534, 536, 547, 600, 608. A related point is made by Richard Sennett, *Respect* (London: Allen Lane, 2003), p. 5, pp. 90–3.
[22] *Emile*, IV.470.

'désœuvrés' in their respective academies, perhaps they have earned the right to be.[23]

Emile's case is very different. What we take to be his inherited wealth might give him some protection against his want of professional self-sufficiency, but lacking the right kind of active proficiency could also leave him dangerously exposed, as proves to be the case when we meet him in *Emile et Sophie*. Then, like the adolescent Rousseau in Turin, he finds the unfinished nature of his apprenticeship(s) a grave check on his earning power, which he needs to maximize because he does not wish, even if he were able, to be ranked with those 'que l'Etat paye pour ne rien faire'.[24] He must, in simple terms, find his place among that number who by their independent effort ensure their future as useful human beings; he must become an artisan 'qui ne dépend que de son travail'. It is at this point, however, that we suddenly learn how consummately skilled a carpenter he is despite having never finished a proper craft training (it has been calculated that about 10,000 hours of experience are required in the real world to produce a master in this trade).[25] His creator Rousseau, more realistically, discovered that his failure to finish qualifying as an apprentice left him ill-equipped to make his way in life as a watchmaker's engraver.

When Emile remarks that for the child engraving is a useless art, at least in comparison with the skills of pastrycook or confectioner,[26] he is simply reminding us how taste, or tastes—among the most basic of sensory responses to all products of nature and humankind, as to creations of art—, vary over the ages of man. The child's taste for sugar, it is implied, normally shades into a more mature one, for example that for savoury things; eating well, equally, may become less important to him or her than the desire for satisfaction through intellectual, aesthetic, or other pursuits, such as collecting engravings. The art of engraving may serve a useful purpose too, as the young Rousseau discovers with Mme Basile, though it is also a decorative art, offering a non-essential, visual, delight rather than a gustatory one. All delight involves taste—sensation and/or aesthetic response—, but the assessment of different types of delight can alter with the passing years. (Delight itself is never the essential thing; the baseline quality is simple acceptability. Delight marks refinement, acceptability merely need.) As for horology, Rousseau has already made it clear

---

[23] An analogy might be drawn with the ancient concept of 'otium cum dignitate'. On the various possible meanings of the phrase see Charles Wirszubski, 'Cicero's *cum dignitate otium*: A Reconsideration', *Journal of Romance Studies*, 44 (1954), pp. 1–13. I am grateful to Katherine Clarke for referring me to this article.
[24] *Emile*, IV.470.   [25] See Sennett, *Craftsman*, p. 20.   [26] *Emile*, IV.459.

that the child's timepieces are his stomach and the degree of bodily fatigue he experiences; even adults, he thinks, may dispense with a watch.

The element of need is often taken to distinguish the arts from the crafts. The former are unconnected with the basic requirements of living, serving to enhance rather than merely support human existence; they make it possible to *live*, not minimally subsist, their province that of the pleasing, not the functional. The hierarchy of genres in painting, as Diderot's aesthetic writings remind us, presented a set scale of values within the art of painting that itself seemed to distinguish useful types from beautiful ones, ranking the former below the latter in academic, though not pragmatic, terms: thus sign painters typically belonged to the trade academy or guild, the Académie de Saint-Luc, and painters associated with the concept of beauty rather than utility to the Académie royale de peinture et de sculpture. Without quite arguing in the spirit implied by the *Encyclopédie*'s subtitle that craft guilds were equal in status to academies, Diderot advanced the view that categories established by the liberal arts tradition were insufficient to settle hierarchical distinctions between painters; genre painters as good as Chardin, he thought, should simply be rated as highly as artists working in the Grand Style.[27] This creates a new democracy of taste and practice, one that explains why the different royal academies should have been dissolved with the Revolution of 1789. In axiological (not practical) terms, craft can be, should be, and *is* properly indistinguishable from art, and in utilitarian terms surpasses it, though art conventionally surpasses craft in the aesthetic sense. One illustration among many of the consequences that flow from this is the following: in 1766 members of the Guild of Painters and Sculptors who thought themselves genuine artists complained at their implied subordination in the administrative hierarchy, accorded the rank of 'mere' artisans doing a purely mechanical job. Honour was important in the craft culture, as was the recognition that craftsmen could be as innovative and original as the creator-genius in the liberal arts.[28]

As Rousseau points out, the criterion of utility is often perversely taken as demeaning whatever practice or situation it is associated with. The work of a sign painter is more useful, but probably gives less pleasure,

[27] See also Chapter 1, f.n. 49, and Philippe Minard, 'Trade Without Institution? French Debates about Restoring Guilds at the Start of the Nineteenth Century', in Gadd and Hollis, *Guilds and Associations*, pp. 83–100; and especially Michael Sonenscher, *Work and Wages: Natural Law, Politics and the Eighteenth-Century French Trades* (Cambridge: Cambridge University Press, 1989), pp. 239–40.
[28] See George J. Sheridan, Jr, 'Craft Technique, Association and Guild History: The Silk Weavers of Nineteenth-Century Lyon', in Gadd and Hollis, *Guilds and Associations*, pp. 147–68, esp. pp. 164–5.

than the painting of a mythological subject (then ranked within the grand genre of 'history' painting), hence is conventionally consigned to the realm of craft rather than that of art. The history painting may, but may not, inspire those who contemplate it with 'good', heroic, useful thoughts; if it does, may it be called partly craft-like, or does it remain 'purely' artistic? What are we to say in general of a period, such as the age of Rousseau and Diderot, that emphasized the desirability of paintings, literature, and other arts of imitation being moral? That its novels, plays, and paintings are 'partly' craft-like as a consequence? These are delicate, perhaps overdelicate, matters to resolve. Rousseau's *Projet de constitution pour la Corse* makes clear that in certain cases what his age usually named craft might instead be called art: 'Plus on doit écarter avec soin les arts oisifs, les arts d'agrément et de molesse, plus on doit favoriser ceux qui sont utiles à l'agriculture et avantageux à la vie humaine. Il ne nous faut ni sculpteurs ni orphèvres mais il nous faut des charpentiers et des forgerons, il nous faut des tisserans, de bons ouvriers en laine et non pas des brodeurs ni des tireurs d'or'.[29] His more specific enquiry in *Emile*, in the spirit of encyclopaedic revisionism, calls into question those categories first proposed in classical antiquity that placed art as well as craft in a lowly rank because of their purposiveness, their occupying time that free men could more fittingly have devoted to disinterested thought. The Renaissance then elevated painting and sculpture above craft by calling the former alone liberal arts, that is, arts of the free. Yet according to *Emile*, only the crafts, by combining social usefulness with independence, truly free the individual from want: it is through his efforts as a craftsman that the enslaved Emile of *Emile et Sophie* gains liberation. Craft products are vital to life as most artefacts are not, so ensuring the subsistence of those who make them.[30]

Emile was revolutionary in facing issues such as these squarely. Emile himself is not prepared to accept existing notions and categories unquestioningly, having been trained by his tutor always to seek the first principles behind things: 'd'instrument en instrument, il voudra toujours remonter au prémier', and 'refuseroit d'apprendre ce qui demanderoit une connoissance antérieure qu'il n'auroit pas'.[31] Had the apprenticeship with Ducommun not been tainted by what the *Confessions* calls the master's monstrous cruelty, it could have been an effective illustration of this concept.

Rousseau's theme of enquiry followed by performance on the basis of answer given echoes Defoe's description of how the solitary Robinson Crusoe, after encountering problems that threaten his subsistence, gradually con-

---

[29] *Constitution pour la Corse, O.C.*, III.926.   [30] *Emile*, IV.418.
[31] *Emile*, IV.460.

trives to solve them in the most efficient way. Orthopraxis before orthodoxy is Emile's byword, because right doing shapes right thinking. He will,
we know, succeed according to these principles (at least for the duration of
the completed novel: *Emile et Sophie* shows their breakdown), because the
mode of enquiry he has been taught will save him from dangers that constantly beset his creator. Rousseau's habitual state, at least according to the
Dialogues, 'fut et sera toujours l'inertie d'esprit et l'activité machinale',[32]
the word 'machinale' implying much less than Defoe's use of the etymologically related term in describing Robinson Crusoe's ambition of becoming 'master of every Mechanick art',[33] and in Rousseau's case perhaps
signifying simply that which attends the involuntary motions of living.
Whatever we may think of his self-assessment, it is beyond question that
laziness compromises the production of useful craft articles as well as of
superfluous things. It does not settle the question whether it is better, and
in what sense better, for mankind that more people should actually want
or be able to do craftwork than create or enjoy art, unless the art is, as it
was then taken to be, that of agriculture. The world, as Diderot remarked,
pays less to those who make themselves useful than to anyone else; Rousseau
says the same. And there are less than useful craft products—Rousseau's
ribbons, perhaps—as well as essential ones.

Is the useful, whether or not it inheres in art as well as craft, incompatible with the luxurious? Surely not: a winter garment made of expensive
fabric may be warmer and therefore 'better' than one made of commonplace, though still serviceable, stuff. (One wonders precisely where Rousseau's Armenian kaftan would fit within this category.) Luxury almost
always implies something distinct in rarity, complexity, or cost, and
distinct from general needfulness, the elemental and strictly utilitarian.
The luxurious usually arouses the senses, and also perhaps the mind, in a
pleasant way: there can be luxury versions of what is basic, though the
basic is the essential form, the irreducible minimum. Luxury, too, may
personalize a product, as the craftsman's fingerprint does; but there are
other ways in which a maker marks his work as characteristically his.

The honest craftsman—the epithet is significant, if not inevitable—is
at home wherever a community exists with wants his skill can satisfy; like
the Montagnons described in the *Lettre à d'Alembert*, he may work effectively without any complex tools or elaborate machinery, be functional
with the minimum kit required for doing his job competently. His typical
condition is well described in *Emile et Sophie*, where Emile turns from the
discovery of Sophie's infidelity to experience relief in the satisfying rhythm

[32] *Dialogues*, I.850.   [33] *Robinson Crusoe*, p. 68.

of manual work:[34] he is able to find such employment without difficulty in a master craftsman's workshop, always proving, predictably if unconvincingly, to be better at his job than his employer. The pattern continues satisfyingly for him: he knows his skill is more than marketable enough to ensure that he stays alive, for his hand accompanies him everywhere he goes, and 'Quand je ne trouvois pas à travailler de mon metier, ce qui étoit rare, j'en faisois d'autres.'[35] His mentor has helpfully ensured that 'les outils de tous les metiers lui sont déjà familiers', so that, as Emile comments, 'Tantôt paysan, tantôt artisan, tantôt artiste, quelquefois même homme à talens, j'avois par tout quelque connoissance de mise, et je me rendois maitre de leur usage par mon peu d'empressement à les montrer'.[36] If he ever wondered what he was doing, he had the reassuring answer: 'Je fais ma tâche, je reste à ma place'. No metaphysical Angst, then, just contentment in a well-earned subsistence. 'Je suis donc utile aux autres en proportion de ma subsistence: car les hommes ne donnent rien pour rien.' This comfortingly egalitarian arrangement ends only when he is captured in a sea battle and sold as a slave, though even here he once more finds work at which he effortlessly excels his master.

The functional nature of his craft skills explains the ease with which he manages to subsist. Society has, implicitly or otherwise, defined jobs to be done; artisan workers supply the manpower and the tools (often multifunctional ones) that let the job be done satisfactorily. Crusoe's slow progress on the desert island is caused by his lacking the implements he needs, the materials required for their manufacture and the techniques that may help him overcome this want.[37] This is why he must make himself 'master of every mechanic art', as he gradually does. Crusoe wants simply to secure the maximum utility from his environment,[38] both on the desert island and in the European economic world. Nature, therefore, is for him not an object of worship, but a resource to be exploited, primitivism a state to be bettered according to the spirit of colonial capitalism, where profit—the motivating impulse of the producer—lies in the most efficient generation of material for consumption. Labour is dignified by its (temperate) association with natural resources, corrupted by its association with an alienated workforce. Crusoe's holistic individualism is thus a saving grace, as the industrial maximizing of product and profit according to the division of labour would be its curse. Work is validated by its link with an unexploited earth, an economic fact in Crusoe's case, if an ecological requirement in ours.

---

[34] *Emile et Sophie*, IV.899–900.   [35] *Emile et Sophie*, IV.
[36] *Emile et Sophie*, IV.913.   [37] *Robinson Crusoe*, p. 68.
[38] Watt, p. 100.

Time is also a determining factor in the craftsman's effort to address needs profitably, though less in the slow world Emile and Robinson Crusoe inhabit than in the hurried universe of civilized man. The passage of time helps establish how satisfactorily an object has been manufactured—how durable it is, and how effectively it does the job for which it is intended. Journeymen craftsmen working 'au jour la journée' may of course escape the further consequences of poor workmanship; like them, Emile frequently moves from place to place, but it is his good reputation that will follow him, at least in an environment possessing the means for comparatively speedy and effective communications (as much of France did then, if Switzerland did not). The craftsman as well as the product needs resilience. The former has to be able to perform an often physically demanding task effectively and maintain his credit in an economic world in which not only must he sell his labour, but rivals may try to undercut him, to some degree the situation Rousseau would find himself in as a music copyist. The best object is often, though not necessarily, the most useful one, and Emile proves able to supply such objects reliably. His work is the product of discipline, vision, and integrity, and so appears to guarantee him a future of consistent employment.

CRAFT OPTIONS AND ESSENTIALS

Crafting in Rousseau's day, unlike more modern times, was rarely the optional way to make a product, that is, the way chosen in preference to some other, probably mechanized, one, but for the most part the only way; craft techniques had not yet taken second place behind the methods of industrialism, and the use of the internal combustion engine to power agricultural equipment was still some time away. It would take a future of rampant mass production for craft to designate the sometimes luxurious, always distinctive, often more ethical, and generally more expensive 'other way' for consumers to choose (at least consumers with sufficient income). While the fact that the most-needed products have to sell at the lowest possible prices is beneficial to the consumer, it may not guarantee the profitable survival of the maker or seller unless he can manufacture or market the requisite object quickly and in volume, or successfully demonstrate the superiority of his more expensive model to cheaper ones. It is a point that hardly needs to be laboured in a Western world in which juggernaut multinationals edge out small producers and suppliers, and where only the gradual development of a post-industrial ethics offers hope for the legacy of one of environmentalism's earliest and most important writers. For we have been, not so much powerless, as disinclined, to restore the balance that a slower and less capitalist economy once provided. Switzerland itself has often been reluctant to see the full force of Rousseau's socialist argument that one man's prosperity is tainted when it rests on the impoverishment of others.

There are, of course, various reasons for living at a gentler pace, not all of them deliberately chosen. Crusoe's slow production of staples, for example, may not be inherently better than some quicker means, even though the swiftly-produced is often shoddy or otherwise unsatisfactory, not 'craftsmanlike', in other words; had he the ability to manufacture things fit for his purpose more rapidly, he would. Thus it is no virtue that making bread takes him months: it simply reflects the fact that the process of creating anything has to start from scratch on a desert island. We, on the other hand, might reasonably expect any disciple of Rousseau's to protest at the fast and, by implication, often bad manufacturing practices and production processes of modernity: we are heirs of the craft movements of the late nineteenth and early twentieth centuries, and understand, even if we do not support, the 'Slow' and 'Green' ethos of the present day. Rousseau's world moved according to those older rhythms.

In keeping with this gentle tempo, skills that take time to develop were nurtured, apprenticeships were still served, and the rapid advance of industry had not blighted the countryside and town, or not conspicuously so. Nature was left intact as the industrialized world has refused to let it be, not *exploited* in either of the French senses of the word: as far as we know, Rousseau cultivated no allotment, except perhaps at Les Charmettes, grew little of his own food, killed no flesh, and caught no fish to eat. He was, however, no vegetarian, as Emile is taught to be by a mentor who still recommends hunting to him as the best means to work off his surplus energies and, by implication, protect his chastity.[39] Earl Marshal Keith would try to tempt his protégé to Scotland or Potsdam with the promise of natural and plenteous sources of sustenance—fish abounding in loch and stream, vegetables thriving in kitchen garden, fruit burgeoning in orchard, and so on[40]—but to no avail. Superior sustainability was not then a strong enough motive to prompt a change in lifestyle or environment when so much of the natural world remained intact and productive, a fertile source of staple products: Boswell's account of the simple, delicious meal prepared by Thérèse and shared with Rousseau at Môtiers makes this plain.[41] Whatever Rousseau says about the starving of

[39] Compare the mythological association of the goddess Diana with chastity as well as hunting.
[40] *C.C.*, XXV.214 (30 April 1765).
[41] Boswell, *Journal of his German and Swiss Travels, 1764*, ed. Marlies K. Danziger (Edinburgh: Edinburgh University Press, 2008), pp. 284–9 (14 December 1764).

peasants and the useless plenty of the upper classes, his world still knew cheap food in another sense than ours.

In that world, craft still enabled humans to use and adapt the products of their environment effectively. Indeed, craft methods, craft work, remained perfectly adapted to man's everyday relations with the phenomenal world. Nothing and no one, however, could feel entirely safe from what became Rousseau's crusade to inspire a counter-civilization ethos, the approach first tried in the *Discours sur les sciences et les arts* and subsequently developed in the *Inégalité* and the *Lettre à d'Alembert*. Yet how confidently could the work of skilling appropriate to an ideal, non-progressivist society be formulated? Did its conception not rest on nostalgia, as the *Lettre à d'Alembert*'s recollection of the Montagnons' past virtues suggests? Not solely. Learning manufacture from scratch, as Emile is taught and Crusoe obliged to do, seemed a positive step towards reconnecting with a world not yet alien, but threatening to become so, the world that Rousseau called enchanted, and which implicitly opposed (and still opposes) the rationalistic structures of modernity. Craft may seem divorced from reenchantment in virtue of its pragmatism, its essential link with the world of manufacture, but its opposition to the soullessness of automation was both vital and redemptive. Certainly, many *philosophes* shared some at least of Rousseau's views about the urgency of returning to the heart of things, the soul that craft principles seemed to embody. The problem was to persuade society in general that some form of rehabilitation was both needful and desirable. Necessity, Rousseau believed, spawned the right kind of adaptation. He had to believe it, although the price demanded would be high.

The solution he adopted, that of curbing imagination, promoting practicality, and withdrawing from the terrible seduction of literature, has been outlined. The theme continues in the story of his crafting new writing as well as writing old craft, copying music and thus returning to a form of artisanship, even one combining art and craft, as a penman driven by an exquisite aesthetic sense and a practical need to earn money. One difficulty attending this interpretation has already been noted: did supplying non-essential goods to those wealthy enough to pay for them really qualify as a craftlike activity? Music, after all, was, and is, not self-evidently useful, though it may unquestionably be beautiful. At best, perhaps, Rousseau was craftsmanlike simply in combining the beauty (in a different medium) with utility at a remove (the need for handwritten scores where music stayed unpublished). Craft in general spelt utility with beauty, or perhaps utility with love: the craftsman takes pride in his work, whether that work is aesthetically pleasing or not, and never intentionally produces an inferior product: for to craft something is in a special sense to be engaged by it.

The craftsman may also be an artist, or have an artist's sensibility, which explains why Rousseau wrote Rey letter after letter, often in reproach, about the physical look of his works: if they were written by an author whose celebrity guaranteed sales independently of advertising or subscription, the 'package' of ink, paper, type, and binding that presented them was overseen by an author-connoisseur who knew, as Emile might have done had his mentor not taught him to hate books, about every aspect of their production, and thought them all important. It is a concern we may well understand three centuries after Rousseau's birth, as the proliferation of ebooks spawns a countervailing (and strategic) concern with making its physical equivalent an object of beauty and value that advertises, more widely than to existing specialist markets, the virtues of such things as cloth-slip covers, designer jackets, numbered limited editions, artwork that truly *is* art, superb print quality, and paper so exquisite that it draws the reader as a sensuous, special material quite beyond its utilitarian function of carrying text. Although Rousseau would have deprecated the notion that any reader might buy his works simply because they looked elegant, his artisan background was such as to make him mind acutely about production values.

Yet the principle of usefulness has been so firmly impressed on Emile that he constantly sets utility above aesthetic appeal, iron above gold, glass above diamond,[42] with all the consequences already noted. (This is when he has overcome his childlike preference for cake over potentially useful things.) The hierarchy remains whatever the relative complexity of making materials ready for human use—whether mining diamonds, for example, is easier than making glass, the first process more straightforward than the second, irrespective of the rarity or otherwise of the substance obtained. Glass is in most practical respects more useful than precious stones, though mirror glass may not be. Rousseau's focus is on need, on what serves a purpose beyond that of (dispensable) ornament, which means, in some cases inconveniently, that the useful substance is more highly valued even when readying or 'outing' it involves more costly human processes; yet it needs or deserves to be sold more cheaply than the useless substance whose price is high because it is comparatively rare. The fact that craft and functionality belong together may, from a manufacturing and retailing point of view, sometimes be inconvenient.

---

[42] *Emile*, IV.459.

NATURALISM

Is it significant that the refuge Rousseau sought during his illumination on the way to Vincennes was underneath an oak tree? The cuckolded Emile will later be restored by the experience of working for a master carpenter, practising a trade that is, as his mentor anticipated, absorbing enough to ward off melancholy thoughts during the hours of work, yet tiring enough for the mind to return to reflection at the day's end when contemplative rest helps restore the body. *Emile* calls carpentry the craft most suitable for its young charge to adopt because it is skilled, respectable, clean, useful, and creative.[43] Its substance is a material that is inherently or potentially beautiful, but also practical, adaptable, long-lasting, and usually in plentiful supply. One of its greatest advantages, furthermore, is that preparing it for use need involve no invasive or unnatural procedure: wood is generally sustainable except in certain industrialized circumstances that Rousseau's century was in little danger of encountering, renewing itself, slowly or not, after humans have turned it to their purposes. Wood rarely has to be 'outed' as kaolin, for example, does, though the carpenter's and cabinet-maker's expertise may enable latent beauty in the wood to become more visible than in its untouched state. Carpentry skills relate both to craftsmanship and to artistry: they depend on eye and hand, and at their highest level involve the mind as well. Rousseau's draft constitution for Corsica of 1765 would recommend that the natives train extensively in woodwork because it offers scope for creativity along with possessing a gratifying and valued utility. The objects that wood may be made into, furthermore, are wide-ranging enough for its very substance to be seen as universal: in the eighteenth-century world it supplied the basic material for houses, boats, carts, and machinery, as well as all kinds of furniture, paper, and (occasionally) timepieces. Cultivating carpentry skills was, then, a sound investment for any state to make.

The simplicity of preparing wood for use, besides, stood no comparison with the complex business of extracting minerals from the earth in order to provide alternative materials—forged iron and steel, for instance—to furnish houses, tools, and machines. Yet it is a substance that men conventionally worked and work on, not women. When Sophie unexpectedly arrives at the workshop where Emile is practising his trade,[44] she feebly attempts to use a plane with her 'blanche et débile main' after feeling the smoothness of the planks stacked ready for working. (We may

---

[43] *Emile*, IV.478.   [44] *Emile*, IV.808.

remember the enormous effort it cost Crusoe to turn trees into planks, 'with no more tools than an adze and a hatchet'.[45] Much the same is implied in Emile's case.) Rousseau chooses not to examine the ways in which the female's natural delicacy and debility might be channelled in other, positive, craftlike directions, even though according to Diderot he had once thought of setting up in Paris a school for teaching girls the art of floral arrangement.[46]

What is certain is that Sophie is no match for Emile in quiet, serious application: when she and her mother arrive unannounced he is too absorbed with his carpentry to notice, while Sophie is highly self-conscious. Yet Rousseau is careful not to present her as coquettish; initially, indeed, she strikes the onlooker as modest and physically unremarkable. (Rousseau regards coquetry as a natural female trait, one to be responsibly schooled rather than eradicated.)[47] So while Emile's self-presentation as he applies himself in workshop after workshop is simply what the task demands, Sophie is attentive to the fact that the graceful curve of her body as she sews displays it to best advantage, as Rousseau's compatriot and contemporary Angelica Kauffman suggests in the picture of an embroideress dating from about this time.[48] Sophie sews because she must, but enjoys lacemaking because there is no other type of needlework 'qui donne une attitude plus agréable et où les doigts s'exercent avec plus de grace et de légéreté'.[49] Later, as machinery took over old hand practices, such female attitudes were idealized as testaments to a positively virtuous occupation. Yet some writers argued, as Rousseau did of scholarship in men, that the postures needlework encouraged weakened women's 'machine', imperilling soundness of mind as well as body.

Like others of her sex, however, Sophie will learn practical skills too[50]—how to cut fabric and make garments as well as how to embroider, talents whose desirability becomes apparent to her as she dresses first her dolls and, later on, herself. But she has none of the emancipated craft skills that would later let women bash brass and hack wood; it is for men alone in *Emile*'s universe to work on hard, resistant substances, stone and metal as well as wood, for women merely to make and handle softly pliant or accommodating things—the textiles and the decorative materials that could be further prettified by the delicate craft of needlework, an occupation Rousseau regards as befitting women's limited strength. The fifth book of *Emile* contains much reflection of this kind, and has duly enraged feminists from Mary Wollstonecraft[51] onwards. For Rousseau,

---

[45] *Robinson Crusoe*, p. 68.   [46] See Chapter 7.   [47] *Emile*, IV.703.
[48] *Morning Amusement* (or *The Embroideress*), 1773, Pushkin Museum, Moscow.
[49] *Emile*, IV.747–8.   [50] *Emile*, IV.707.
[51] Mary Wolllstonecraft, *A Vindication of the Rights of Woman*, ed. Sylvana Tomaselli (Cambridge: Cambridge University Press, 1995), esp. pp. 156–73.

who says that man has capacities the opposite sex simply lacks, nowhere considers whether society has created the latter's deficiencies. He simply concludes that woman stands defined by physical debility, the natural inequality his second *Discours* had addressed.

There is an anticipation of this doctrine, fully developed in *Emile*'s fifth book, in book III, before Sophie has been discovered and identified as a suitable future partner for Emile. At this stage Rousseau unsurprisingy refers to sewing as an activity particularly suited to the female hand: 'Si j'étois souverain je ne permettrois la couture et les metiers à l'aiguille qu'aux femmes, et aux boiteux réduits à s'occuper comme elles',[52] or effeminate men, even eunuchs reduced to sedentary occupations, as the female is. Yet in Môtiers, after the condemnation of *Emile* and *Du contrat social*, he himself would plan to make various kinds of silk and lace;[53] and he had his Armenian costume made by a male tailor, although needlework and the activities closely related to it were regarded as properly those of the opposite sex. But why? Although embroidery has been seen for centuries as addressing the female's sense of vanity, and its products as purely ornamental, as far from the functional as a painted face, in earlier ages both male and female were employed with threadwork in guild workshops and noble houses, with monks even embroidering in monasteries. Up to Rousseau's day, indeed, most 'brodeurs' to the king were men.[54] Were his own theory and practice in this regard consistent? It hardly seems so. 'En voyant [in Italy] des marchands de modes vendre aux Dames des rubans, des pompons, du rezeau, de la chenille, je trouvois ces parures delicates bien ridicules dans de grosses mains faites pour souffler la forge et frapper sur l'enclume', he announces;[55] yet he himself took needlework into company in his dotage, much as women then did tatting, knotting, or tapestry.

THE MORALITY OF MAKING AND DOING

Rather than wonder whether it is wrong to share Rousseau's sense of values, we should perhaps consider the matter from another point of view. What gave such crafts—often, significantly, called pastimes—a potential moral force, as opposed to a general utility, was their capacity to save those who practised them from the threat of idleness, as all domestic tasks allegedly saved women from promiscuity. It seems fitting, then, that when

[52] *Emile*, IV.476.
[53] *C.C.*, XII.256 (Julie de Bondeli to Johann Zimmermann, 21 August 1762).
[54] See Roszika Parker, *The Subversive Stitch* (London: Women's Press, 1984).
[55] *Emile*, IV.477–8.

Rousseau died noble ladies should have sewn silk and chenille pictures of his tomb, as they had once stitched portraits of his heroines.[56] Perhaps in so doing they were implicitly confirming the justice of his view that femininity was both innate and itself capable of embellishment by the right kind of training. 'Jeune homme', Emile is urged, 'imprime à tes travaux la main de l'homme. Apprends à manier d'un bras vigoureux la hache et la scie, à équarrir une poutre, à monter sur un comble, à poser le faîte, à l'affermir de jambe-de-force et d'entraits; puis crie à ta sœur de venir t'aider à ton ouvrage, comme elle te disoit de travailler à son point-croisé.'[57] Had Rousseau kept his own children, might he have appreciated what the female hand can do? Presumably Thérèse Le Vasseur's, unlike Sophie's, was neither white nor nerveless, though Maman's might have been. Even the virile Emile is to be spared exercising professions such as blacksmithing or metalwork that are unclean, despite their being 'utiles, et même les plus utiles de tous', for what counts is that he should consider no trade beneath him rather than that he should actually engage in them indiscriminately.

This inconsistency is no more resolved by Rousseau than is his attitude towards men who sew, his last word on the matter being that 'Il faut que tous les metiers se fassent; mais qui peut choisir doit avoir égard à la propreté', and as far as Emile is concerned 'je n'aimerois pas à lui voir dans la forge la figure d'un Cyclope'.[58] Yet if the male hand's lack of delicacy makes it suited to rough trades—in *Emile et Sophie* Emile is an enslaved member of a road gang—it is still to be spared activities that demean it in other ways. 'Enfin je n'aimerois pas ces stupides professions dont les ouvriers, sans industrie, et presque automates, n'éxercent jamais leurs mains qu'au même travail. Les tisserans, les faiseurs de bas, les scieurs de pierre; à quoi sert d'employer à ces métiers des hommes de sens.' The slave, of course, has no choice, whether or not he is a man of good sense. The aside on brutish physical work begs the question whether a musician's nimble hand is essentially different from that of the cabinetmaker, and the latter's from the woodman's.

A different, equally fundamental problem is touched on in the novel, that of the division of labour[59] which, in removing from the worker variety and the satisfaction attendant on creating an object from beginning to end, would make ever greater inroads into industrial life as the age of Rousseau passed and that of the factory began.[60] It is something of a paradox that the growth of specialization may weaken the individual's

---

[56] Parker, pp. 124–5.   [57] *Emile*, IV.477.
[58] *Emile*, IV.477.   [59] *Emile*, IV.460.
[60] See, on this general matter, Jacques Proust, *Diderot et l'Encyclopédie* (Paris: A. Colin, 1963), p. 170.

sense of involvement in making a product by removing integrity from the manufacturing process, even though there is evident cause for pride in his doing specific tasks others cannot do. This matter does not relate solely to what we call machine-made objects, clearly. Emile will learn to value a meal where the food has been grown and prepared in its entirety by a peasant family above all the delicacies of a richly supplied banquet sourced from other lands and made ready by other hands, and where no individual enterprise can be directly identified.[61] He may draw the same lesson from *Robinson Crusoe*, where total origination or creation such as the solitary Crusoe is reduced to contrasts with another sort made up of endless discrete processes: 'Que pensera-t-il en voyant que les arts ne se perfectionnent qu'en se subdivisant, en multipliant à l'infini les instrumens des uns et des autres?'[62]

We may not regard this as a negative aspect of making things, but it perhaps becomes so when the consequence is to dis-arm the individual, easily persuaded that his own creative input can similarly be delegated, with no perceptible loss, to other beings or to tools; and 'plus [les matiéres premiéres] changent de mains, plus la main d'œuvre augmente de prix et devient honorable'.[63] This can be an impoverishing process, Rousseau suggests, with individual involvement sacrificed to plural manufacture at the inevitable cost of integrity. An undesirable consequence, too, may be to push up prices for reasons unconnected with inherent value, though not when supplying more of the required article is the natural outcome of employing exponentially more workers to make it. 'Good' division of labour occurs as the necessary process of pooling resources, the second *Discours* had already noted,[64] but the good comes at a human price.

Emile's story has demonstrated in a variety of ways that a certain breadth of education is necessary even for the artisan who lacks his privilege; and we recall Rousseau's letter to Théodore Tronchin of 26 November 1758 commenting that 'L'éducation d'un ouvrier tend à former ses doigts, rien de plus. Cependant le citoyen reste'.[65] This citizen's education is, of course, what Emile receives, and it is one that does not minimize the importance of educating the senses most useful to any artisan or craftsman, especially touch and sight. Emile must develop eyes at the end of his fingers as though he were genuinely blind, we are told,[66] an observation that may remind us of the *Encyclopédie* article 'Invisible', with its rhetorical question 'L'aveugle voit-il les objets dans sa tête ou au bout de ses doigts?' It may

---

[61] *Emile*, IV.465. See also undated letter from Louis d'Escherny on Rousseau's simple tastes in food, *C.C.*, XIX.104–5.
[62] Emile, IV. 460.   [63] *Emile*, IV.459.   [64] *Discours sur l'inégalité*, III.173.
[65] *C.C.*, V.242.   [66] Emile, IV.381.

also recall the eighth addition to Diderot's *Lettre sur les aveugles* concerning the blind young woman whose realm begins where it ends for the sighted, with darkness. As *Emile* comments, 'Nous sommes aveugles la moitié de la vie; avec la différence que les vrais aveugles savent toujours se conduire, et que nous n'osons faire un pas au cœur de la nuit'.[67] Deprivation of this sense, then, helps sharpen another or others, qualifying the everyday belief that, for example, in obscurity we need the help of artificial light: 'Eh quoi! Toujours des machines! Qui vous répond qu'elles vous suivront par tout au besoin?' It may be safer to make more intelligent and probing use of those senses that are unaffected by temporary or permanent blindness.

This notion supports the rather obvious argument Rousseau advances later in *Emile*, that achieving whatever independence man can is desirable for his general wellbeing and prosperity because it enables him to avoid appealing to his fellows in ways that diminish his sense of personal worth (another illustration of the potentially pernicious effects of the division of labour). The ever-presence of the tactile sense—not necessarily that identified specifically with the hand—during our waking lives explains its primacy for the blind, and perhaps suggests that it should have the same significance for the sighted. After all, touch is so ubiquitous in our bodies that when called upon to do so it can act as substitute for the other senses: by placing our hand on the violin we may be able, not merely to 'hear' the tune being played, but also to determine whether the sound it has produced is flat or sharp.

What we might call Crusoe's venture capitalism, finally, is alien to Emile's creative spirit, which conceives of all activity in terms of practical sustenance and the general good. In light of the education he has received we cannot feel surprised at his rejection of work that deliberately moves beyond sufficiency to superfluity: if on Robinson Crusoe's island excess goods are pointless, similarly in the more peopled universe Emile comes to inhabit the norm, as at Clarens and in Rousseau's own small world, is to produce only what subsistence requires. Exchange, nothing else, is seen as the proper response to individual over-abundance. The arts (including agriculture) Emile desires to master prefer substance to representativeness: wheat and wood, not intangible profit. His universe, like Crusoe's, is one of things, a world in which practicality is king. It may seem impoverished in ways that have sometimes shocked *Emile*'s readers, especially in its comparative illiteracy, but the argument it advances from material wealth to necessary sustenance is unimpeachable. Craft anchors them in both substance and soul.

---

[67] *Emile*, IV. 381.

6

Crafting a Self

THE AGENCY OF HANDS

One of Plutarch's *Famous Lives* reveals that Cicero's hands—or head and hands, according to a different source—were posthumously chopped off as punishment for his attack on Anthony in the *Philippics*. A more familiar episode from Roman history describes how Scaevola plunged his sword arm into the fire for having failed to kill Porsenna, an act of Stoic heroism the young Rousseau once threatened to imitate.[1] His watching family was horrified, and understandably so: not only might the boy have hurt himself seriously, but his whole future could have been compromised. In a craft milieu, damaging the hand imperils, if not life itself, at least the worker's livelihood.

Yet the hand's adaptability is endless. Other body parts may seem to equal or exceed it in expressiveness or sensitivity, sometimes even separating the human from the animal in ways more distinctive than digital flexibility,[2] but there is every reason to privilege the hand in Rousseau's case. The story of Scaevola reminds us of various episodes in Jean-Jacques's life associating hands with misdeeds, ignoble and degrading acts rather than mock-heroic ones. There was the hand that stole—fruit, asparagus, a ribbon—, though it stole for others, not for Rousseau, so he claims; or the hand involved in sexual pleasure, other people's and his own, either in revulsion (Rousseau's feeling when a 'filthy' fellow seminarian asked him to perform a sexual act in Turin) or with guilt, the guilt that masturbating always filled him with. In none of these cases, it is true, would hands themselves be punished, as with Cicero and Scaevola; for Rousseau, transferred penalties suffice.

The stories of the Romans may make us think of other instances in literature and life of actual or figurative dismemberment, punishment for something more than manual transgression: Abelard's castration for

---

[1] *Confessions*, I.9.
[2] Anaxagoras remarked that 'It is by having hands that man is the most intelligent of animals', an observation quoted by Aristotle (*The Parts of Animals* 686a).

seducing Heloise, perhaps, or Saint-Preux's effective emasculation in *La Nouvelle Héloïse*, first with Julie's marriage, then through Wolmar's efforts to desexualize her union with her former lover. But sexual hands may also be transfigured, thus 'saved'. Thérèse shows how when she tells Boswell about Rousseau's manual skill at pleasuring her, a skill that trumped the younger man's intrusive efforts over the five days of his escorting her to England. Given Rousseau's abandonment of all the children Thérèse bore him, we may think this less consequential form of lovemaking one he should have stayed with from the start.

Whatever he might feel about these things—of hands as guilty or as harmlessly caressing—, it was his writing hand Rousseau was punished for in life, the writing hand that drove him under cover for the best part of a decade and made him think recurrently about the 'better' craftsman's life he could have led had he not been an author. Punishment, of course, could not undo the books already written, although authority would carry on suppressing them and chasing him. Nor could it prevent him writing in his head, as he did through sleepless nights or out on botanizing rambles, where, he claims, his best work was conceived. The sense of touch, the grasp or clasp of hands, though meant in friendship or support, often seemed to him as threatening as the urge to write, and he always feared the world's attempts to capture him. The hand that 'caught' in the most simple sense had punished him for playing with machinery at Pâquis, but 'caught' him more alarmingly in later life, or so he says: 'Je tiens Jean-Jacques Rousseau!', he claims the sleeping Hume cried out in Senlis on their way to England, though his benefactor had no notion why Rousseau thought he had pronounced these words, especially not in French.[3] Paranoid or otherwise, Rousseau always had the arm, or weapon, of his words to fight the enemy with; it was the words and acts of others that disquieted him.

How active he thought different types of eloquence could be—the artist's, not the writer's, for example, the power of images, not words—, how compromising to him, how eager to entrap him just when he needed freedom, emerges indirectly from the play he finished at about the same time as *Emile*, *Pygmalion*, switching medium, effectively, from words to stone, the object shaped from text to statuary. The story of Pygmalion's sculpting Galathée may simply seem to show that art is dangerous because of its material reality, as Diderot thought the chiselled form, the 'thing itself', potentially more corrupting than the painted one,[4] with danger

---

[3] *C.C.*, XXX.44 (10 July 1766). Hume himself pointed out that the phrase could have been borrowed from Plutarch's *Lives*, where Xerxes cries out that he has 'got' Themistocles.

[4] Diderot, *Pensées détachées sur la peinture*, *Œuvres esthétiques*, ed. Paul Vernière (Paris: Garnier, 1968), p. 769.

lurking when what have been figments become flesh (Pygmalion wills the statue into being, from idea into substance, from substance into life), especially when the trick of art makes alien things familiar, naturalizing non-selves or the marble image. But most art forms that seek to represent reality do this in some way or other; it is, indeed, what troubled Rousseau's enemies the most. We may also think *Pygmalion* is saying the opposite, that what it emphasizes is aesthetic error, or the way art fools us by its tendency to make illusion real (as Plato argues in the *Symposium*). Such a view may help explain the acts of those who do as Rousseau's persecutors did, censoring the work of art for embodying a challenge or professing dissidence.

WORD AND IMAGE

The boundaries that separate reality from figment always exercised him. *Pygmalion* presents them with a special clarity, as might any work whose medium re-presents (substantially)—the plastic and pictorial arts, then, rather than the verbal ones. It is unsurprising that these issues surfaced when Rousseau, in English exile between 1766 and 1767, found himself depicted in a portrait Hume commissioned from the artist Allan Ramsay, and which the subject hated. He loathed it in particular because he felt that portraiture, however close its superficial likeness to the sitter, never captures all the complex 'story' of his mind and character: Diderot agreed with him, to judge by what he wrote about a portrait Michel Van Loo painted of him at that time.[5] Rousseau, then, was joining a debate about the shared and separate capacities of word and image just when persecution drove him far from literature and its analytical potential, pushing him to other modes and mediums of expression.

When painting was at issue, and the problem was another person's version of the subject, all the limitations of the visual seemed offensive. Yet the half-length portrait Ramsay did of him in 1766 is one of the artist's finest, plumbing all its subject's troubled depths.[6] Most who saw the work, accordingly, appeared to rate it highly: George III expressed the wish to see the picture (Ramsay was official painter to the King),[7] and engravings done of it were popular and widely circulated. It is a fascinating study of

---

[5] Diderot, *Salon* of 1767, *O.C.*, XVI.82–3, observes that he had a hundred different expressions every day, and Van Loo had chosen an untypical one. He also protested at being painted in uncharacteristic finery.

[6] See Alastair Smart, *Allan Ramsay: Printer, Essayist and Man of the Enlightenment* (New Haven and London: Yale University Press, 1992), p. 93.

[7] See Rousseau's letter of 29 May 1766 to DuPeyrou, *C.C.*, XXIX.72.

a misfit in Armenian mufti, with set mouth, baleful look, and glowering eyes that burn the gloom around him.[8] Was this mistrust linked with the beliefs Rousseau had formed concerning Hume's duplicity, or with something deeper? Did he feel particular ill-will for artists, men whose trade involved (or so it seemed to him) the speciously direct attempt to copy an observed reality, the facile re-presenting of abhorred materiality rather than abstraction or the half-intuited perception? His loathing for reductive physicalist thought was generally known and lifelong, although he usually expressed it in connection with contemporary philosophy, not painting. Painting, on the face of it, should have seemed attractive to him as a hands-on trade involving the long-practised skills of trained and sober artisans; portraiture was tolerated even in most Puritan societies for its documentary aim and distance from the realms of fancy. It might, indeed, pass muster in the same way as the genre Rousseau said his *Confessions* established, even though it lacked—or so it seemed to him—the latter's narrative and analytical potential.

But the memoirs (as the *Confessions* was initially called) he would set about in England give the most compelling explanation for this distaste: Rousseau simply would not grant that any outside witness could present him as he truly was, *intus, et in cute*,[9] and disliked the Ramsay picture so intensely as to break off all relations with acquaintances who praised it. A M. Bret, for instance, had told Rousseau that his wife possessed a picture (presumably an engraving) of him that she loved, which showed him dressed as an Armenian: this may be a print of Ramsay's painting or the modified version of Latour's earlier pastel that substituted kaftan for original frock coat. 'Sortez de chez moi, répond Rousseau furieux, un portrait fait pour me déshonorer, pour m'avilir, je ne veux jamais voir la femme capable de regarder, d'aimer, de conserver ce monument à ma honte: dîner aver elle, j'aimerais mieux mourir. La pauvre Mme Bret s'arra[ch]e les cheveux ne peut se consoler d'avoir offensé Jean-Jacques. Quelle brute que cet homme d'esprit.'[10] The second *Dialogue* would later draw atten-

---

[8] In a letter to d'Alembert of 27 July 1766 Hume reports that the very excess of his attentions has seemingly aroused Rousseau's suspicions of a plot against him. Rousseau regarded Hume's eagerness to arrange for the portrait to be painted as resembling that of an impatient lover (*Dialogues*, I.779). His claim was always that he possessed an open and trusting character, and that his suspicious nature had revealed itself only as a result of the treachery of others. Hume was forewarned about Rousseau's habit of picking quarrels with benefactors, as well as his mistrustfulness: see Ernest Campbell Mossner, *The Life of David Hume*, 2nd edn (Oxford: Oxford University Press, 1980), p. 571. Rousseau's dislike for the portrait may have been accentuated by the engraving David Martin did of it.

[9] Persius, *Satire III*. Rousseau uses the phrase at the head of Book 1 of the *Confessions*.

[10] See Mme Riccoboni to David Garrick, 1 October 1770 (*C.C.*, XXXVIII.119–20); also the letter from Mme Alissan de La Tour to Rousseau on 9 July 1769: 'J'ai votre portrait

tion to the engraving of Latour's portrait, which Rousseau claimed to like in its original form, but which he anathematizes here because it makes him look deformed, 'un petit fourbe, un petit menteur, un petit escroc, un coureur de tavernes et de mauvais lieux', and finally a man with a treacherous sardonic smile 'comme celui de Panurge achetant les moutons de Dindenaut', or of those who casually met Rousseau in the street.[11] He had, in other words, been made an object of derision.

He said a great deal more about the world's determination to traduce him, openly or otherwise. The companion portrait Ramsay did of Hume, so Rousseau thought, made the subject seem a handsome man in contrast, an opinion contradicted by the evidence: it seemed impossible to make Hume's kindly, moon-like face, which Diderot was struck by,[12] look intelligent[13] (Lord Charlemont said that what it most resembled was a turtle-eating alderman).[14] Profile studies of him, like the one by Carmontelle in Scotland's National Portrait Gallery, more effectively convey Hume's mental powers; his corpulence, already showing in a portrait Ramsay did of him in 1754,[15] was a matter he himself made light of,[16] and it is accentuated in the later picture by the richness of the garments that encase his frame. When the King passed comment on his splendid scarlet costume, which had been Hume's uniform as secretary to military missions in Vienna and Turin, Hume said he wanted future ages to realize that one philosopher at least had had a good coat on his back in George's reign.[17] Rousseau's claim, conversely, that the plot to ridicule him had begun when he was made to wear the Armenian costume Ramsay showed him in[18] cannot be sustained: it was known that he had worn it from his Môtiers days because loose clothing gave him some relief in his physical afflictions. The engravers of the Ramsay portrait were as far from being party to an anti-Rousseau plot as Ramsay was himself.

---

gravé à Londres d'apres l'original de Kamsay [Ramsay], et je l'ai placé au dessus de la table qui me sert de secrétaire, précisément comme une dévote place au dessus de son oratoire l'image du Saint à qui elle a la plus fervente devotion' (*C.C.*, XXXVII.109).

[11] *Dialogues*, I.781–2.

[12] In a letter to Hume of 17 March 1769, Diderot refers to the latter's 'face ronde et riante': Diderot, *Correspondance*, ed. Georges Roth and Jean Varloot, 16 vols. (Paris: Minuit, 1955–70), IX.39.

[13] Smart, however, regards the portrait as an effective presentation of interior thought, highlighting Hume's reflective mood (*Allan Ramsay*, p. 210).

[14] *Memoirs of the Political and Private Life of James Caulfield, Earl of Charlemont*, 2nd edn, ed. Francis Hardy (London: Cadell and Davies, 1812), quoted in the *Dictionary of National Biography*.

[15] Private collection. [16] See Mossner, *Life of Hume*, pp. 233–4.

[17] See Smart, *Allan Ramsay*, p. 210. [18] *Dialogues*, I.779.

Rousseau's hatred of the picture and its reproductions rested on a set of complex factors bound up with their philosophical times, and sheds light on what the self-account begun in England would eventually become. Through all the correspondence dealing with the Ramsay picture, as throughout the second *Dialogue*, runs the thread of Rousseau's attitude to self-depiction, the self's attempt to capture its 'reality' objectively (the thorny question of what constituted personhood), and some other issues with a central place in eighteenth-century thought. Hume's engagement with them was well known, but it is unlikely Rousseau ever had a philosophical debate with him[19] or had read his works:[20] the seminal *Treatise of Human Nature*, in particular, was not translated into French until the mid nineteenth century. As Rousseau insisted that humanity traduced him and betrayed his noblest impulses, never understanding how his nature could be captured both as essence and as image, he remained convinced that he, and only he, possessed the key that might unlock his personality. The world's presumption as it tried to explain him stood revealed as arrogance and error, he declared; what it saw, the evidence on which it built its Rousseau, was incomplete. Only he knew how to penetrate his personality *intus, et in cute*—inside *and* out, rather than (simply) inside out.

Other witnesses might disagree with Rousseau's view of painting as non-analytical, taking Ramsay's image as both 'in the flesh' and subcutaneous: painters have to show the surface, certainly, but may also seek to go beneath the *cutis* just as writers do, if differently. Whether Persius' phrase was clear to him or not, however, Rousseau knew how hard it is to grasp and then reveal what may be felt but cannot be straightforwardly presented; visual images, as Lessing's treatise *Laokoon* argued that same year, invariably fall short of showing temporal processes that define the person and his inner motive forces, even though their power to show extent is endlessly superior.[21] So when, in the *Confessions*, Rousseau sees himself as standing in God's presence, book in hand, he thinks that only written words can tell his history ('ce que j'ai fait, ce que j'ai pensé, ce que je fus'), since only language lets us show the way we pass through time and how the impulses that make up personal psychology are successively experienced. Yet to focus merely on a sequence of phenomena may mislead as much as showing just one moment: point of view, in all the senses of the phrase, is paramount.

---

[19] See A. J. Ayer, *Hume* (Oxford: Oxford University Press, 1980), p. 37.

[20] Hume remarked in a letter to Hugh Blair of 25 March 1766 that Rousseau had 'study'd very little: and has not indeed much Knowledge' (*C.C.*, XXIX.58).

[21] *Laokoon*'s subtitle is 'On the Limitations of Painting and Poetry', where 'poetry' is taken as signifying literature in general. The question of the similarities and differences between artistic media was a constant topic of discussion in eighteenth-century aesthetics.

In the fragment *Mon Portrait* Rousseau wrestles with the problem of establishing the inner motives that determine conduct, and concludes that those who stand outside the self invariably mistake the evidence: 'Je vois que les gens qui vivent le plus intimement avec moi ne me connoissent pas, et qu'ils attribuent la plupart de mes actions, soit en bien soit en mal, à de tout autres motifs que ceux qui les ont produites.'[22] The Neuchâtel preamble to the *Confessions* rails against the habit of presenting character as 'des histoires, des vies, des portraits', which can do no more than try to show a subject through external acts: the enterprise must fail because externals barely hint what a person truly is, and the inner model, Rousseau thinks, can be seen by no one but the individual and his all-knowing God.[23] The *Confessions* proper puts the latter point explicitly; but although its subject first tells God: 'j'ai dévoilé mon intérieur tel que tu l'as vu toi-même', he then remarks that 'Nul ne peut écrire la vie d'un homme que lui-même.'[24] What he means, presumably, is not that God is lacking in sufficient insight for this task—God has total insight into everything—, but that he simply does not write biographies, whether because he is too busy, has no inclination for it, or on some other grounds that Rousseau does not specify. The important point is Rousseau's firm conviction that only writing lets the individual life be re-presented, not because a life consists in words, but because the word alone can mirror life's essential element of time.

There is, then, no mystery in his rejecting Ramsay's art of portraiture as a means for rendering the human subject, first because he thinks artists too distant from their subjects for truth, confined as they are to an external view (this appears to Rousseau a straightforward and incontestable fact), and second because painting's temporal limitations pose insuperable difficulties in terms of scope (a matter already dealt with by Lessing and, if less publicly, Diderot). Together these observations seem to Rousseau to possess unanswerable force. We may, however, take issue with the first, that portraitists are fatally hampered in lacking the power of what is now called psychological analysis, or what Rousseau describes as the presentation of 'internal' truth. Quite apart from the tendentiousness of the notion that painters cannot probe beneath the surface, it seems evident that even an external view may tell the subject something he did not know about himself (as those who stand outside the self see it from angles inwardness denies). The second objection is no less questionable, or, rather, what it leaves unsaid requires an emphasis Rousseau withholds: for while the factor of time is undoubtedly central to our concept of the human life, any life, so is that of space and the apprehension it alone permits. Words may be elastic and rich in implication, but they cannot present the direct image, the *eikōn*.

[22] *O.C.*, I.1121.   [23] I.1149.   [24] I.5.

Rousseau's comparative indifference towards visual art in comparison with the arts of literature and music, which helps explain the partiality of his words on Ramsay's picture, is matched by his (select) disdain for circumstantial truth. What he strains for in his writing is a form of moral truth that emerges only with the process of interpretation, and which, so the fourth *Rêverie* will claim, should be trusted more than what appears objective evidence. For this moral truth to show with clarity, for this 'histoire de mon âme' to be convincingly narrated, more is plainly needed than external fact. Yet the introspective will not grant that others may have access to his inner self, or at least have a perception that matches or exceeds his own; and Rousseau denies it most vehemently when the medium in question lacks the temporal dimension. There was more behind his frank hostility than this, however. Ramsay's portrait, so he came to think, gave substance to a myth whose propagation was the work of tireless enemies, the myth that he was not a single person but a plural and disjointed one. Yet pictures surely give a substance, hence a kind of unity or resolution, words can never match.

THE ELUSIVENESS OF BEING

What he wanted to attempt in England, by contrast, was assembling and describing patterns of successive states and thoughts that would convey his self through time, his own identity. When others drew attention to his instability, they meant to highlight his divided person. This split, they said, showed through in all his inconsistencies: inventing social contracts but refusing to live socially, anathematizing art but writing plays and novels, proffering theories of education but casting off his children. Rousseau knew much better, and came to think that going back in time would let him give a truer image of his person than the present and apparently disjointed one, a solid resolution linked with family background and tradition. He also knew that words alone were capable of joining past to present, and that only someone who was once the boy could give the lessons of his early life a narrative form. There was no other way of showing how the fact of being spanked by Mlle Lambercier—'Qui croiroit que ce châtiment d'enfant receu à huit ans par la main d'une fille de trente a décidé de mes gouts, de mes desirs, de mes passions, de moi pour le reste de ma vie'[25]—had helped to shape his present personality. Such truths as this meant only one thing, he concluded: that although he had been made

---

[25] I.15. As is often noted, Rousseau was in fact eleven at the time, and Mlle Lambercier about forty.

to mistrust writing for its link with persecution, writing must now be his sole resort.

Narrative alone could track the multiplicity of Rousseaus, all the inconsistencies of someone who had been protean from childhood. He knew that what he showed to casual onlookers might mislead: 'J'aimerois la societé comme un autre si je n'étois sûr de m'y montrer [...] tout autre que je ne suis', he would announce.[26] Ramsay's crime, it seems, was to intuit, then depict, the otherness of his subject, but in different ways from those Rousseau desired. For Rousseau thought that it was possible to see oneself, if not see others, with dispassion, from a scientific point of view, a theory implicit in the so-called 'morale sensitive' mentioned in book nine of the *Confessions*, which describes how people change in temperament, and 'semblent se transformer en des hommes tout différens'.[27] Hume, though of a more settled disposition than Rousseau—the brief self-account he wrote shortly before his death describes him as 'not [...] very irascible in my Temper', and 'ever more disposed to see the favourable than unfavourable Side of Things'[28]—, would probably have seen such waywardness in terms of personal discontinuity: since the unity of our selves is an assumption, not a fact, he says, we should not be surprised by evidence that calls it into question. Rousseau, on the other hand, like *Emile*'s 'vicaire savoyard', abhorred all scepticism; certainty, not doubt, was what he needed, even at the cost of system-building dogmatism.

For these reasons, it might seem that reverie was the only state in which, from Rousseau's point of view, the artist could have painted him reliably, since reverie is timeless, touched by neither past nor future.[29] Yet it is also a state whose beatific qualities most resist depiction, depending as it does on absence, not on presence: for absence means suspension and abstraction, things alien to representational art. The companion piece of Hume Ramsay painted that same year comes close to capturing them, however, wonderfully depicting the serene half-indolence that the Scotsman said could give him total happiness, his tranquil goodness imaged in the gentle, musing gaze some likened to a cud-chewing cow's. All the same, this calm, unthreatening stare caused Rousseau deep discomfort, as he wrote to French acquaintances. '[Il] me fut impossible de soutenir son affreux regard', he told the Marquise de Verdelin, and even when he fled in tears to Hume's embrace he saw in horror that the latter kept his sang-froid[30]

---

[26] I.116.   [27] I.408.
[28] David Hume, *My Own Life* (appendix to Mossner, p. 613).
[29] *Rêveries du promeneur solitaire*, I.1046–7.
[30] *C.C.*, XXIX.99–100 (9 April 1766); see also his immense letter of recrimination to Hume of 10 July 1766 (*C.C.*, XXX.35).

(a charge Hume denied). Hume in turn would feel unsettled by this
mistrust: 'What! Because sometimes, when absent in thought, I have a
fixed Look or Stare, you suspect me to be a Traytor [...]. Are not most
studious Men (and many of them more than I) subject to like Reveries or
Fits of Absence, without being exposed to such Suspicions?'[31] But even
d'Alembert, whom Hume respected most among the *philosophes*, warned
him not to gaze so fixedly at those he was addressing.[32] Rousseau always
felt unsettled at the thought of other people staring at him,[33] apprehend-
ing his defenceless being, 'taking' it as a painter might catch a likeness,[34]
almost snatching it away: it seemed as threatening as the public confisca-
tion of his works, or his enemies' attempts to catch him out. Hume's look,
for Rousseau, matched the bid for seizure he had blamed him for at Senlis, where *regarding* seemed equivalent to guarding, keeping hold of him,[35]
hence challenging his autonomy. How could any individualist permit it?
Rousseau's sense of the assaulting gaze stayed with him like a retinal per-
sistence, like arrested vision, making him 'feel' a look that was no longer
focused on him. Why, we wonder, in that case did he so blatantly attract
attention with the outlandish clothes he wore, the outfit that defined him
so precisely? Did he, as Hume thought, in fact enjoy his notoriety?

Discontinuous selfhood, as debated by philosophers and occasionally
suggested by portraitists, might be resolved by the projection Hume saw
as central to epistemology, one dependent on imagination. Its theory is
set out in the *Treatise of Human Nature*[36] in terms of intuition, the sympathetic understanding Ramsay's paintings predicate of the beholder; but
Rousseau rejected it outright as a false bid on fancy's part to secure what
it does not and cannot know. Imagination had no part to play in truths
about the self, he thought, because he linked it with disaster, *his* disaster:
hence the embargo on its use by others as an interpretative tool, and the
observations in the draft introduction to the *Confessions* on the comprehensive picture, good and bad, he would paint, so full it would preclude
the need for any outside speculation. Yet the second *Dialogue* calls for
imagination in its readers, seeing it as a precondition of the fellow feeling
Rousseau wanted to be lavished on his shadowy self. Surely, though, this
is nothing other than the sympathy Hume proudly showed his fickle

[31] 22 July 1766, ibid., p. 138.
[32] Mossner, *Life of Hume*, pp. 476–7.
[33] Jean Starobinski, *L'Œil vivant* (Paris: Gallimard, 1961), pp. 100–3.
[34] A notion literally conveyed by the Italian word for portrait, 'ritratto'.
[35] Starobinski, *L'Œil vivant*, pp. 11–13.
[36] See Duncan Forbes, *Hume's Philosophical Politics* (Cambridge: Cambridge University
Press, 1975), p. 15, and John Mullan, *Sentiment and Sociability: The Language of Feeling in
the Eighteenth Century* (Oxford: Oxford University Press, 1988), p. 30.

protégé, thinking, just as Rousseau did, that only thus can personal substantiality be made manifest.[37] Such, at least, is what Hume argues in the *Treatise*, stating all the limitations of our understanding and the need for goodwill in the way we deal with others, a concessive mood that alone permits us to project and round out individual natures on the basis of the sketchy clues we have. Such intuition paves the way to that aesthetic which, in visual art and literature, champions the spontaneous, imaginative impulse against rationality. In portraiture we think perhaps of Raeburn; in literature, of the Romantics, with their emphasis on all that cannot be observed or grasped by ordinary intelligences; but also of their precursor Rousseau, so critical of reason's dryness, so passionate for the values he associates with feeling.

In responding to the Ramsay portrait Rousseau, suspicious of another person's view of him and already mistrustful of imagination, denies collusion of the kind that art has always asked of its consumer. As the eyes must see a third dimension in the two the canvas offers, so we have to read the dark and light in pictures as somehow more than they really are. Yet as Locke said, and as the Rousseau verdict on the portrait shows, vision is subjective; or, in Blake's words, 'As the Eye, so the Object.'[38] In other words, the distance separating Rousseau from the painter, in both moral and aesthetic matters, was much less than either may have thought. Both, like Hume, had moved beyond the tenets of a Lockean empiricism that took the sensorily perceptible as being like material a maker works upon, substance that is physically altered in the studio or workshop, like the reality an artist tricks us into seeing on the painted canvas or in sculpted marble. Despite the implications of his 'morale sensitive', Rousseau knew that he was more than just a sensory object; but he still perversely took exception to the art of one whose work suggested truths that went beyond conventional perception, and who remained dissatisfied with the lessons of an ordinary vision. Rousseau himself, as *Dialogues* and correspondence make apparent, also wanted recognition from those able to probe more deeply than other people, and who could read the soul as well as the physiognomy: initially he thought that Hume, the prophet of benevolence, might plumb his depths, and therefore tried extracting from him all those demonstrations that the 'âmes sensibles' of *La Nouvelle Héloïse* make manifest. When Hume's response proved insufficient, he saw no option but to call this kindly and benevolent man devoid of feeling and morality.

---

[37] *Dialogues*, I.800–2.
[38] Compare Martin Kemp, *The Science of Art* (New Haven and London: Yale University Press, 1990), p. 252.

Given his mistrust of visual images, it is not surprising that deficiencies of sight should figure in his work. *Narcisse* made a portrait, *Pygmalion* a sculpture, triggers for the blindness of their central characters, both 'accidents' that stem from mimesis. To judge by what he says about engravings of his portraits, Rousseau set great store by representational accuracy both because he thought most types of visual art not true enough and because he was a man of vanity; perhaps he should have pondered Diderot's words on how resemblance in the portrait matters only to the sitter and all or some of those who know him. Ramsay had a gift for catching likeness, and his image of Rousseau seemed to its beholders faithful. But he was the painter of inwardness too; and while many contemporaries thought that likeness mattered in portraiture (as the *Encyclopédie* entry 'Portrait' puts it), others valued mental truth more highly.[39] It is surely because he believed in psychology's claims as much as surface resemblance that Ramsay's later work moves behind outwardness to 'thicker' zones of subjective depiction. Ironically, so does that of the hostile Rousseau, particularly the *Confessions*.

The Enlightenment, in Scotland as elsewhere, valued subjectivity as highly as the common good, twin ideals converging in the eighteenth century's efforts both to understand the individual and to develop a 'science' of his general type. This concern was current in contemporary philosophy as in portraiture. Hume writes in the *Treatise* that everything in nature is particular, and thought it worth his while devoting time and effort to the welfare of a single, troublesome person, Rousseau, because he believed that care for the particular is merely a modality of concern for the general. Rousseau, social theorist as well as proud individualist, might have learnt much from the philosophy and personal example of his host, but preferred to see Hume as the representative of a more dubious society, allegedly bent on plotting his shame and downfall. In his defiant subjectivity and inbred tendency to extremism, indeed, he ironically epitomises the character Hume's *History* judges most severely, one who turns away from nature and performs deeds stemming from a culpable excess of imagination—the very instinct on which Rousseau blamed his persecution and exile.

His conviction, expressed throughout his personal writings, that all who 'explained' him did so wrongly made him instinctively hostile to an art form in which the neutral or the noncommittal is almost impossible, and which, as Valère discovers in *Narcisse*, can strikingly mislead. Ramsay,

[39] For this distinction, see *Conversations of James Northcote R.A. with James Ward on Art and Artists*, ed. Ernest Fletcher (London: F. Muller, 1949), p. 57.

a 'peintre habile, ne reconnoissant d'autre guide que la nature', with his 'goût raisonnable de la fidélité', bore witness in his work to an 'esprit juste et ferme'[40] of that drily Scottish kind apparent too throughout Hume's writings. It was perhaps inevitable that these qualities should displease a man known to mistrust wit, which he saw as an adulteration of the authentic and true. But Rousseau's dream of a pre-intellectual, pre-artistic, and pre-civilized age is of a time that never was. He believed in the innocent eye and the absence of distorting point of view, but failed to realize that they were as mythical as Golden Ages of the kind the *Discours* predicate. Artists can no more project the signs of nature in a pre-interpretative stage than authors write without an attitude. Rousseau had his theory of nature, as Hume and Ramsay did; perhaps theirs simply stood the test of scrutiny better.

PRACTICAL INTEGRITY

Although pictures might traduce, as Rousseau thought the Ramsay portrait did, they scarcely had the power to endanger. Words, while unquestionably more treacherous, were the only tools at his disposal. So he had to find a way of using them that challenged the untruthful image, but did not betray him further; words to rebut the falsehoods (painted or professed) without imperilling his life. Such words must be pragmatic implements, not servants of mere fancy, tools that copied down without invention, reconnected with his craftsman forebears in their frank reality, telling the straightforward story *intus, et in cute*. Invention or imagination had no part to play in this, he thought, having more than once betrayed him; the material or pattern of his humble life was something only he was master of, knew intimately as no looker-on could do. The self-inscription flowing from this knowledge would be graphic (too graphic, as some readers said), a new form of mimesis, a text devoid of pomp and glory, plain as the ancient *sermo humilis*, a sober narrative of life experience, the only writing he could trust; in other words, a form of representing done with perfect and unshowy expertise, like the humble still life of the 'tradesman' painter Chardin or the parables of common life that Diderot meant his *drames* to be. Rousseau knew he had betrayed his principles in writing the inventive works that followed on the first *Discours*, though there was no justice in the punishments that France and Switzerland decreed. It

---

[40] The quotations are from Jean-André Rouquet, *Etat des arts en Angleterre* (Paris: Charles-Antoine Jombert, 1755), p. 58.

might be wholly true, as *Julie*'s second preface says, that writing fiction was an inconsistency in anyone so hostile to the arts and sciences, yet the real offence, if that was what it was, had gone unpunished: while Julie's statement of religious faith matched *Emile*'s 'profession de foi', only *Emile* was condemned for heresy. This might, he thought, if encouraged, mean no more than that 'good' writing (safe inscription) had to hide its principles, deny its artistry, as the Elysée of *Héloïse* had done. Such purity would be echoed in the plain, straightforward style he thought appropriate to his background and his roots.

Yet it was a form of safety he had not before seen as essential, not before the burning of his books; until then he simply went along with what imagination prompted. Making Claire and Julie, for example, turned him into a Pygmalion, successfully endowing fictive creatures with substantial life. We know too how imagination let him translate given states into their opposites, absence from Maman ensuring he would feel her presence more completely than he did when really with her, 'living' summer best in winter months, feeling liberated in confinement, and so on, just as he had understood mankind best when far from human contact, wandering in the woods of Saint-Germain and dreaming up the second *Discours*. But there was more to it than that. Memory for him, he said, was only ever of the pleasant things he had experienced, not the painful ones (a statement that unaccountably ignores the paranoia which from middle age would make him see neutrality as hostile, friends as enemies, kindly folk as ill disposed): this power of transformation had seemed positive in earlier life, with the disparate selves created from his childhood on as though they were heroic figures drawn from Plutarch's *Lives*, the Englishman Dudding and the music-maker Vaussore de Villeneuve, along with many others. But no one else could really 'fix' him in all his complex truth.

Settling what he must do now, quite independently of Rey's proposal, therefore seemed straightforward. Although the punishments inflicted on him for his writing seemed to show that he should write no more, self-narrative, self-presentation, was different—almost like his own fair copying of *Julie* (for all the ambiguity of 'fair', hinting at an ornamental purpose) or the transcripts he had done for Mmes de Vercellis and Dupin. Going even further back, he could invoke the imitation he had learned as an apprentice, doing work that made no call on the inventive faculty, but which needed simple care together with a sense of balance: beauty with fidelity. If the question then arose as to what necessary writing was, the kind the *Dialogues* explicitly envisages, writing done in an enchanted world, when both his most important and potentially most useful works had been rejected by authority, Rousseau had this answer: the kind that formulates those truths the individual alone, as writer, may relay. This is what the prefaces to the *Confessions* attempt to crystallize, his need to write an ordinary account, exemplary[41] as truthful self-recounting is, a faithful, not an idealized, re-rendering (unlike other writers' self-depictions), exemplary both in the sense evoked by Scaevola's self-immolation and in that of exemplarity: ordered with perfection, copying more truly than the Ramsay portrait did, capturing his self as only he could do, setting down a fuller record than those offered by the fabulists, or by fauxnaïfs (Montaigne especially) who only showed their better side.[42]

This origin would guarantee a truth that words alone, without support from deeper knowledge, strained to capture, tokens of convention as they were, but which the fact of self-report authenticated. The punishable hand—Scaevola's, Rousseau's own as thief of orchard fruit or ribbon— might be saved if turned entirely to this new account, an enterprise 'qui n'eut jamais d'éxemple',[43] exemplary, that is, in all its intimate unsparingness. The copying, he claimed, was innocent retrieval of matter laid out plainly for transcription, the only beauty it contained that of fidelity. We know this was not wholly true, that Rousseau sometimes altered fact according to desire (of a moral or artistic kind), but we also see the power of his claimed disinterestedness: the clarity of truth works best when told with beauty. Yet the *Confessions* lays bare a further paradox—which the *Rêveries* pursues—of recreating through remembrance a past enhanced by retrospection, an enterprise that cannot therefore be a simple act of reproduction. What stands revealed instead is the elusiveness of personhood, the self that Hume had called a bundle of perceptions: no unity, still less a universal truth. Rousseau had already felt its slipperiness, proposing to address the matter in the 'morale sensitive', although he never did; *Emile* similarly warns against the imagination because it is a power that makes us long for things rather than live them, so that we lose touch with practicality, the very sense that Emile's craft apprenticeship is meant to guarantee. Thought, it says, is dangerously abstract, hence impractical; but this had not always been Rousseau's view. *Julie*, for all its high craftmindedness, proposes a quite different notion, seeing in the power of thought a force that can inspire in practical terms, draw us closer to a socialized ideal.

---

[41] On this concept, see Kelly, *Rousseau's Exemplary Life*.
[42] *Ebauches des 'Confessions'*, *O.C.*, I.1150: Montaigne is the leader of those 'faux sincéres qui veulent tromper en disant vrai', and only gives himself 'd'aimables fautes'. The fourth Promenade of the *Rêveries*, on the other hand, concedes that Rousseau may sometimes have hidden his own 'coté difforme', *O.C.*, I.1036.
[43] *Confessions*, I.5.

CURIOSITY

Rousseau's circumstances had been changed entirely by the time he set about his 'memoirs'. Though many other difficulties attended it, English exile would not make him feel the same degree of social and political disfavour as France and Switzerland had done; even so, when passing through the streets of Paris on his way to London he was greeted as a man of truth and genius, holding levees to which his admirers flocked to fête and flatter him, celebrating him for writing both a novel of heart-stopping sensibility and a treatise on progressive education. England too would laud him, though occasionally with *Schadenfreude*, pleased to seem more tolerant than benighted foreigners.

His future hosts might have been less generous had they known how hard he fought against migrating to their country, harassed as he felt by bossy interventionists and managerial females, unsure too of Hume's support. He also feared a loss of favour when the English came to know him better, knew the insults *Emile* hurled at them (especially his digs at native bloody-mindedness), his ignorance of English, his fear of ridicule (the Armenian outfit), and his sense of alienation from a nation prone to xenophobia and triumphalism, particularly, perhaps, towards all those it—often wrongly—classified as *French*. At one stage, Rousseau says, he had considered settling in Scotland rather than England, possibly for its links with his protector Earl Marshal Keith and its craggy landscape, which would, he thought, remind him of his homeland. (From his time in Chambéry, Rousseau always claimed that flat terrain was charmless—he needed peaks and chasms, raging torrents, fir trees, black woods, towering mountains above all.)[44] Supporters such as Keith who knew him better tried to disabuse him, partly by informing him how very cold the country was; Rousseau, who had suffered greatly from the climate when he lived in Neuchâtel, took fright at this, but stayed irresolute, at which point the Earl Marshal tried to settle things by telling him that Scotland was in some unspecified particular exceedingly unpleasant. When he himself was invited by the King of Prussia to reside in Potsdam, he urged Rousseau to join him there; Rousseau was uncertain, wondering if he should not rather move to Italy. In the end he went to London, then lodged in Chiswick with a grocer, Pulleyn, in whose shop he sat exchanging baffling pleasantries with customers and admirers, insisting that he could fix no English words or grammar in his head[45] (the grocer's regulars were

---

[44] *Confessions*, I.172.
[45] He could, however, apparently read the language (Ritter, *Famille et jeunesse*, p. 225).

probably equally ignorant of French). Even so, these meetings seemed in some strange way fulfilling to a man who always said he felt much closer to the humble than to their social betters.

Whatever fear past criticisms of England made him feel—a fear of which he told the largely sympathetic Hume—, he did suppress it long enough to bask in London's praise, although he then attacked the place for being both a city and a capital. If the native bigotry that Hume had feared for him was not apparent, he still went on to find most kinds of Englishman distasteful, saying that the moral qualities they claimed were far from evident to others. Later on he would regret this criticism. In any case, he also felt a certain admiration for the Anglo-Saxon virtue of directness, a fondness for plain speech that some had thought he would take umbrage at, and after his return to France in 1767 would even feel nostalgia for both England and its Englishness, although the plans he made to go back never came to anything. The preference for country over city was natural in a man of Rousseau's stripe, eventually prompting him to move to Wootton Hall in Staffordshire, a country mansion separated by the valley of the river Dove from Derbyshire, which a rich admirer, Richard Davenport, had put at his disposal, but where Thérèse succeeded in antagonizing all the staff. And yet the 'gouvernante' would gain some sympathy among the villagers for her apparent suffering at Rousseau's hands: one day after a beating, so the story goes, Thérèse—known to them as Madam Zell—appeared amidst the women uttering the few words of English she had learnt: 'Never marry! Never marry! You see! You see!'[46]

If this spell was more disquieting than other periods in Rousseau's life, it still confirmed his preference for rural ways, underlining his belief that people in the countryside possessed integrity that city dwellers lacked. In Wootton he acquired a name for necromancy among those who watched him come and go on botanizing rambles through a landscape partly tamed but still preserving natural form, the grounds of Wootton Hall particularly. He later noted all the pleasure to be found in scrutinizing mosses in the cold and rainy season, carefully making 'moussiers' that elevate these modest products by exquisitely displaying them on sheets of coloured card and annotating different types with scholarly and calligraphic care.[47] The villagers could never quite grow used to this strange man in odd exotic robe and fur-brimmed hat who roamed around the area, frightening the children, but was taken as a sage who knew, as an apothecary might, how to find and name, and even use, a range of 'yarbs' to

[46] William Howitt, *Visits to Remarkable Places* (London: no publisher, 1840), p. 511.
[47] The Musée des arts décoratifs in Paris possesses an example.

medical ends. (He had dabbled in this art before, when living at Môtiers.)[48] Mme de Warens would have been surprised, but also, surely, rather proud of him.

The task that writing the *Confessions* set him might be likened to this pastime, the gathering of specimens, then classifying, and displaying them; or, perhaps, the tracking down, acquiring, and exhibiting of those *curiosities* beloved of eighteenth-century connoisseurs, owners of the 'cabinets' that summed up the part-scientific, part-aesthetic spirit of the age.[49] Just as Rousseau's English friend the Duchess of Portland, visiting near Wootton while he lived there, obsessively assembled naturalia—her cabinet of shells at Bulstrode became legendary, but her mania meant she died consumed by debt[50]—, so he himself would try to put together bits and scraps of truth for others to examine, driven by what the *Rêveries* would liken to a scientific process of collecting, followed by the publication that let the truths uncovered be diffused. He wanted, like Linnaeus, to scrutinize an area of nature, but an intangible one, laying bare its secrets as the botanist displays his specimens. It would be a personal presentation, yet complete, he thought, as few florilegia or 'Kunstkammer' aimed to be.

For all that, he broached the writing of this personal account with quite different motives from the common one of personal curiosity. The narrative would be extracted from him less because he knew Rey wanted it than because Voltaire's anonymous attack had so grossly challenged his integrity by revealing the abandonment of his children. Rousseau was a man who needed to defend himself: hence the *Confessions*' claim to 'vitam impendere vero' in the writer's self-account. Hume's view that no man knew himself as little as Rousseau did had not, presumably, by then been spread abroad; if it had, Voltaire would surely have pounced upon it.[51] So DuPeyrou was asked to send to England such documents as this enterprise required, and Rousseau carried on the job he had begun to think about at Môtiers, if now with greater urgency.[52]

He wanted to present as organized a picture of his person as the *Encyclopédie* gave of human knowledge, as complete an image as seemed in practice possible. Readers such as Mme d'Epinay might query (and they did) the need for a collection of what Rousseau called facts, but others

[48] Letter to Malesherbes, *C.C.*, XXII.44 (11 November 1764).

[49] See Arthur MacGregor, *Curiosity and Enlightenment* (New Haven and London: Yale University Press, 2007). On the lexical history of 'curiosité' and its cognates, see Neil Kenny, *Curiosity in Early Modern Europe: Word Histories* (Wiesbaden: Harrassowitz Verlag, 1998).

[50] MacGregor, *Curiosity and Enlightenment*, p. 139.

[51] *C.C.*, XXVIII.203 (Hume to Comtesse de Boufflers, 14 July 1766).

[52] *C.C.*, XXXIII.65 (Rousseau to General Conway, 18 May 1767).

named his fantasies, and the view inevitably prevailed that the work was biased in his favour. When he told a pretty woman, 'J'y ai dit tout le mal qu'on ne sait pas de moi, et tout le bien que je sais des autres', she allegedly replied, 'En ce cas le livre sera fort court'.[53] Part of the work's interest rests on paradox, its author's strange attempt to write a book about himself, the man who, having written other books, had said that he would write no more of them, but whose life could be described through writing and no other means. Many of the other oddities his life presents stem from one or another version of this fact.[54] Yet he chose to discontinue the confessions when he settled back in Paris in 1770, though after leaving England in 1767 he had carried on the project first at the Prince de Conti's château at Trye, then at Monquin in Dauphiné. Book XII, which breaks off at the point where Rousseau, driven from the île de Saint-Pierre and from Switzerland itself, envisages settling in England, seems to promise a continuation, but it never came. Fearing that the manuscript might be impounded, he made copies of it in a fine and regular hand; and Part I of *Les Confessions* was published posthumously in 1782, followed by Part II in 1789. For all his insistence that he lived by copying music, not writing books, he was relying on an edition of his other collected works to support him in old age, while Thérèse's widowhood would be eased by Rey's pension, the sum that he, made prosperous as Rousseau's publisher, had settled on her. (In the event, she remarried soon after her first husband's death.)

With this, Rousseau's wanderings seemed concluded, flux resolved, though hardly on the *terra firma* he had then attained, beyond provisionality. Or did the book instead depict a world whose psychological equivalent would be found in another work of self-imagining, the tortured *Dialogues*? Rousseau went further, translating and recording his life's moves in solitary reveries, where thoughts conveyed a Montaignean sense of human instability against a backdrop of the down-to-earth and practical, mirrored in the calm routine of daily life. This pattern showed him how to reconcile the making and imagining of things, the hand's and mind's combined creation. If mental processes could be resolved by writing, some physical ones were also subject to his own control. When, back in Paris, he botanized, he realized that the flora he pursued were curiosities like any object in collectors' cabinets, but representative of something more, of permanence in change; he sought to image or depict them, first by naming, then by pressing and displaying them on paper. Walking

---

[53] *C.C.*, XL.215 (quoting Métra's report on 12 May 1778).
[54] See, e.g., *Lettre à Christophe de Beaumont, O.C.*, IV.928.

would become his trusted means to such an end, giving him profound experiences that might otherwise be fleeting, the walker's pace permitting intimate examination that ensured he stayed in touch with nature through all the vehicles of sensory perception—hands, eyes, feet, and nose. Plant-hunting took him to a plane almost beyond self-reference, where what mattered was less his reality than nature's. Flowers changed preoccupation with identity, or sameness, into more disinterested reflection.

7
The Order of Insight

NOVEL THOUGHTS

Before leaving England in 1767, Rousseau made new two acquaintances: one with a Midlands naturalist, the other with an East Anglian vicar. Together they illuminate some aspects of the scientific rationalism of the age, a movement towards which he was less hostile than is often thought.

The naturalist was Erasmus Darwin, who lived in Lichfield, twenty-five miles from Wootton, and whose trip to Wootton Hall in hopes of seeing Rousseau is recounted by his grandson Charles. The latter writes that the two men met and conversed, then corresponded over several years, though there are no letters to bear witness to the exchange or reveal its nature. Botany was surely among the subjects they addressed, however, perhaps the only one. According to the anonymous author of *The History and Topography of Ashbourne* Rousseau had intended to avoid his visitor, who used a harmless subterfuge to gain his attention;[1] other sources claimed they met by accident.[2] In any case, Rousseau could hardly have denied the interests they shared. For Darwin was the founder of the Lichfield botanical society, which published a translation of Linnaeus's *Genera plantarum*,[3] and his strange erotic poem *The Loves of the Plants* of 1789 was loosely based on Linnaean taxonomy: unpublished until 1789, it reflected a long-term interest in the Swedish botanist and his groundbreaking classification system. Rousseau too revered Linnaeus, whose doctrine he expounds in the *Lettres sur la botanique* of 1771–4.

Darwin would also found the Philosophical Society of Derby, one of the provincial gentlemen's associations of the day whose regular meetings

---

[1] *History and Topography of Ashbourne, the Valley of the Dove and the Adjacent Villages* (Ashbourne: Dawson and Hobson, 1839), p. 248.

[2] See J. H. Broome, *Jean-Jacques Rousseau in Staffordshire, 1766–1767* (Keele University Library Occasional Publications, I, 1966), p. 12.

[3] Eric Robinson, 'The Derby Philosophical Society', *Annals of Science*, 9 (1953), pp. 359–67, esp. pp. 359–60.

became forums for debating and discussing the experimental and 'natural' sciences, including botany. Although provincial academies devoted primarily to deliberating on the arts and sciences also existed in eighteenth-century France[4]—that of Dijon had effectively stimulated the works ensuing on Rousseau's 1749 illumination—, their members enjoyed much less freedom than contemporaries in England. Intellectual culture seems always to have been less constricted in Protestant communities than Catholic ones,[5] and men belonging to the English philosophical societies (for these were gentlemen's societies, never gentlewomen's) were seldom hampered by entrenched establishment hostility, religious and lay, towards a range of modern scientific discoveries. These were matters regularly debated in the Derby fraternity and others like it, especially in the Midlands and the industrial North. But it was to another Gentlemen's Society, that of Spalding, that Rousseau had his entrée, indirectly, it is true. Given the apparent clash between the aspects of modernity these brotherhoods explored and his essentially negative or regressive theory of the arts and sciences, the fact is noteworthy.

His arrival in England also coincided with the genesis of some important works of art combining this forward-looking scientific mood with the spirit of imagination. Wright of Derby's picture *The Orrery* (1766), for example, painted and exhibited in London precisely when Rousseau was living there, captures the contemporary thirst for scientific discovery and its promotion by laymen interested in 'natural' philosophy (as science was then called). Its complement *The Alchemist* (1768),[6] dating from the year after Rousseau left England, epitomizes what would later be termed Romantic science, an outlook uniting the spirit of empirical investigation with a note of counter-rationalism.[7] Wright's *Experiment with a Bird in an Air Pump* (an object that had apparently keenly interested members of the Spalding Society some thirty years earlier),[8] also of that year, shows the same complex synthesis of art, science, and philosophy, and owed much to Wright's membership of what would later be called the Lunar Society, a group to which Erasmus Darwin also belonged: it was formally established in the 1770s to represent a distillation of the European Enlightenment then much engaged by developments in chemistry, physics, engineering,

---

[4] Daniel Roche, *Le Siècle des lumières en province: académies et académiciens provinciaux (1680–1789)*, 2 vols. (Paris and The Hague: Mouton, 1978), I.329–43.

[5] Trevor-Roper, *Religion, the Reformation and Social Change*, p. 195.

[6] On both paintings see David Fraser, 'Joseph Wright of Derby and the Lunar Society', in Judy Egerton (ed.), *Wright of Derby* (London: Tate Gallery, 1990), pp. 15–23, esp. p. 15.

[7] See Holmes, *Age of Wonder*.

[8] See Michael Honeybone, 'The Spalding Gentlemen's Society: The Communication of Science in the East Midlands of England, 1710–1760', PhD thesis, Open University, 2007, p. 418.

and other fields relevant to science and industry.[9] Wright is said to have painted a portrait of Rousseau during the latter's stay in England, possibly while he was living near Derby, though no record of it or any reliable contemporary or later reference to it appears to exist.[10]

The various Gentlemen's or Philosophical Societies of the eighteenth century all in their different ways captured the essence of these thrusting, visionary times, and Rousseau's contact with one of them links him with the new progressive spirit. This is less surprising, perhaps, than initially appears: a certain openness to aspects of the new knowledge sweeping Europe was evident, after all, in his attendance at the scientific lectures and courses offered in 1740s Paris. It was in Rousseau's day, we hardly need reminding, that a few poor craftsmen in the north of England were devising apparatus for mechanized spinning, and Watt was completing the invention of the steam engine.

The Spalding Gentlemen's Society was the first provincial association of the new 'scientific' type in England, and was originally created as an assembly of like-minded men who gathered regularly to read and discuss the Whig journal the *Tatler* after it arrived in the town on the coach from London. Although at the time of the Society's foundation Spalding's population numbered only 500 families or so, an astonishing 374 men joined it between 1712 and 1755.[11] Nearly a quarter of them were clergymen, the rest being drawn from the professional classes and some of the trades. Josiah Wedgwood of Barlaston, about fifteen miles from Wootton, was both a member of the Derby Society and a friend and colleague of Erasmus Darwin's; he epitomized this breadth of appeal, remarking in a letter of 1765 that 'I scarcely know without a great deal of recollection whether I am a landed gentleman, an engineer or a potter, for indeed I am all three and many other characters by turns'.[12] Like other industrialists of the time he read the *philosophes*, including (or, depending on point of view, as well as) Rousseau.

[9] Uglow, *Lunar Men*; also Golinski, 'Barometers of Change, in Clark et al., eds., *The Sciences in Enlightenment Europe*, 69–93, pp. 70–85.

[10] John Morley, *Rousseau*, 2 vols. (London: Chapman and Hall, 1873), II.282–3, refers simply to a portrait of Rousseau done in England by a provincial artist, and at that time owned by Sir Maurice Boileau, Bart., whereas, J. Churton Collins, *Voltaire, Montesquieu and Rousseau in England* (London: E. Nash, 1908), p. 185, referring to Morley's description of the painting, declares that Wright of Derby did it in Spring 1766. Collins's plate of the engraved portrait bears no resemblance to Wright in style or Rousseau in appearance, however.

[11] See Jacob, *Cultural Meaning*, p. 157.

[12] *Letters of Josiah Wedgwood*, 3 vols. (London: Women's Printing Society Ltd, 1903–6), I.54–5, quoted in Jacob, *Cultural Meaning*, p. 136.

OLD PREOCCUPATIONS

The latter's agitation on leaving Wootton Hall, in a state of hypertension mixed with bitter recrimination towards its blameless and hospitable owner, can be traced in a series of wild letters written to his French acquaintances and to Davenport himself. But if the tone and content of these seemed inexplicable, what followed the departure was equally bizarre: for from Staffordshire Rousseau headed for Spalding, where he apparently knew no one, and where he put up at the White Hart Inn. Davenport, who excoriated the little Lincolnshire town, was at a loss to explain his motives in travelling there, worrying with typical generosity how the former protégé would survive. In fact Rousseau seems to have done so surprisingly comfortably, not least through the friendship of the vicar of Spalding, John Dinham. It is the latter's association with the sciences of man and matter through his membership of the Spalding Gentlemen's Society that, like the acquaintance of Erasmus Darwin, links Rousseau's experience of the English provinces with the wider world. Yet despite the comforts he seemingly enjoyed, Rousseau declared his unhappiness in his new home, writing to Davenport on 11 May to complain that his situation was hideous, and intimating that returning to Wootton would be infinitely preferable to it.[13] Davenport responded by inviting him back to Staffordshire, but by the time his letter arrived Rousseau had moved on.

Although he had not, apparently, come to Spalding to see Dinham, the two men seem to have spent much time in each other's company once he had arrived there and settled at the inn. There is no evidence that Rousseau attended any of the society's meetings, despite the fact that natural history was among the topics discussed there, and that the members even maintained a herb garden;[14] but Dinham must have spoken to him of the regular proceedings. Worldwide trade links between India, the Americas, and Europe had led to an increasing interest in outlandish flora, the exotica Rousseau so greatly disliked and which had been extensively advertised half a century earlier in the work of his compatriot Maria Sibylla Merian, the artist; other interests of the society, on the evidence of documents and library holdings, included mechanics and experimental science, as well as such 'useful' matters as were then conventionally ranged among the arts.

In a letter of 9 October 1767 Hume reported that Rousseau, despite his claims to the contrary, had been quite at ease in his East Anglian retreat,

[13] *C.C.*, XXXIII.54.
[14] Jacob, *Cultural Meaning*, p. 157; Honeybone, 'Spalding Gentlemen's Society', p. 416.

'cheerful, good-humoured, easy, and enjoyed himself perfectly well, without the least fear or complaint of any kind'.[15] (This report may be inaccurate: Hume was not always reliable in what he said and wrote about Rousseau.) Davenport, meanwhile, had written to Hume on 6 May that year about a letter Rousseau had left him when he bolted from Wootton that it had been 'every jot as odd a letter as he formerly sent you [...] without openly saying it, I can easily perceive him to be uneasy and infinitely suspicious of my having any sort of correspondence with Mr Hume'.[16] According to one commentator, the reason for Rousseau's sudden disappearance was the 'insulting' discovery that Davenport had been letting him the house at a reduced rent.[17] As for Rousseau's purpose in making for Spalding, Davenport continued as mystified as he was uneasy, not least because, as he wrote in the letter of 18 May 1767 intended for Rousseau, but never received by him, 'I have always understood it to be one of the most Cursed disagreeable places in England. I cant conceive what could possibly make you go there, and all that flat Country is reckoned very unwholesome, especially for those who are not natives. For God Sake return out of it as soon as you can'.[18] Rousseau did not, instead making for Dover, and from there sailing back to France. He never said why he had gone to Lincolnshire, though the trip may have been linked with his desire to entrust the papers sent to Wootton by DuPeyrou to a contact of the latter's, an émigré of Swiss extraction called Cerjat who lived in Louth, near Spalding. (On the other hand, there is some evidence to suggest that Cerjat had received these papers before Rousseau left Wootton.) Another possibility is that Rousseau believed he could cross the Channel from Louth and discovered his error only on arrival at Spalding.

The *Confessions* finished, or as finished as it would ever be, he weighed up his options. After the period in the French provinces he returned to Paris in 1770, living once again in the rue Plâtrière (now the rue Jean-Jacques Rousseau), still renting rooms in the hôtel Saint-Esprit, as he had done in the late 1740s, and still mistrusted by authority, as he had been since 1763. Yet he was made to feel a social success: the Prince de Ligne, Goldoni, and other notables crowded to his apartment asking him to copy music for them, and Bachaumont's *Mémoires secrets* for 1 July 1770 observes that he was far from courting obscurity, instead enjoying his celebrity status as he presided at the café de la Régence just as he had done in 1766 on his way to England. Late in 1770 he moved to a two-room apartment in the same street, which he would change once more for a different lodging in the rue Plâtrière before the end of his life.

---

[15] *C.C.*, XXXIII.46 (to Adam Smith).   [16] *C.C.*, XXXIII.47–8.
[17] *History and Topography of Ashbourne*, p. 248.   [18] *C.C.*, XXXIII.71.

Persecution still seemed to court him to a degree, or he it: the prefect of police Sartine stopped the public readings from the *Confessions* Rousseau had begun at the end of that year and continued in May 1771, a prohibition that fed his tortured sense of still being defamed and misunderstood by his fellows. It culminated in his trying to circulate by hand an open letter on his plight written 'à tout Français aimant la justice', and, from 1772, in his composition of the *Dialogues*, whose first book he vainly tried to deposit on the altar of Notre-Dame. This letter made three observations: the first, that Rousseau was alone and misunderstood, persecuted without reason, the second, that no proof of any of his 'crimes' had ever been presented by his enemies, and the third, that the French people had been duped by those hostile towards him, but would one day see reason. The *Dialogues* comments similarly. The *idée fixe* pervading these writings is that of upset against settledness, the seeming stability in a world that denies that quality to Rousseau himself, a fixedness paradoxically conveyed by its opposite, mobile words arguing a consistency of character traduced by his enemies and which in the *Dialogues* is expressed through the 'otherness' of the Rousseau of the popular imagination.

Throughout his life Rousseau had felt a sameness or identity that his assumption of other personae from boyhood onwards only thinly veiled. The task of the *Dialogues* was to retrace inwards the foundation of this unvarying self, substituting right for wrong interpretation, refusing to see fracture where continuity existed, guaranteeing the correctness of his interpretation against the unreliable testimony of the ill-disposed. At first this procedure looks the opposite of that adopted in the *Confessions*, a work emphasizing successivity, an accumulation of stages in life rather than the assertion of what is moored and motionless. Its reverse explains how Rousseau's writings came to seem so dangerous to the authorities that they ordered them to be publicly burnt; for what has been made stable, fixed in print, may somehow seem exemplary, however great its deviation from the norm. The seduction of Rousseau's style, besides, makes the forbidden alluring, the imprint of his certainty contrasting with the mere 'sentiments' of citizens (as Voltaire had entitled his vicious attack on Rousseau).

His claimed detachment from the act of writing also looks, at least in some respects, a little like Montaigne's: both formulate in style and theme an art of lowering expectation in order to exceed it, just as Julie's Elysée disguises all its artfulness in order to win over those who value the appearance of the natural. Like Montaigne, Rousseau will emphasize his 'paresse', his 'désœuvrement', in a bid to forestall criticism; but we know the meaning of his professed inattention, of statements such as this: 'l'indolence et l'oisiveté, qui dans la société sont un si grand vice, n'en sont plus un dans quiconque a su renoncer à ses avantages pour n'en supporter ses travaux'.[19] Is writing to be similarly disengaged, like daydreaming? We cannot yet be sure, but there are many such assertions in the *Rêveries*. In Montaigne the disengagement is of someone socially above the need for pedantry, for whom manifesting learnedness or schooling is simply bad form. Rousseau's statement that he, descended from a line of craftsmen, finds writing of whatever sort an unnatural act is similarly meant to disarm his reader, if by the opposite means; yet the beauty and importance of the prose he wrote in the course of what in authorial terms is a brief lifetime is provocative, to say the least. We understand the motive, however disinclined to take it seriously. The doxa, the doctrinal work, dismissed, he had to emphasize the practicality of what remained for him to do. Yet praxis still fell short of practicality, the work before him still less useful than an artisan's toil, harder to shape into a real purpose. So Rousseau emphasizes his 'désœuvrement', as though retreat were all remaining to him.

BOTANICAL RECREATIONS

We are familiar with the *Dialogues*'s comments on his fastidious care in the making of herbaria,[20] a topic also covered in the *Lettres sur la botanique*. Its interest is, again, in the implied contrast—in fact more like an affectation—between this focused, practical activity and the idleness that governs the actions of his mind, including the occasional writing. And yet, like Diderot (implicitly) or Stendhal (openly), he writes purposefully, with an eye to the future, the time of the happy few who will read him without the prejudice that dogs the writer in his own day.[21] In real life Rousseau found writing, and loving, in absence, removed in space or time, the only true and fulfilling kind. Wandering or botanizing that might to onlookers appear purposeless, mere 'divagation',[22] was in fact a goal-directed enterprise, however insignificant it seemed, however distant from the writing it would furnish.

He calls his 'travail dans la retraite' meaningful, then, in its removal from the world of sociability and its dubious pressures, things that alienate by fostering intrigue. Can this claim of Rousseau's be justified? The music copyist must, after all, work for and in the world; his performance cannot meaningfully—that is, profitably—exist in isolation, which is why Rousseau did almost none of it away from Paris (Montmorency and

---

[19] *Dialogues*, I.824.   [20] *Dialogues*, I.832.
[21] See his letter to Malesherbes of 28 January 1762, *O.C.*, I.1145.
[22] *Dialogues*, I.824.

Montlouis being close enough to the capital for this purpose, but far enough away to deter most time-wasting visitors). The writer, on the other hand, may serve the world at large, or do so for as long as publication remains unrestricted: as the peasants of Montmorency are more useful than academicians who produce mere words, so Rousseau's words, conceived and set down in isolation, may be propagated far beyond their primitive reach. When that happens, what appears 'oisiveté' is anything but.

But is botanizing, as opposed to the peasant's cultivation, not separate from practical utility? Mme de Warens would not have agreed, nor any other apothecary. The second *Dialogue* emphasizes the beauty of the herbaria Rousseau makes after his botanizing walks as though their purpose were simply aesthetic, but fails to record their usefulness to him: for if 'il en a *donné*, envoyé à diverses personnes',[23] some at least were sold for money, however meagre their yield. Botanizing was no disenchanting, rationalizing profession for all that, merely an interest; what sustained the household was his copying of music, along with the sums realized by his literary œuvre and whatever money he would take from well-wishers. Writing the second *Dialogue*, however, he claimed to devote all his time to studying plants, a passion so demanding as to leave no space for other things. The care he lavished on herbaria proclaims the all-absorbing nature of this enthusiasm: 'il a fait une immense collection de plantes; il les a desséchées avec des soins infinis, il les a collées avec une grande propreté sur des papiers qu'il ornait de cadres rouges. Il s'est appliqué à conserver la figure et la couleur des fleurs et des feuilles, au point de faire de ces herbiers ainsi préparés des recueils de miniatures'.[24] The fact that it was a disinterested study for Rousseau emerges from his focus on the object's inner purposiveness, in Kant's phrase, the plant as structural system in and for itself.[25]

It was a personal obsession, then, not a trade or weapon. Could an obsessive concern not still be a disinterested one, a *pure* study of *pure* curiosity? Or does the true obsessive, however solitary by nature, want to bring others round to his fixation, convert them to his cause? The fact that Rousseau botanized in packs as well as on his own seems to answer in the affirmative: his Bernese friend Julie de Bondeli would claim in 1765 that the then fifty-three-year-old Rousseau was creating a band of new Emiles as he led men from Neuchâtel in their late thirties and early forties, entirely unused to walking, on ambitious botanizing rambles.[26] We cannot know,

---

[23] *Dialogues*, I.832 (emphasis added).   [24] *Dialogues*, I.832.
[25] See David Cantor, 'The Metaphysics of Botany: Rousseau and the New Criticism of Plants', *Southwest Review*, 70 (1986), pp. 362–8, esp. pp. 371–2.
[26] *C.C.*, XXVI.72 (3 July 1765), to Zimmermann.

however, if the same Rousseau ever seriously envisaged another form of induction for a different constituency—whether he ever really meant to start the school for flower girls referred to in the third *Addition* to Diderot's *Lettre sur les aveugles*. He might well have thought learning how to do the flowers a wise option for their sex, particularly in light of the women's issues raised by his writings in general, but floral science was quite another matter; for if, according to tradition, flower arranging was a woman's work, botany belonged to men.[27] True, it had been a woman, Mme de Warens, who taught the young Rousseau 'mille choses curieuses'[28] about plant structure, just as it would be a woman, the Duchess of Portland, who botanized with him in the English shires; but both were members of a social elite, which gave them certain freedoms. The curiosity of less privileged females, to whose number 'bouquetières' belonged, was contained within tighter limits. The only proper concern of humble flower girls, surely, was the immediate and seemingly intuitive one of beauty. Or could their judgement of a flower's appeal be based on other principles, a different order of sense impressions from those the eye receives? The fact that Diderot's *Lettre sur les aveugles* alludes to such matters suggests it might.

According to Bernardin de Saint-Pierre, Rousseau had an 'odorat fort subtil', all the keener for the fact that he had never smoked or taken snuff; he never dug up a plant or picked a flower for his herbarium without first sniffing it, and, according to Saint-Pierre, 'il aurait pu faire une botanique de l'odorat s'il y avait eu autant de noms propres à les caractériser qu'il y a d'odeurs dans la nature'.[29] Linnaeus divided plants into a mere handful of smell types—the aromatic, the fragrant, the ambrosiac, the allinaceous or garlic-like, the hircine or goat-like, the foul, and the nauseous. But Rousseau was a veritable gourmet of aromas, good smells satisfying him almost as much as tasting the substances that produced them. Saint-Pierre writes of a walk they once took in the Tuileries gardens that 'il sentit l'odeur du café. *Voici*, me dit-il, *un parfum que j'aime beaucoup. Quand on en brûle dans mon escalier, j'ai des voisins qui ferment leur porte, et moi j'ouvre la mienne*'.[30] All these matters are raised, at least implicitly, by the idea of a school for flower girls, whether or not Rousseau ever seriously entertained it.

If such an institution had existed, what would its students have been taught first of all? Possibly, at least judging by a famous passage in the *Confessions*, simply to look harder at commonplace things. The periwinkle

[27] See Londa Schiebinger, *Nature's Body* (London: Pandora, 1993), especially pp. 35–9; Uglow, *Lunar Men*, p. 271.
[28] *Confessions*, I.245.
[29] Bernardin de Saint-Pierre, *Vie*, pp. 50–1, n. 1.
[30] Bernardin de Saint-Pierre, *Vie*, p. 35.

Rousseau noticed on a botanizing trip in old age famously returned him to the moment in his youth when Maman pointed one out to him on a walk:[31] this revelation caused an explosion of interest in the tiny flower among Rousseau's lady readers, who flocked to the Paris Jardin des plantes to see one *in situ*. That may tell us many things potentially useful to the future 'bouquetières', among them the remoteness of the worldly from nature and everyday life; but it also highlights the influence of fashion on the florist's trade, including the fashion for artlessness as well as artfulness. And it may, most pertinently, make us question why someone of Rousseau's bent should ever think the assembling and arranging of flowers an accomplishment that needed to be taught. A 'beau désordre' like that of nature itself was surely more appealing to him, as to the cultivated eighteenth century generally.

If flower girls had actually needed serious instruction in botany, in any case, contemporary science might not have offered them the right kind of help. On the one hand, the Linnaean revolution meant that no student of botany could properly—that is, defensibly—stay ignorant of the sexual system of plant classification he had introduced.[32] On the other, propriety might actually prevent the 'bouquetière's' sex, not just the 'bouquetière' herself, discovering secrets about propagation that would make it blush. Given, as Linnaeus had shown, that the whole of nature was suffused with sexuality, it seemed quite obvious that no nice girl (or respectable matron) could decently investigate the plants he had endowed with *labia minora* or *majora*, or flowers possessing *clitoria*. Was it not inevitable that applying a Linnaean taxonomy based on the number of male stamens and female pistils should appear a lewd method, even a loathsome form of harlotry? The persuasiveness of the new binomial classification, where the one-word generic term was followed by a single specific epithet, was evident, but it meant, strictly speaking, that no flower could ever again be seen as chaste, no violet as shrinking, no rose as blushing. Yet plants seemed so unthreatening, so innocent! In *Emile* Rousseau writes with pity, not approval, of the man unstirred by the sight and smell of a bunch of (shrinking) violets in his lover's corsage.[33] Can the sensual ever be excluded, though? Linnaeus's English translator was Erasmus Darwin, whose *Loves of the Plants* seemed to suggest otherwise.

---

[31] *Confessions*, I.226.
[32] See, for example, Gunnar Erikson, 'Linnaeus the Botanist', in Tove Frängsmyr (ed.), *Linnaeus: The Man and His Work*, rev. edn (Canton, MA: Science History Publications, 1994), pp. 63–109, esp. p. 63, p. 74.
[33] *Emile*, IV.416.

Ambitious women artists, their sex debarred from studying the nude, were instead directed to the polite art of botanical illustration, at which many of them, unlike Rousseau, excelled. Even so, a different order of propriety still dictated that although they could gather flowers in the garden or countryside, arrange them tastefully in the house, sketch and paint them, or dry them for their *hortus siccus*, they might only exceptionally go further: for no woman ever became a great naturalist. The *intendants* of the Jardin du Roi were all male, either trained scientists like Buffon or men more informally interested in flora, like Bernardin de Saint-Pierre;[34] and when Mme de Warens planned a physic garden in Chambéry, it was her steward Claude Anet she meant to make the demonstrator there, not herself and certainly not Rousseau.[35] In the *Confessions* Rousseau reflects that if he had himself become interested in botany, then, he too might have become an expert; but the time was not ripe.[36] Only when the condemnation of *Emile* and *Du contrat social* drove him to settle in the canton of Neuchâtel, leaving him without appetite for any further writing, did a passion for botany finally seize him, making him a mere 'machine ambulante'[37] to whom 'il [était] interdit de penser'. Yet knowledge still came slowly, always hampered, so he claimed, by his poor sight.

A further frustration was the lack of illustrations, especially colour illustrations, in the standard botanical books available, though friends sometimes supplied him with alternatives. The *Confessions* traces his interest in botanical illustration much further back, however, to the time in his youth when, living once more with Mme de Warens in Chambéry, he had worked as a secretary on the royal survey.[38] 'Le lavis des mappes de nos geometres m'avoit rendu le gout du dessein [*sic*]. J'achettai des couleurs et je me mis à faire des fleurs et des paysages. C'est dommage que je me sois trouvé peu de talent pour cet art; l'inclination y étoit toute entiére.'[39] The pleasure principle, whatever its precise expression, remained paramount: Rousseau's botany must be without purpose, but aesthetically delightful or charming in some other way. This suggests, not unexpectedly, that in their imagined Paris school his 'bouquetières' would be taught to treat flowers as pleasing above all in their beauty, whether or not they were also

[34] See, for example, E. C. Spary, *Utopia's Garden: French Natural History from Old Regime to Revolution* (Chicago and London: Chicago University Press, 2000), p. 1.

[35] *Confessions*, I.204–5.

[36] *Confessions*, I.245.

[37] Rousseau to Coindet, 27 April 1765, *C.C.*, XXV.186; he uses the same phrase to many other correspondents.

[38] *Confessions*, I.174.

[39] *Confessions*, I.180. Rousseau apparently resumed drawing flowers and plants on the île de Saint-Pierre, taking the same childlike pride in his performance. See von Wagner, *L'Ile Saint-Pierre*, p. 39, and Gavin de Beer, 'Jean-Jacques Rousseau: Botanist', *Annals of Science*, X, 3 (1954), pp. 189–223, esp. pp. 192–212.

of scientific interest.[40] Rousseau's anti-utilitarianism is not absolute, however. The fourth Promenade of the *Rêveries* describes how, as a boy, he had once used moss to stanch the flow of blood after injuring his hand, and on another occasion had a poultice of lilies macerated in spirits ('vulneraire excellent et très usité dans notre pays') applied to a cut on his head.[41] His general reluctance to see flowers functionally echoes his disapproval of manipulating nature to other ends. The world of plants, he thought, should generally be left to itself, not adapted for some alien purpose, which meant respecting the integrity of creation rather than making a new flower by means of human ingenuity. Such a procedure was, for him, to *denature* the proper order of things, as he emphasized in a letter to the Duchess of Portland: 'Les végétaux dans nos bois et dans nos montagnes sont encore tels qu'ils sortirent originairement de ses [God's] mains.'[42]

One of the lessons taught to the 'bouquetières', we may therefore suppose, would be that of responding to the products of the natural world, which man's alleged mastery of creation tempts him to slight, in a spirit of humility—recognizing its organizing principles, then letting be. Letting be[43] means not allowing wilderness to claim what may usefully be cultivated, but refraining from giving alien form to what grows satisfactorily of its own accord: we may think of the eighteenth-century English landscape garden in this connection, and its antithesis in the formal French creations of the seventeenth century. On the other hand, the logical extension of the laissez-faire aesthetic might be to leave all growing things *in situ*, untended and not dug up, pruned, or cut and made into bouquets. The botanist Rousseau did indeed express a preference for nature's garden over man's,[44] but serious botanical investigation of the kind he had begun in Môtiers and continued to the end of his life required dissection, an apparent intrusion into the *hortus vivus* of nature

[40] See Jean Starobinski, *Jean-Jacques Rousseau. La transparence et l'obstacle* (Paris: Gallimard, 1971), p. 280, for the idea that in botany Rousseau sees nature as the Garden of Eden before the Fall, too beautiful and intact to be exploited to medical ends; also David Scott, 'Rousseau and Flowers', *SVEC*, CLXXXII (1979), pp. 73–86. But Rousseau advances a different view in the letter to Malesherbes of 11 November 1764: 'Je suis tenté d'essayer de la Botanique, non pas comme vous, Monsieur, en grand et comme une branche de l'histoire naturelle, mais tout au plus en garçon apothicaire, pour Savoir faire ma tisanne et mes bouillons' (*C.C.*, XXII.44). This is surely meant as a joke.
[41] *Rêveries du promeneur solitaire*, I.1037.
[42] *C.C.*, XXXII.135 (12 February 1767).
[43] 'Letting be' is a central preoccupation in Heidegger's philosophy, part of the state of 'relaxedness about things'. See Heidegger, *Discourse on Thinking*, pp. 45–56; also Michael Zimmermann, *Heidegger's Confrontation with Modernity* (Bloomington, Indiana: Indiana University Press, 1990), p. xvi. More generally, see Jonathan Bate, *The Song of the Earth* (Cambridge, MA: Harvard University Press, 2000), pp. 253–4.
[44] Rousseau to the Duchess of Portland, *C.C.*, XXXII.135 (12 February 1767).

that necessitated uprooting or at least picking its products. A letter to
DuPeyrou rather unexpectedly shows him delighting in this aspect of
plant study, though provoked by his lack of tools: 'je vous avertis que le
charme de cette science consiste surtout dans l'étude anatomique des
plantes. Je ne puis faire cette étude à mon gré faute des instruments
nécessaires',[45] which he asks his friend to get for him. The plan of opening a flower girls' school in Paris expresses a natural human desire to find
rus in urbe by whatever means possible, whether bouquets in boudoirs or
(in the case of Rousseau's humble Paris flat) pot plants in parlours.[46]

It is obviously a matter of opinion whether a flower is better living in a
field among other flowers or set off to advantage in a bunch or bouquet.
In neither case will it last for ever, though duration of a kind is guaranteed
by pressing: 'Les herbiers servent de mémoratifs pour celles [plants] qu'on
a déjà connues; mais ils font mal connoitre celles qu'on n'a pas vues
auparavant'.[47] The Prince de Ligne was privately contemptuous of Rousseau's dried displays, dismissing one he had inspected as 'recueil très peu
intéressant, et le plus commun du monde',[48] but Rousseau's Geneva friend
Pierre Prévost disagreed: 'Jamais herboriste n'a poussé plus loin la délicatesse et la propreté dans l'arrangement des plantes sur le papier [...]. Son
Moussier [...] était un petit chef-d'œuvre d'élégance.'[49] To impenitently
urban sorts, painting pictures seemed a better way of preserving the transient products of nature: Diderot's 1759 *Salon*, for instance, praises Mme
Vien for executing studies from natural history that would last as long as
the contents of any collector's cabinet.[50] The achievement of the 'fleuriste
artificiel', according to the *Encyclopédie* entry of that title, was similarly to
fix fleeting time, to 'rendre les fleurs fragiles de tous les temps et de tous
les pays'; but his skills were scarcely turned to purposes Rousseau could
countenance, focused as they were on luxury and ornament—flowers for
banqueting halls, nosegays for corsages, posies for hairpieces.

Was the beauty of flowers just an 'ornement indifférent'?[51] What should
we make of Rousseau's creating a *hortus siccus*[52] as opposed to a *hortus*

---

[45] Rousseau to the Duchess of Portland, *C.C.*, XXV.204 (29 April 1765).

[46] Bernardin de Saint-Pierre, *Vie*, p. 33, reports seeing there 'des pots remplis de plantes
telles qu'il plaît à la nature de les semer'.

[47] *Lettres sur la botanique*, IV.1191.

[48] Ligne, *Lettres et pensées*, I.237.

[49] *C.C.*, XL, Appendix, p. 267 (*Lettre sur Jean-Jacques Rousseau*, in *Archives littéraires de
l'Europe*, Paris and Tübingen, vol. ii, 1804, pp. 201–9).

[50] Diderot, *Salon* of 1759, *O.C.*, XIII.79.

[51] *Confessions*, I.5; the fourth Promenade of the *Rêveries* makes a similar observation, I.1035.

[52] The eighth *Lettre sur la botanique* gives detailed instructions for drying flowers. On
the contrast with the *hortus vivus*, see Gerda Calmann, *Ehret, Flower Painter Extraordinaire*
(Oxford: Phaidon, 1977), p. 48.

vivus, a herbarium rather than a garden of growing things? Perhaps simply that his philosophy of nature was governed by a rational intelligence as well as by a feeling heart. If the former spelled a dislocation from the source of beauty, the latter seemed to guarantee the possibility of reconnection; yet the herbarium, the collection of dried specimens, was also a 'signe mémoratif' that showed how nature can be preserved in its apparent absence, if in less vivid and less vital form.

The modern herbarium is part of a vast electronic store of floral information, a huge agglomeration of the different types of plant whose purpose is to make man better understand the balance of the world he lives in. Rousseau's efforts at making a 'pasigraphic'[53] alphabet of plants was an eighteenth-century forebear of the modern computerized database of types and samples, and his handwritten labels for the hand-picked species precursors of the digitizing of our electronic era, laden, of course, with all the digit's ambiguity, the lingering testimony of the 'doigt' whose intimate connection with the human body has almost been severed.

Was botany pure 'désœuvrement', crucially devoid of purposiveness or intentionalism? Was it a study, a form of repose from study, or the two together? Rousseau's botanizing never precluded the operation of intelligence, a fact that needs recalling every time we feel the urge to call him the hater of science and scourge of system-building, or argue for his sentimental vision to the exclusion of all rational method. We need, besides, to recollect that he was not merely the author of a philosophy that negatively ascribed the denaturing of original man to the discoveries of science; for *Emile* calls denaturing the process that lets us fruitfully proceed from individuality to a sense of community, a bond with others that includes the brotherhood of scientific understanding.[54] No periwinkle or other flower loses individuality for being set within a taxonomic system of genus and species

LIVING BY THE HAND (AND FOOT)

However fulfilling this occupation, it could not meet Rousseau's and his household's need for sustenance. In the *Dialogues* the 'Jean-Jacques' figure convinces 'Rousseau' that music copying is vital, does support them, lets them live, and not simply because his writings do not yield enough for the

[53] See Matthey Jeantet, *Ecriture*, pp. 38–9. The unfinished schema he devised is reproduced in *O.C.*, IV.1196.
[54] *Emile*, IV.249. See also *Lettres sur la botanique*, IV.1188 (letter 7).

purpose.[55] He was far from enjoying austerity for its own sake, or because it seemed morally preferable to real financial ease, though he certainly, and Calvinistically, liked making do with little. He never missed the inherited wealth he silently attributes to Emile, though he was well aware that his own father had for years lived off the interest of those parts of his wife's estate meant for her sons. Yet Boswell's account of the meal he enjoyed *chez* Rousseau in Môtiers shows the great man as, within limits, a 'bon viveur', not an ascetic.

The charge levelled at 'Jean-Jacques', that his great talent might be put to some more useful purposes than the copying of music, is barely considered[56]—perhaps surprisingly, given the urgency of Rousseau's arguments for overhauling education, reforming the arts, and establishing rational and morally defensible political structures. On the other hand, he could be said to have dealt with them sufficiently in the past, when he lived in what he called a magic world.[57] Whatever the case, 'Rousseau' agrees that 'Jean-Jacques' does the scribe's work he claims to do, but does not ask whether it is a worthwhile activity: it is, professedly, simply one that suits him and does not tire his lazy mind. His enemies may dismiss this and other manual activities as degrading and only moderately remunerative,[58] but 'Rousseau' knows otherwise, rehearsing the meagre income he could count on from alternative sources:

> avec quelque argent comptant provenant tant de son accord avec l'Opera que de la vente de ses livres de botanique et du reste d'un fond de mille écus qu'il avoit à Lyon et qu'il retira pour s'établir à Paris, toute sa fortune présente consiste en 800 francs de rente viagére [probably from the Earl Marischal] incertain et dont il n'a aucun titre, et 300 francs de rente aussi viagére mais assuré[59]

He needs work for material reasons, then, but also to stave off boredom, with all the temptations of idleness that accompany it. Positive 'désœuvrement' is quite different. It lets him savour disengagement as a state in which the balance between activity and non-activity, when freely struck, creates a perfect harmony. Given this, he is now quite at ease with himself and the world: 'après le travail le simple repos a son charme, et suffit avec la promenade pour l'amusement dont j'ai besoin'.[60]

So we have no reason to doubt the sincerity of his next remark, that 'travailler de la main et laisser ma tête en repos me recrée et m'anime', when the animation is that of the calm soul distant from the artificial

---

[55] *Dialogues*, I.837–8.   [56] *Dialogues*, I.837.   [57] *Dialogues*, I.672–3.
[58] See *Dialogues*, I.843, for his rate, ten sols per page.
[59] *Dialogues*, I.838; also p. 1873, n. 1.   [60] *Dialogues*, I.839.

stimulants and adulterated pleasures of civilization. And 'Si j'aime quelquefois à penser c'est librement et sans gêne en laissant aller à leur gré mes idées sans les assujettir à rien.'[61] Certainly, the need to think as a matter of duty (rather than, for example, out of inclination, as he did when meditating on useful matters such as Poland's constitution) was always repellent to Rousseau. But his sweeping claim to dislike making what he writes grammatically correct as well as readable in other ways does not always ring true, nor does the statement that manual work leaves the brain delightfully free and at repose always square with the evidence provided by the *Dialogue* itself, which reflects the author's torment as he fights to uphold his reputation in the face of public and private attack. Certainly, working as a copyist saves him from the prostitution he observes in contemporaries, and which Diderot describes in *Le Neveu de Rameau*, but it does not block out invasive thoughts.

Is that why the state of seeming indolence he loves demands of him a physical engagement tailored to the demands of mental vacuity?—'il est vif, laborieux à sa manière. Il ne peut souffrir une oisiveté absolue: il faut que ses mains, que ses pieds, que ses doigts agissent, que son corps soit en exercice et que sa tête reste en repos.'[62] It represents an ideal fusion in which each of the two opposing quantities guarantees, then cancels out, the other. But it is an ideal equilibrium, not a given; for although Rousseau's hands and legs must work for his head to be able not to, the perfect balance of reciprocity is hard to achieve. The state most conducive to such harmony is that of walking; yet walking is not a paid activity, merely one most favourable to reverie (the fifth *Rêverie* later suggests that floating gently on the water may match it). If the hand's work pays, later, for the brain's inactivity (and activity), is the paying, the price, ever a source of disharmony? Apparently not: while creation may be disruptive, paid for dearly, the calm rhythm of calligraphy can somehow almost literally compensate. What mental state should we attribute to Rousseau as he copies? Still one of peace, but apparently enhanced by a temporal, and probably also geographical, distance?

Since discarding his watch he had found it possible to live in a world without time; or, rather, a world without *others'* time. We know that the watch, by making time graphic, makes it intrusive; it shows ('montre'), pragmatically, without respect for individual will or desire. A watch, we also know, may be a vigil as well as a device, a state demanding that sense of alert responsibility and duty Rousseau finds oppressive. The clock commands attention in both auditory and visual ways, insistently intruding on our disengagement; the 'horloge' lodges the hour, enframes it in a tangible, visible, and auditory form. It has its pattern, to which it tries to make us attentively obedient. The pattern Rousseau willingly respects, rather, is one of unreflecting regularity, where repetition occurs because it avoids enforcement, or is enforced only by our grateful indolence. So in his walks he 'répétera toujours la même jusqu'à ce que quelque motif le force absolument d'en changer: ses pieds le reportent d'eux-mêmes où ils l'ont déjà porté. Il aime à marcher toujours devant lui, parce que cela se fait sans avoir besoin d'y penser.'[63] But also without any need to obey a higher authority: so he dislikes gardens where every path has a definite end, making him take a new direction.

'La vie ambulante est celle qu'il me faut. Faire route à pied par un beau tems dans un beau pays sans être pressé, et avoir pour terme de ma course un objet agréable; voila de toutes les maniéres de vivre celle qui est le plus de mon goût.'[64] Rousseau's ideal of freedom of course demands that others submit to obligation, as Thérèse awaits his return from a day-long ramble with food ready prepared, waiting in ignorance of his inner clock. For what could her inconvenience be when set against her master's? Rousseau admits more than he realizes when he remarks: 'L'homme en qui l'amour-propre ne domine pas et qui ne va point chercher son bonheur loin de lui est le seul qui connaisse l'incurie et les doux loisirs, et Jean Jacques est cet homme-là autant que je puis m'y connoître.'[65] A kind of self-regard is involved, clearly, in following one's desires, things that are both outside and within oneself. Egoists are people who rely upon the willingness of others to serve those desires: it is, despite appearances, a supreme form of egoism to 'fai[re] sa tâche quand et comme il lui plaît',[66] even if the word 'tâche' attempts to disguise the fact.

To treasure regularity is to possess the craftsman's nature, content to live within and by what is tried and tested; not to address the *cosa mentale* that may entail pursuing something boundless, but to cherish sameness, as the craftsman's changeless tools reflect it; to be a jobbing worker, not an artist dealing with imagined quantities and products of the mind. Art may breed disturbance, the nightmare that still torments Rousseau,[67] not confirm consolingly familiar things, the things, moreover, that society most needs. The writings that had caused his persecution contrasted with this kind by urging revolution—less radical than his opponents thought, perhaps, but still enough to defamiliarize the world. To be a craftsman was to replicate, not primarily to generate, or not to generate contentiously. Copyists were craftsmen, following this definition, dealing with no perilous initiative. Obedience to pragmatic laws defined them, respect for matter, practical endeavour.

---

[63] *Dialogues*, I.846.   [64] *Confessions*, I.172.   [65] *Dialogues*, I.847.
[66] *Dialogues*, I.851.   [67] See *Rêveries du promeneur solitaire*, I.995.

Nor, it seems, can Rousseau be trusted to do what manual work he does precisely as others might desire; it must be accepted that he will do it slowly, but also possibly inaccurately.[68] And yet his scores are sold at a higher price than the norm (Rousseau adds those touches he has already described in the *Confessions*, 'des attentions qui ne sont pas sans effet, et qu'on attendrait en vain des autres copistes'). We remember his half-joke about being tolerated as a poor copyist because he was also a famous, even an infamous, author—and here a further reason for his high prices is offered: he charges more on account of the endless interruptions he has to endure, as well as because some clients pay him either too little or nothing at all. Another observation he makes at this point is poignant, given the financial straits he and Thérèse were reduced to towards the end of his life, and which prompted him to take the previously unthinkable step of asking for help;[69] for, as he wrote the second *Dialogue* (within only a few years of having to give up his profession), 'sa main déja tremblottante lui refuse un service aisé [...]', to the point where he envisages being reduced to 'un tardif et dur apprentissage d'une frugalité bien austère'.[70]

The last entry in his register of copies is 22 August 1777, but as early as February that year Rousseau made a call for help because he and Thérèse were 'Réduits à vivre absolument seuls et neanmoins hors d'état de nous passer du service d'autrui.'[71] Being Rousseau, he also notes that his sad situation is possibly the most unfortunate ever known to man. According to the register he had been keeping over a period of five years from 1 April 1772, he copied 9,236 pages of music at ten sous per page during that time, which yielded a total of 4,618 francs; from 1774 his income increased, thanks to dues paid by the Opéra for works of his performed there.[72] His long-lived aunt Suzanne Gonceru eventually died at the beginning of 1775, but from April 1776 Rousseau had to convert the allowance he had previously paid her into wages for a servant. A much earlier document, a letter from Môtiers of 18 March 1765, records that Rousseau spent 1,600 francs per annum; in the second *Dialogue* he remarks that it is impossible to live 'comodément' on 1,100 francs a year,[73] and the need to reside in Paris to earn a living certainly cost him more than life in the French provinces or in Switzerland ever did.

Rousseau declared, and his friend Corancez would later confirm, that he had an almost childlike temperament, docile often, working mechanically, thinking always the same without tiring of those thoughts, and happier

[68] *Dialogues*, I.848.
[69] See *Mémoire écrit au mois de février 1777, et depuis lors remis ou montré à diverses personnes*, *O.C.*, I.1187–9.
[70] *Dialogues*, I.848–9.   [71] *Mémoire*, I.1188.
[72] *Mémoire*, I.1873, n. to p. 1187.   [73] *Dialogues*, I.838.

in retreat than he had ever been during his years of public success. 'Les hommes, le figurant toujours à leur mode, en ont fait tantôt un profond génie, tantôt un petit charlatan, d'abord un prodige de vertu, puis un monstre de scélératesse, toujours l'être du monde le plus étrange et le plus bizarre.' But 'La nature n'en a fait qu'un bon artisan.'[74] Does he admit the charge of egoism? It might seem surprising in light of the great works of public doctrine he had written; less so, perhaps, when we reflect that 'amour de soi' was a virtue in his eyes, only 'amour-propre' a vice. Thus it is to concede nothing damaging to observe as he does that 'son vice dominant est de s'occuper de lui plus que des autres, et celui des méchans, au contraire, est de s'occuper plus des autres que d'eux; et c'est précisément pour cela qu'à prendre le mot d'*egoïsme* dans son vrai sens, ils sont tous égoistes et qu'il ne l'est point parce qu'il ne se met ni à coté, ni au dessus, ni au dessous de personne, et que le déplacement de personne n'est nécessaire à son bonheur'.[75] The egoist, he believes, desires to sacrifice others to his own interests; Rousseau is the 'natural' man living for himself. But why in that case did he write so much *at* and *for* others?

The older Rousseau, in society, was a living advertisement for the fact that to be surrounded by what the world values may be to suffer visibly: the individual becomes a 'montre' to the world, presenting the sight of his 'maigreur', his 'teint pâle' and the 'air mourant qu'il eut constamment dix ans de sa vie pendant tout le temps qu'il se mêla d'écrire, métier aussi funeste à sa constitution que contraire à son gout'.[76] And we also remember that living within oneself, not egotistically, but with a sense of personal fulfilment, was for him to live in the special world where people write few books, and do so only when inspired by a desire, not for honours, celebrity, or riches, but simply for communicating something vital. Such men, having said what they must say, then feel at rest, 'sans s'aller fourrant dans le tripot littéraire, sans sentir cette ridicule démangeaison de rabâcher, et barbouiller éternellement du papier qu'on dit être attaché au metier d'Auteur'.[77] When Rousseau 'scrawls', by contrast, it is either because the fever of inspiration makes him do so or because his indolence and inattentiveness as a copyist put him in a distracting world of dreams or music; for he could slowly sight-read and could therefore 'hear' music as he copied it, if less easily than he claimed he would have done had his new system of musical notation been adopted.

As 'Rousseau' comments in the first *Dialogue*, 'Jean-Jacques' adored this sublime art, wrote as well as copied it, spent his time with musicians, gave lessons in composition, and generally showed himself a more competent

[74] *Dialogues*, I.849.   [75] *Dialogues*, I.851–2.
[76] *Dialogues*, I.865.   [77] *Dialogues*, I.673.

musician than many of his fellows.[78] (Even Rameau had denied Rousseau's authorship of the music for *Les Muses Galantes* on the grounds that it was too good for an amateur.) What possible comparison between this Jean-Jacques and the man described in the *Confessions*, maligned in society, incapable of composing music or even reading it, and reduced to copying *faute de mieux?*[79] No man unable to write either libretti or music could have composed *Le Devin*; therefore Rousseau could not have done so, any more than he could have written the *Lettre sur la musique française* of 1753 or the *Dictionnaire de musique* ten years later. Hence the sarcasm of his letter to Sartine on 15 January 1772: 'j'ai laissé débiter, parmi cent autres bruits non moins ineptes, [...] que je ne copiais de la musique que par grimace, que j'avais de quoi vivre fort à mon aise'.[80]

We remember his assertion that the quality a music copyist needs above all else is invisibility; his copying, transparency; that a single error in the score may sabotage an entire performance.[81] Mistakes in copying literary manuscripts are different; they can be mentally corrected by the reader, and pauses either for reinterpretation or because of some other need for interruption are a normal part of the consumption process. Reading time, so different from performing time or playing time, resembles what might be called the loose time Rousseau reserved for his favourite 'activity' of disengagement: a sense of leisure, focused or not, infuses both. Loose time may or may not be filled with a nameable activity, such as walking; its nature is to be unspecific, and the question whether it contains any substance is misdirected. Loose time is its own substance, its very definition to be shapeless; that is why reverie fits it so well.

When he observes in the first Promenade of the *Rêveries* that his duty is to abstain from action, Rousseau also notes that he fulfils this duty—a negative fulfilment that 'fills' the void by adding further emptiness to emptiness. This is not really true, though; the body is inactive ('désœuvrement' contains a stronger contrast with work or labour than any English translation can convey), but the soul still feels and thinks, so reenchanting the experience of life itself by affirming the reign of what is weightless and invisible. This is the reverse of what the artisan conventionally experiences, or perhaps it is only near the end of a life containing its degree of suffering that Rousseau really feels entitled to put (most) action by: he owes it to himself, though the necessities of living mean that he cannot afford to be earning nothing. What he seems to refer to is less the act that has earned him a living, music copying, than the act of writing that had spelled disaster and offered him a lesser living than it might have done. And it

---

[78] *Dialogues*, I.677.   [79] *Confessions*, I.334.   [80] *C.C.*, XXXIX.12.
[81] *Dictionnaire de musique*, V, 'Copiste'.

is hard to see that Rousseau's later years were free from this activity, given that his great autobiographical works were all written long after the censored *Emile* and *Du contrat social*. Botanizing, besides, involved far more activity on Rousseau's part than the first Promenade suggests, even if he counts it among the leisure activities still permitted to him. He is able to range it among the empty arts (or crafts) only because he regards it as a subject of mere curiosity. As a hobby of Rousseau's, however, it effectively disproves his claim to have achieved the state of being 'mort de tout interest terrestre et temporel' in old age,[82] unless we take 'interest' simply to mean self-concern.

Walking, in any case, cannot but draw his attention to the phenomenal world, whether or not the ravishments and ecstasies it causes also carry him beyond it. The first morning he spent at the Hermitage, book 9 of the *Confessions* recalls, was taken up not with arranging his possessions, but with giving himself over to the impression of the 'objets champêtres' around him, the 'touching beauties' scarcely found in towns.[83] We may think ahead to the fifth Promenade of the *Rêveries*, and Rousseau's reluctance to unpack his books before grounding himself in repeated forays outside the house on the île de Saint-Pierre. Even so, as he retrospectively surveys the list of works written either as Mme d'Epinay's lodger or in the Petit Château at Montmorency, it is clear to him that if he wasted any time over the six-year period, 'ce n'a pas été du moins dans l'oisiveté'.[84]

The *Confessions* had touched upon the theme of pleasurable perambulation much earlier.[85] Rousseau's delight in journeying on foot was such that arrival did not seem to matter very much to him, the principle of unhurriedness preferred even if duty dictated otherwise.[86] As with his return from Turin with Bâcle, or his accompanying Mme d'Epinay to Geneva for a medical consultation with Tronchin, he on foot and she in a carriage, this was a constant in his life. *Emile*, too, rehearses the reasons for travelling as a pedestrian rather than on wheels. Slowness is part of the good life, speed its thief; happiness consists in savouring the present, not anticipating some future of imagined prosperity or note. 'Je n'ai point élevé mon Emile pour desirer ni pour attendre, mais pour joüir',[87] an ambition best achieved by the person who lives for the moment, exploring what surrounds him and drawing what good he can from it. If Emile's feet hurt, 'Il porte par tout de quoi s'amuser. Il entre chez un maitre, il

---

[82] *Rêveries*, I.1000.   [83] *Confessions*, I.403–4.   [84] *Confessions*, I.404.
[85] *Confessions*, I.172.
[86] *C.C.*, XXI.53 (21 August 1764, to Earl Marshal Keith), and XXII.175 (Keith to Rousseau, 5 December 1764).
[87] *Emile*, IV.771.

travaille; il exerce ses bras pour reposer ses pieds'.[88] The last thing we should ask of our legs, Rousseau thinks, is speed.

Perambulation and insight went happily together, although any kind of gentle movement yielded certain gains. He was far from being alone in arguing the close connection between walking and health; it was a commonplace of this as of other ages,[89] recommended by doctors such as Samuel Tissot—who wrote a tract on the dangers of sedentariness that chimed precisely with Rousseau's views[90]—and Théodore Tronchin, the Genevese physician whose friendship with Rousseau would sour over the years. Tronchin won great influence in the social circles Rousseau (selectively) despised, so much so that well-born women started to adopt the healthy type of gait and general locomotion he prescribed, and for which the verb 'tronchiner' was coined. Rousseau himself, though temperamentally given to striding out in the open air whenever possible, often claimed to be too ill to move, though at the very times when acquaintances and observers were commenting[91] on his extraordinary vigour in climbing mountain paths and crossing alpine pastures in pursuit of botanical specimens, leaping like an ibex from one rock to another. At the same time he excoriated the 'spies' who in some mysterious way prevented him from walking in the countryside, or blamed his health for keeping him confined indoors. When he was on form, he told Deluc on 7 June 1764, he could hardly keep still.[92] Yet a few months earlier he had assured another correspondent that although he was keen to walk to (or around?) Scotland, 'mon état actuel ne m'en laisse guère l'espérance'.[93]

What are we to make of all this? Partly, as Hume had commented, that Rousseau knew himself very little in some respects; besides, he had been inclined to hypochondria from his youth onwards (if not from birth: the Confessions notes that he had been born practically dying and since then had always carried the germ of 'incommodité' which the years accentuated).[94] He also disliked other people telling him what to do even when he could see the advisability of doing it, which did not stop him prescribing something similar for others. So he told DuPeyrou on 29 April 1765 that botanizing was the latter's best weapon in fighting gout,[95] an observation he would also make to Davenport in England. A well-wisher admired him for walking like Plato and Pythagoras, the model of locomotion prescribed in book 5 of Emile, but made the mistake of offering

---

[88] Emile, IV.772.   [89] See his letter to DuPeyrou of 2 May 1764, C.C., XXV.223.
[90] Samuel Tissot, De la santé des gens de lettres (Lausanne: François Grasset, 1768).
[91] See Bernardin de Saint-Pierre, Vie, p. 47; C.C., XX.149 (Jakob Heinrich Meister to Johann Heinrich Meister, 6 June 1764).
[92] C.C., XX.160.   [93] C.C., XVIII.11 (to Usteri, 3 October 1763).
[94] Confessions, I.7.   [95] C.C., XXV.203–4.

Rousseau the use of his wife's carriage all the same, an offer to which Rousseau disdained to respond.[96] To travel by coach, after all, was to ignore the lessons in agriculture, natural history, and natural science that the simple expedient of keeping one's feet on the ground made available. It also condemned the traveller to a hateful 'oisiveté'.[97] These were compromises Rousseau refused to make.

So his hand did not simply give way to his legs, as he had playfully suggested much earlier in his working life, when in a letter to the Chevalier de Lorenzy of 21 May 1759 about the surroundings at the Petit Château he was renting from the Luxembourgs he declared that 'mes pieds me font perdre l'usage de mes mains, et le métier n'en va pas mieux'.[98] It is more that the hand's activity was now very specific. We remember his observation in the letter to Malesherbes of 28 January 1762 that, lacking the health and stamina to do manual work, he had withdrawn from the world in order to tell society painful truths about itself, contrasting his situation with that of the useless layabouts and tittle-tattlers of Paris whom 'on devrait tous renvoyer labourer la terre dans leur provinces'. However useful Rousseau's own hands might have been for labouring the fields, their default activity of writing was obviously considerable. Yet this, so he claims, would have been inconceivable without the limbs on whose resilience in carrying him around outdoors the very concept of his last great work was predicated.

Throughout his life, particularly the latter part, the legs had helped disengagement, as certain benign forms of stasis also did: reverie might ensue on one's walking to a pleasant place, or on abstraction from the negative forces life could generate, and which brought the 'trouble' and 'inquiétude' whose opposite was calm and peace. Yet rootedness in a *locus amœnus* reached by walking yielded only semi-permanence: it would be destroyed by enforced removal, the exile he endured from the early 1760s. Good wandering meant moving soul and body to a refuge in which stillness could be found and reverie unfolded. Bad wandering was physical or (in Rousseau's frenzied paranoia) mental; whatever form it took, it marked the end of peace. Although the 'délices internes' of ultimate repose had been captured in Diderot's *Encyclopédie* entry 'Délicieux' decades before the fifth Promenade, Rousseau's presentation of it now seems archetypal. Not only is the rush of cities hostile to serenity; all kinds of progress, literally the act of stepping forth, rub against its grain. Another kind of stepping forth, the botanizing Rousseau does in later life, permits the inactivity he loves, not stillness of a physical kind, for the second *Dialogue* tells us that

---

[96] *C.C.*, XXXV.19 (Geffrard de La Motte to Rousseau, 7 January 1768).
[97] *Dialogues*, I.845.   [98] *C.C.*, VI.102.

'il faut que ses mains, que ses pieds, que ses doigts agissent, que son corps soit en exercice',[99] but alertness of a higher form, played out, as he proceeds, against a background 'oisiveté' that botany first focuses and then contains[100]—a conscious relaxation of the mind and body. The *Confessions* describes something similar in the 'loisirs champêtres' experienced at Les Charmettes,[101] and later in the rambling he enjoyed in Môtiers.[102] Later still, confinement as he knows it on the île de Saint-Pierre generates a new and intoxicating delirium in which he lives life most intensely through disengagement and contemplation. 'J'aurois voulu être tellement confiné dans cette Ile que je n'eusse plus de commerce avec les mortels.'[103] Calvin, we remember, had attempted to ensure that men and women, denied idleness, would also be preserved from vice. Work was the discipline whose ultimate development would be the workhouse, an institution entailing the division of labour as a way of life, and where profit and productiveness were all. Puritanism took matters further, declaring that extracting all possible profit from manufacture—no longer the literal making of things by hand, perhaps, but fabricating by machine—would leave a surplus for godly benefaction, so reconciling wealth with conscience. (*Robinson Crusoe*, it is true, draws different conclusions.) The first *Discours* saw leisure as promoting literacy in ways that harmed mankind,[104] as machinery weakens bodies; the second *Discours* concludes similarly.[105] *Emile* insists that where bodies are idle a taste for meditation must be cultivated: it is essential that the pupil 'pense en philosophe pour n'être pas aussi fainéant qu'un sauvage',[106] a statement that contextualizes the attractions of an immobile life.

The calm that Rousseau sees as ensuing on detached reflection and occasional vacancy is different. It may need to be disturbed for safety's sake: the individual's own contentment might not be respected by his fellows, who covet it for its enriching properties (mental state or physical possession). Thus the second *Discours* recommends alertness that runs counter to repose and the state of pure divestment. Or is this really what it counsels? Rousseau still sees self-divestment as a form of bliss, but only when it frees man from the nagging urge of egoism. This ultimate state is the one he experienced most fully on the île de Saint Pierre; but his life-long freedom from the 'civilized' vulgarities of material desire made it easier of access than his enemies imagined. It has been the zero state of sages throughout culture, recurrently admired, if not achieved, against a

---

[99] *Dialogues*, I.845.   [100] See the seventh Promenade, *Rêveries*, I.1069.
[101] *Confessions*, I.401.   [102] *Confessions*, I.601.   [103] *Confessions*, I.638.
[104] *Discours sur les sciences et les arts*, III.18, n. 4.
[105] *Discours sur l'inégalité*, III.135.   [106] *Emile*, IV.480.

background of advanced technology and crass money-mindedness. In 1764 Rousseau would write to Mme de Boufflers about a self-preserving state of seeming emptiness, promoted by indolence but not caused by it, and which created in him the radical, yet positive, disenchantment with life that mystics know. It does not mean disaffection with the energies of life itself, however; Rousseau will die when his 'machine' is terminally weakened, not seek to end his life (though some contemporaries believed he did). There is no second meaning in his words to Mme de Boufflers that 'Il y a longtemps que je cherche à déloger',[107] simply a realistic and far from negative evaluation of the state to which 'désœuvrement' has brought him: fruitful nullity.

Self-divestment of the kind he said he practised in England meant getting rid of material objects such as books (later on he would sell much of his botanical library to Daniel Malthus, the father of the economist, whom he met in England),[108] not ridding himself of life.

> Cette vie oisive et contemplative, que vous n'approuvez pas et que je n'excuse pas, me devient chaque jour plus délicieuse. Errer seul sans fin et sans cesse parmi les arbres et les rochers qui entourent ma demeure, rêver ou plutôt extravaguer à mon aise, et, comme vous dites, bayer aux corneilles; quand mon cerveau s'échauffe trop, le calmer en analysant quelque mousse ou quelque gramen; enfin me livrer sans asservissement, sans gêne à mes fantaisies, qui, grâce au Ciel, sont toutes en mon pouvoir: voilà, Monsieur [Mirabeau], pour moi la suprême jouissance, à laquelle je n'imagine rien de supérieur dans cette vie, et même dans l'autre.[109]

Daydreaming is his keenest pleasure, emptying his head, wandering as the very word 'rêver' defines it, 're-ex-vagari', the etymological wandering away from (something or oneself)—these are his only 'actions'.

But the activity he engages in, from and after England, belies this account. From Bourgoin he tells Moultou on 14 February 1769[110] that he feels closer than ever to the natural end of his life, yet not, as he suggests it, in a spirit of equanimity: the business of self-justification has intervened, writing his life has become an absorbing purpose, and it remains alive as long as Rousseau himself does (so the unfinished tenth *Rêverie*, the last thing he wrote, will break off with his death). To Rey as well[111] he calls it his new duty, one owed to himself alone. Thérèse will be untouched by it, though she does arrange the posthumous publication of the *Confessions*, and there are no known children to benefit from what he means to be the re-writing of his life story. The imagined plot necessitates this clarification

---

[107] *C.C.*, XXI.72 (26 August 1764).   [108] *O.C.*, I.1687, n. 5.
[109] *C.C.*, XXXII.82 (31 January 1767).   [110] *C.C.*, XXXVII.56.
[111] *C.C.*, XXXVII.177 (23 November 1769).

of the record, this end of 'oisiveté', though he had seemingly abandoned writing. This, he implies, is why he will likewise abandon botany (though he does not), an idle pastime that deflects him from the task at hand. So he drops the alias under which he has been living since his return to France, returns to Paris, and resumes the writing of his life, the truth he has to recreate.

The *Dialogues* then re-approaches it in another way than that adopted by the *Confessions*, and the *Rêveries* differently again. The latter both recalls the past and lets the writer/dreamer reexperience it, a double delectation different in kind from that of religious doctrine, but similarly aimed at victory over time. Rousseau has moved away from the ideal inactivity he once tried to embrace, but to the same good 'end' of utter repose: passionlessness is freedom from suffering as well as freedom from intense feeling, from invasive want. A new kind of copying has taken over, a copying *of* life whose benefit to Rousseau is as radical, as rooted, as the copying *for* life of his former profession, or the stylized copying *from* life of his plant pasigraphy. The question of whether this focus on the self may also give a model for others to observe—so giving the copy an exemplary force, a third dimension—now seems less important to him than it once did; it has, perhaps, acquired an aesthetic rather than a moral slant. What his late writing does is remind us of the world, one he had invoked twenty years and more earlier, in the two *Discours*, where something we have lost still lives—where technology does not challenge or mould nature, but leaves it intact: not turned to human ends, like coal and ore torn from earth and rocks, but simply left and let to be.[112] The *Rêveries* describes wandering in this ample world, though we may see it now as narrow and constricted, lost to meddling and machinery: in telling us what life was like before the land was scarred, it may help end our alienation. For language is the tool by which we reappropriate the natural world, as we gained it once by simply naming, like the periwinkle suddenly revealed to Rousseau and thus his reader.[113] Naming, writing, tell us of the limits to our ownership, but let us see afresh.

[112] See, again, Bate, p. 254.

[113] Compare Bruno Latour's theory of 'bringing back' in this connection: Bruno Latour, 'Visualization and Cognition: Thinking with Eyes and Hands', in Henrika Kuklick and Elis Long (eds.), *Knowledge and Society: Studies in the Sociology of Culture Past and Present*, 6 (1986), pp. 1–40.

Conclusion

THE ARTISAN'S TOUCH

Rousseau had two signatures, the craftsman's fingerprint and the writer's eloquence; the hand of praxis and the voice of doxa. This is, of course, to over-simplify, since not all of his handwork was craftsmanlike or practical, nor all that he articulated meant to teach. But hand and voice converged in complex, masterly inscription, writing that had beauty both as script and as expressive text. Though censorship might check the eloquence, it could not wholly silence it: for Rousseau knew that what has once been thought can never be beyond conception, nor what has once been said or written quite forgotten.[1] Repression drove him back to craftsmanship, but also generated art.

His copying took many forms. Early on it was a simple kind of make-believe, remembered scenes from literature enacted as a childhood game; later it became another kind of mimicry, as he took on different personae—a semi-literate composer, an Englishman who did not know his language, a mental retard whom his family disowned. There was more useful copying than this, however: the engraving of inscriptions onto metal plate, writing letters for the rich or idle, transcribing papers for a diplomat, or making literary extracts for a wealthy bourgeoise. From his middle years other kinds of copying filled his time, initially that of music: the copyist's life in Paris drew on many of the manual skills he had developed earlier on, letting him charge premium rates for the special beauty of his work. Later still, when botany became his passion, pictographic schemas let him represent the range of floral types concisely and with clarity. Finally, *Confessions* and *Rêveries* show him using language as a way of capturing memory and emotion, evocatively, not exactly, tracing in, as he relived them, different kinds of past reality.

---

[1] Kelly, *Rousseau as Author*, p. 175, refers to Starobinski's observation in *Le Remède dans le mal* (Paris: Gallimard, 1989), pp. 187–200, on Rousseau's telling his anonymous correspondent 'Henriette' on 24 August 1751 that the effervescence of thought changes the thinker radically: having once discovered a mental world that took her beyond her old preoccupations, she could never be made happy again by returning to a simple domestic life of crocheting and knitting (*Corr.*, XX.19). Clearly the same was true, *mutatus mutandis*, of Rousseau himself.

He saw the crucial moment of his writing life in epiphanic terms, the visitation near Vincennes that told him what he had to say and do to save mankind. The first *Discours* records the only matter from that moment that stayed clearly with him; further works of doctrine followed, built on other notions briefly glimpsed in 1749, books the state suppressed for their alleged unorthodoxy, but which he regarded as his *necessary* writings, things that had been dreamt of, thought about, and copied up in the special place where authors say what they must say and then fall silent. Prohibition pushed him back into the world of praxis, that of deeds, not thoughts, of artefacts, not words, a shift that may be closer to the mood of Rousseau's time than we readily imagine: for if the age of sensibility gloried in emotional affect, sentiment was always linked with the material world, sensory contact shaping inward states in various expressive ways. It cannot, then, be separated from the world Rousseau was born into, the world of artisanship, not of art. While art's links with concrete matter cannot be denied—making images with tools and substances, paintbrushes and colours, pens and inks—it is quite different from the making of things with matter in the world of craft.

Replicas are rarely sought in visual art, except, perhaps, by pupils learning from the work of earlier masters, or by forgers; craft, conversely, seeks equivalence to prototype, identity to established patterns, although there are exceptions—the shaping of a unique object, the original and distinctive bowl or piece of weaving, for example, still called a craftwork because of other features it possesses, such as functionality. What art objects 'do' is seldom something functional; they attract, not users, but beholders. Art generally has an immaterial, mental, aim, craft a physical, utilitarian one. Craftworks are not often viewed as thought-objects, as works of art may be (and from the Renaissance were extolled as being), but instead as bits of useable matter. This difference has had both negative and positive consequences in the world of man, underlined in debates about the range of sciences and arts both in Rousseau's day and in ours, science taken as of this world and real, art as connected with the imagined and unworldly; science with need and progress, art with timelessness and beauty.

Of those three fields advertised in the *Encyclopédie*'s subtitle, 'sciences', 'arts', and 'métiers', craft undoubtedly seems nearer to the first than the second. Yet its association with the functional may be closer still than science's, craft objects serving an occurrent purpose, science objects (or thoughts, or theories) purposes that may as yet be undefined. Craft appears the most immediately pragmatic, in the senses outlined here: it takes existing matter with and upon which to work. In art and science we shape, and sometimes make, materials, but may still be dealing with and through abstractions. In craft the theme of making, of solidity, is always there.

Does art seem more dispensable than craft because it does not (usually) deal with practicality, or address the purposes of life? Common sense says yes, aesthetic feeling no. Even at its lowest level human life involves the need for basic products, natural not manufactured; elemental life must always, so it seems, be thought of in organic terms. We die for want of food and water, not of books. Yet in another sense the book is vital, or seemed so to Rousseau in 1749 (*Emile* says something different: 'Je hais les livres').[2] It is this notion of primal need that the first *Dialogue* alludes to when it speaks of writers who articulate essential truths. Rousseau did not give up writing after 1763, but thought nothing he produced thereafter necessary to the world or to himself. We might disagree, thinking differently of what that word implies in his case, the literary indispensability of almost everything he wrote. Yet his life support from the early 1750s was work that should have seemed impossible to justify in one who had inveighed against the arts, and whose political beliefs conflicted with the social privilege of most of those for whom he copied. It was all most puzzling, and thus rather typical of Rousseau.

FREE AGENCY

No professional activity, not writing words or copying musical notes, gave him all the liberty he asked for. That came with movement. From the start of what he felt to be his free existence, before familiar constraints set in— from childhood to apprenticeship, from Geneva to Turin, from Annecy to Paris, from Hermitage to Neuchâtel, from lac de Bienne to Staffordshire—, he spent his time enjoying independence, clear of the constrictions he associated with professional writing, despite all his literary celebrity. Even back in Paris in what he called his old age, he had worked as his own master, though such mastery had its price. He had no taste for anything imposed on him from outside, just as he disliked forced fruits or unnatural hybrid flowers brought on artificially by man's pernicious meddling with the natural order.

This is why his written 'lives' stayed dangling, *Confessions* unfinished, as *Rêveries* remained, both because the writing of a self must close before the self's end and because he had a need to live his idleness as well as his profession. Leisure was a guiding principle before old age imposed it, for it alone permitted the unhurried flowering he wanted. To break the pact of slowness he had made with life would be to make him truly alien in the

---

[2] *Emile*, IV.454.

world; writing and then copying kept him literally in touch. Yet intactness
of the kind he needed to preserve required renunciation, as the *Rêveries*
makes clear—losing freedom of movement and some friendships, forfeit-
ing small pleasures. It had its compensations, even so: when artistic life
was over, or appeared to be, practicality could take its place. All retreat
and loss were relative, and despite denials he continued writing; yet he
also said he needed company, even company that annoyed him, to stop
him dreaming fruitlessly. Hence his unguarded expression of delight, as
the seventh *Rêverie* records it, when he comes upon the signs of human
presence, human (cottage) industry, as he walks and botanizes in what
seemed to be the wilds of nature.

This sense of deep connection is in part why craft's materials and actions
matter, continuing age-old methods and techniques, making objects that
we feel we have, in some sense, always known and always needed. Art's
objects, on the other hand, may unsettle, both the artist and the public,
sometimes through their novelty: so *Du contrat social* articulates new
thoughts on statecraft, politics, religion, and other kinds of doctrine that
were challenges to orthodoxy. In some of what he wrote Rousseau's inven-
tiveness would signal for his enemies a kind of cleverness (or craftiness)
beyond the proper limit, alien to the honest and familiar world of making
things by hand. This daring meant he would encounter obstacles that forced
him from creating things to copying them, from first- to second-hand
engagement. Often he was happy with this outcome; his craftsman ancestry
had, after all, made natural the learning of a trade through imitation, re-
presenting tried and tested matter through established methods for the purpose of utility. Such functional work must surely guarantee integrity.

Perhaps it only seemed to do so, though: there is no certainty about the
status various kinds of scribal work enjoy. The trade Rousseau had started
learning in his youth seemed more obviously pragmatic, since watch dials
need their numerals, medals their inscriptions; despite the pride he took
in his fine penmanship, he knew this work was simply presentational, the
copying done in Paris, then Turin and Venice, later on at Chenonceaux.[3]
It showed less skill than the apprentice's as he honed his craft until the
work he did could stand as an original, like a master's master piece. Rousseau's most original, creative work came later.

When it did, it won him far more fame and (sometimes) favour than
the copying or other second-hand inscription ever did, but it also damned
him. That explains why scribal work became a refuge—earlier it had just
been a resort—, even though his exile after *Emile* and *Du contrat social*

---

[3] See A. Sénéchal, 'Jean-Jacques Rousseau, secrétaire de Mme Dupin', *Annales de la Société Jean-Jacques Rousseau*, XXXVI (1966), pp. 173–288.

were banned made music copying hard to live by. Yet Rousseau had earlier seemed to choose this status of outsider freely, and when called to live in the real world again would do so with reluctance, feeling he could not be *of* it, out of step still more, in some ways, than when officially outlawed. He might have managed comfortably had he agreed to live off others, taken pensions offered him by monarchs, for example: Diderot did this, in effect, by mortgaging his library to Catherine of Russia. But Rousseau's independence, a product of Genevan birth, said otherwise.

The most original writing came last, and was new in a particular sense. Rousseau's paradoxical achievement near the end of his career was to move beyond the use of language as a referential means,[4] a merely useful tool (as tools are meant to be), to a form of poetry. The works that won him public fame and infamy referred to a world order readers recognized, but requiring adaptation in specific ways to function better (*Emile*'s blue-print for transforming education, or *Du contrat social*'s for shaping social structures). In such works, clarity of meaning called for clarity of style, though the first *Discours* had blurred its argument, begged the questions it provoked. Functional discourse needs transparency of reference, but Rousseau's last work seems to set clear reference below the claims of sensory appeal.[5] The concept of emotional conviction at the cost of sense, or rule, or reason[6] had been emphasized much earlier on, when the author of *La Nouvelle Héloïse* gave the sound of words priority over grammatical correctness. The *Rêveries* goes further, privileging a poetic language that possesses wholeness almost independent of semantic content, wholeness based on textuality, on a sense of words as being self-reflexive entities that embody what Jakobson called 'le côté palpable des signes'.

Does this signal writing's freedom from a world in which the word is merely a pragmatic tool? Hardly, for the 'old' linguistic signs are always more than workmen's implements; their function of communicating meaning cannot be gainsaid, as *Dialogues* and *Confessions* testify. What makes the *Rêveries* appear different is that Rousseau claims in it, and seems to mean, that he no longer needs to explain or justify his thoughts and actions,[7] has renounced all hope of being understood: he feels, in other

---

[4] See Jean-Louis Lecercle, 'Rousseau critique littéraire. "Le cœur et la plume"', in *Reappraisals of Rousseau*, ed. Simon Harvey et al. (Manchester: Manchester University Press, 1980), pp. 215–28.

[5] On this general matter, see Roman Jakobson, *Essai de linguistique générale* (Paris: Seuil, 1963), p. 218; Lecercle, 'Rousseau critique littéraire. "Le cœur et la plume"', in *Reappraisals of Rousseau*, pp. 227–8.

[6] See Jessica Riskin, *Science in the Age of Sensibility* (Chicago and London: University of Chicago Press, 2002).

[7] The fourth Promenade's distinctively personal preoccupation with the matter of lying qualifies this view, however.

words, as free as other living things—flowers, for instance—that exist both in and for themselves, his words devoid of obvious purpose, 'pur' in both the senses of the word in French, void of meaning and unsullied or intact. They suit a world in which, so Rousseau says, he has no further wish to explain himself or what he does. Focusing on words in their inherent being, in this final work of his, we may also find it imitating the materiality or texture of the substances the craftsman works on: shaping at first hand, then, not copying as machines may do, but handling language as both sound and form, language in its palpability, like the stuff of craftsmanship, matter valued for its own worth—the wood's grain or jewel's iridescence— beyond all practicality of purpose or functional durability.

USE AND FUNCTION

This does not mean that functionality is dead, simply that the point of words extends beyond it. Often, in related ways, the usefulness of things decreases as their poetry unfolds, just as portraits come to matter less as images resembling people than as painted forms. Language too may lose transparency of meaning over time while preserving beauty of both sound and shape. Evidently, these are principles Rousseau cares about. Does that imply that he took the claims of art to be superior to those of craft? Such a view would contradict a long-established and persuasive view of his philosophy. So we should perhaps say that they are only metaphorically the same, since 'tactile' words are never palpable except when carved in wood or stone, while craft objects always are: the 'feel' of language differs from the solidity of matter or the look of beauty (its sensory reality, as empiricists maintained).

The craftsman's fingerprint may matter most in societies rich enough to value craft as beautiful as well as useful, or to need its functionality less; Rousseau speaks for simpler, poorer times, though his age still gave the usefulness of craft a part-aesthetic sense. The hand's work never disappears from culture, but its evidence will vary. Sometimes it is just a light and glancing presence, like the fleeting, disconnected hand of the *Encyclopédie* plates, hinting at an agency it barely still possesses, the hand that is not there because its work is done once wheels are set in motion or warp is put on loom; a tacit hand with faintest fingerprint, lingering by machinery whose operations are so smooth that all their motions seem invisible, things that 'are' and 'are not' there: the lightest hand, as Barthes describes it, with the softest touch.

If we find craft reassuring, it is partly in this lack of self-assertiveness, familiar as its motions are, reliant on a set of practised movements, lacking any grand ambition. It hardly seems surprising, then, that Rousseau should have gone back to a world of minute shifts and actions where what mattered was precise and careful handling of material; for praxis seemed the safest and most obvious retreat when orthodoxy tolerated nothing but compliance. As his blueprints made the world seem other, so his enemies made it alien, turned his life into the nightmare of the first *Rêverie*, in which he sought but found no path or sign to guide him. This is why he made his counter-culture in the world of reenchantment, stressed the principle of other needs—needing to keep old paths open, needing not to tamper with those things that work best left alone, not subject to man's alien, manipulative purposes: woodland privatized or alp industrialized, mountain mined and common land enclosed. Like the modern eco-warrior who denies his fellow men the right to hold the natural world to ransom, Rousseau likes the image of an earth in which environmentalism matters, letting us create (or manufacture) things as craftsmen do, respectfully and from abundant natural sources.

These principles illuminate Rousseau's reflections on the world of proper creativity. They clarify the main distinction in his theory of human agency, between controlling or creative impulses and protective ones, where the first makes and the second takes, or the first shapes and the second soothes. Without such dualities, no balance can be struck between the motive force (man's scientific spirit) and his inclination towards rest. They show us how to deal with living in an impermanent world, using but not diminishing its resources, not manifesting in it an unseemly will to power. Rousseau's thought in this respect rests on an imagined harmony between divergent parts, between man and the universe; his reveries express this balance where all opposing impulses are reconciled. They are mutually supportive acts in which the hand is metaphor and reality.

For in an ideal world, and sometimes in the real one, one hand always knows the other's business: the feeling touch, the writing hand, the thinking brain all work together, fusing sense and intellect, body and mind, experience and record, instincts that define our human lives. Hume had written, though Rousseau did not know it, that men 'cannot reasonably expect that a piece of woollen cloth will be wrought to perfection in a nation which is ignorant of astronomy, or where ethics are neglected'[8]— in other words, that craft and what we call the moral and intellectual life are mutually supportive, cannot be experienced in full without each other. This justifies the *Encyclopédiste* enterprise, but also Rousseau's work of reassessment. The 'jouissance' he wanted at the end of life was found at

[8] Hume, 'Of Refinement in the Arts', *Essays*, new edn, 2 vols. (London: no publisher, 1764), II.196.

second hand, not from reality itself (if that was ever possible) but from the memory of an impression, the grafting of it onto the material present, feeling it translated once again from mental into physical form.[9]

It may seem ironic that the start of Rousseau's writing life should have been so clearly linked, if indirectly, with the hand—his fateful walk of 1749 to see a friend imprisoned for a heresy involving a blind sceptic and the power (or otherwise) of touching God. The story underlines how central to the period's philosophy and culture were a range of theories concerning sense impressions, foremost that of touch. It is in this context, too, that the *Encyclopédie*'s focusing on crafts as well as arts and sciences may best be understood. But was it equally ironic that this walk, or any walk, should lead to an attack on progress, literally the act of stepping forth? Rousseau's perambulations later on, directed as they were towards the world of nature, amplified the paradox, until his final work, the *Rêveries*, made walking seem the very means of self-disclosure. He gives us countless images of goal-directed movement where the sense of 'goal' is unconventional, signifying the aim of going nowhere in particular, slowly. Slowly above all: arrival matters less than what precedes it, starkly qualifying, even nullifying, ordinary principles of progress. Craftsmen might earn more by working faster, but watching clocks—especially if they are horologists—is alien to their spirit.

There were of course advances of quite other kinds in this age of science and discovery. The hand that felt and wrote was also the dissecting hand, performing scientific operations: Rousseau did these partly, it appears, because he was so poor a draughtsman. Whereas the great illustrator Ehret needed only naked eye and magnifying glass to prepare his studies (Rousseau's Duchess hired him to record the English flowers in her vast collection, then to teach her daughters drawing), Rousseau had to use the pen as scalpel, words as lens. It was not Ehret, though, but Redouté who did the illustrations to the *Lettres sur la botanique*, so turning this brief work of Rousseau's into a collector's piece. Even without pictures, the *Lettres* makes what is transient lasting, versions of some past perception brought into the present, as the *Rêveries* records the probing of the self; registering in words what eye and touch, like lens and scalpel, have laid bare. Copying of this kind resembled botany for Rousseau; both were therapies that could engage the mind at a remove and keep the copyist's 'machine' attuned, stretched without exhaustion. Like botanizing, too, for which he said he felt he had been born,[10] reverie might bring surprising clarity, sharpening his sense of beauty by both physical and mental means: unable

---

[9] Compare the first Promenade's formulation of this state.
[10] See Henri Cheyron, "'L'Amour de la botanique'", *Littératures*, 4 (1981), pp. 53–95.

to draw plants or flowers as he wanted to, he found that pressing and preserving them—in language as between the herbal's pages—anchored them by other means. Such re-presentation might translate the evanescent floral form and passing mood no less than musical emotion, given perfect clarity as he set them down on paper, score and book both rearranging the 'signes mémoratifs' for posterity.

The hand was central in this search for meaning and fulfilment, but it was the hand that knew its skill, not doubted it; not the abject hand, but the hand that wrote with beauty, composed passages of prose and music, played the spinet and the pen. The copyist's hand, his focus from mid-century, was not, we hardly need to say, the hand he is remembered for, nor the hand that played a part in certain bodily matters, though that hand had its importance too (Boswell needed wine to 'take' Thérèse, unsatisfactorily; Rousseau, she insisted, trumped him easily by manual means).[11] The hand whose solitary work had been the dangerous supplement of self-pleasuring was redeemed in service of another, just as his own sexual needs had called upon another's hands (in the thrilling spanking by Mlle Lambercier). There were greater manual causes to be served, however.

The greatest of them was his goal of penetrating with the written word as the surgeon's blade would penetrate, 'intus, et in cute', cutting through with clinical precision to the vital organs, not simply piercing flesh, but slicing into it and peeling back the carapace to show the man himself, inside and out, skinned like a hare, flayed like an ox or an artist's écorché, *excoriated*, thus oversensitive, a paranoid; penetrated, but also penetrating, sounding out as though with probes, the 'sondes' Rousseau inserted in himself throughout his adult life (a need for opening and release also answered by the call to literature); opening up as the *Encyclopédie* plates dissect machinery, retention overcome by expert handling, the master operator, like the etcher with his burin, blurring where the mezzotint of vagueness, not the harder clarity of line, was needed, everything dependent on the deftness of the trained manipulator's hand. It all came back to craft, he knew, the writing and the loving, the playing with pens and books and women, and the rest.

This is why he had to warn against modernity's advance, the making of machines that threatened to supplant such vital manual measures. While

---

[11] See *Corr.*, XXVII.348: according to some missing pages seen by Colonel Ralph Isham at Malahide Castle in Ireland, but immediately destroyed, Boswell reported that she called him a very imperfect lover and 'asked him as a man who had travelled more had he not noticed how many things were achieved by men's hands and how she instructed him […]. I felt like a child in her hands, not a lover.' She hurt his feelings by saying, 'Don't imagine that you are a better lover than Rousseau.'

he could, he did so with his pen. When that was impossible, he turned to craft, though for other purposes than those that inspired the *Encyclopédistes* and their modern-minded peers; for it is both a strength and a weakness in the craftsman's world to stand opposed, as Rousseau would have done and *philosophes* did not, to most technology and the streamlined, automated processes it makes possible. Focused on traditional ways, often hostile to machine and manufacture (words uniting handwork and contrivance), craft is based on practicality: what is made by hand is rarely as disposable or blandly uniform as factory products, though it shares their purpose of utility. Craft may keep to long-established ways of making that align it with the modern ethos of the Slows or Greens, but is not deliberately nostalgic: older methods simply give it an integrity in literal terms, a completeness stemming from the involvement of a single maker at each stage of manufacture. It may also have a moral wholeness dependent on accountability: the maker sourcing his material responsibly knows its provenance and sustainability. These issues fit with principles developed in *Emile* and which the Wolmars' homestead tacitly upholds. In essence they reflect the compassionate Puritanism of Rousseau's Geneva background.

THE GOOD LIFE

Rousseau made his literary works and musical scores as he made herbaria, the first and second more closely linked than in other writers of the time to material fabrication (the physical object, the manuscript copies, preoccupied him just as much as invention, argument, and plot), stamped with the mark of Rousseau the craftsman, proud of the distinctness of his scores from those of other copyists. The herbaria were works of hand as well as of perambulating legs, laid-down records of discovery, with all the plants he gathered pressed, arranged, and labelled in his careful script on heavy, costly paper. He 'made' his letters too, inscribing them with tender care, copying them as records in his books of manuscript as Saint-Preux does with Julie's in *La Nouvelle Héloïse*. These were ways in which he could project his person, using them as he might use machines and tools to extend his reach and sight (the lens that let him look at nature microscopically, the files and probes and scalpels that gave access to unimagined scientific truths), but always mindful of the fact that artistry might shade into an artifice of thought or manufacture.

Given these preoccupations, it is no doubt deliberately that he writes in the first *Dialogue* of those who make, not write, books in a magic world, whose acts blend physicality and thought, and whose purpose differs from the wordsmith's. Weightless though the enchantment seems, he gives it substance, even adding on a sense of what is burdensome. Writing that comes painfully may be a practical guarantee, as skills that come with time and effort are. Craft, too, serves our purposes deliberately as well as beautifully. It links morality with enterprise, need with usefulness and honour. Extravagance is foreign to its spirit, and durability implicit in its constructs, things meant to serve a solid purpose. It subtly shows our ingenuity, not bypassing the human factor as technology may do: the Heron's fountain Rousseau got in Italy had symbolized technology as sideshow or as plaything, usefulness ignored for entertainment's sake. Playing with devices without allowing them to serve their function was tedious in the end, as his childhood games with craftsmen's implements made clear.

Boating on the lake in the fifth *Rêverie*, Rousseau thinks of what it is to live a human life, concluding that it means existing deeply, separately from artfulness and ingenuity, from the barren physicalism that defines modernity. They are implicitly opposed to the gentle motion he experiences on water, the kind of letting be or letting go that really counts: taking what technology makes possible (building boats, for instance) while pushing it no further; not writing nor even thinking, though he might do both; simply experiencing.

The retired life he embraced from middle age shocked some of his acquaintances because it seemed to signal his withdrawal from the vital missions they identified with him, saving the world or changing society. They were wrong, however: several of these missions were launched in his 'retirement' (*Emile* and *Du contrat social* most notably); besides, he had always been admired for lighter things as well as serious ones. The tame or domestic Rousseau was content to do things he described as strictly useless—writing on the science of flowers for a mother and daughter, for instance—all the more pleasurably because he called them simple pastimes,[12] things that made no difference to the fortunes of the human race or the planet's health. Was he wrong in this respect?

The friend to whom Julie de Bondeli described the botanizing rambles Rousseau went on with some middle-aged enthusiasts was Zimmermann, whose name means carpenter in German. Perhaps Emile the carpenter, taught by his mentor to be useful, would have taken up botany in middle age too, or even, as Rousseau did, in what he calls old age, because it served real human purpose: Rousseau calls it otiose, yet it is a study useful to medicine and other applied sciences, and learning from it could have

---

[12] See his letter to Mme Delessert, end March/beginning April 1774 (*C.C.*, XXXIX.234); also *Lettres sur la botanique*, IV.1188.

furthered his (and Emile's) urge to serve mankind. We should not, besides, exaggerate the aesthetic thrust of this flower fever. His enthusiasm for Linnaeus's system shows its pragmatism, as does the unpoetic entry 'Fleur' in his unfinished *Dictionnaire de botanique*: the flower is simply 'l'état passager des parties de la fructification durant la fécondation du germe', or, more baldly still, 'le foyer et l'instrument de la fécondation'.

This down-to-earth conception shows a link between the botanical and the philosophical, or at least makes evident that they were happier partners than initially appeared. It intimates that one classificatory system (the Linnaean, for example) is much like another (such as the materialist determinism Rousseau thought the *philosophes* committed to), even that there are ways of linking them with political systems such as those developed in *Du contrat social*. Everything, as the *Encyclopédie*'s tree of knowledge put it, was potentially linked to everything else, all founded on a concept of order.

According to the ancient Greeks, philosophy began with wonder, with the aim of comprehending something either great or puzzling, or both together, often by reducing them to basic principles. Almost everything Rousseau wrote fits within this theory, an ideal order whose pattern shows how best to infuse the objects of the world with life. Human efforts at creative structuring take various forms, art's beauty and the practicality of craft among them. The pragmatism bred in Rousseau as a Genevese found much that was persuasive in creating patterns, reducing different things to rule; the truths he glimpsed on the way to Vincennes attested to it, and the practicality he found in craft and (some of) art confirmed it.

His thought in some or all of these respects made fertile ground for later theorists and makers, the founders of the Arts and Crafts movement, the Deutscher Werkbund, Wiener Werkstätte, and other brotherhoods (and sisterhoods), designers and industrialists who wanted, like the *Encyclopédistes*, to restore the dignity of manual work. There is much, too, that tells us what a Rousseau of the present day might be: an eager conservationist appalled at the despoiling of the countryside and the rape of ecosystems, fighting airstrips and the idiocies of cosmic travel (even though he once attempted to design a rudimentary aircraft),[13] wanderer down private lanes and footpaths, nemesis of second-homers and their anti-rural ways, enemy of freighted food that tricked the seasons and the continents, car refusenik, hater of the cult of instantaneity, Soil Associationist, Third World activist, Green and Slow supporter, pacifist and social

---

[13] See Pierre-Paul Plan, 'Jean-Jacques Rousseau aviateur', *Mercure de France*, 1910, pp. 577–97, and John R. Pannabecker, 'Rousseau in the Heritage of Technology Education', *Journal of Technology Education*, 6, no. 2 (Spring 1995), pp. 46–58.

democrat, Fair Trade preacher, anti-capitalist raging at the cost of mass consumption that is subsidized by the environment (and of human capital thereby squandered), and much more besides. These vices are the product of a degrading human cleverness, of an ingenuity at variance with the meaning of humanity.[14] Some would call the man who warned against such barren rationalism crazy, others honour his integrity and championship of hopeless causes, his hatred of conglomerates and support for all the causes of the little man.

Would other causes, even 'civilizing' aspects of the modern age, have drawn him too? Would he have remained opposed to woman's liberation, for example, a simple freedom to accompany the others he had championed? Would he, a solid Calvinist and craftsman, have cursed the flimsy virtuality of life, however closely it resembled his own mental composition during sleepless nights, followed by frustrated efforts to remember thoughts and write them up in waking hours? Would he have remained a true calligrapher, clinging to the pen (or quill) and paper while all about him others dropped them for the practicality of processed, printed text, mocked them as, with craftsman's touch, he sharpened lead or dipped the nib in ink? Or might he, as a correspondent almost ruined by the cost of franking letters, have been an unlikely convert to the possibilities of electronic mail? In most other ways, in writing as in making, in art as well as craft, he tried to fend off science and modernity's excesses, thinking that new kinds of understanding, the secular and materialist above all, impoverished humanity. The cult they had established was of objects without future, constant obsolescence, offending man's real need to cherish in the long term, all things that are symbolized by craft's commitment to the strong and durable as well as the utilitarian.

His own social-mindedness, together with his distance from the world of sociability, in some respects resembled what he saw in other craftsmen, people practically engaged by matter, usefully concerned for others, but with a certain wise detachment from mankind for concentration's sake; doing work requiring long embedded skills and thought (his years of meditating on *Emile*, for instance), making a real difference to humanity by labour over slow and steady time, reaching back to past and looking on to future. Set against such qualities, the sudden insights, the eureka moments, seemed of secondary importance: although one had sparked off

---

[14] According to Philippe Ariès, the last third of the twentieth century showed the end of the Enlightenment, that is, of the belief in the irreversibility and absolute beneficence of scientific and technological progress ('L'Histoire des mentalités', in *La Nouvelle Histoire*, ed. Jacques Le Goff (Paris: Retz, 1978), p. 411); see also Brewer, *Enlightenment Past*, pp. 199–200.

his entire career as moralist and social conscience, only labour over years could consecrate it. The world of speed, he thought, was generally unsettling; speed become an orthodoxy meant that nothing worthwhile, nothing made with real time, could survive. That is what defines him so exactly as a predecessor of those modern movements that appeal to rootedness, integrity, sustainability, freedom from the urgent pressures of industrial life, from the altering of nature's rhythm and the alienating jargon of time management.

Simple harmonies would always draw him more than magic through machinery, mastery in some new and falsifying sense that contrasted with the latent knowledge of the craftsman, orthopraxis based on deeper time and care. Discovering the craftsman's art of almost standing still needs patience of the kind apprentices may lack, but alone releases the creative virtues Rousseau cares about. His preference for what is fit appears exemplary in this respect, a model like the craftsman's master piece, a product that possesses its own value, and itself conserves time, *keeps* time like the clocks and watches of his family's tradition. Rousseau's life maintains this inner shape as well, whether he is copying or writing (when he takes it up again), or copying *as* writing, blending art and craft harmoniously.

Bibliography

Adams, William Howard, *The French Garden 1500–1800* (London: Scholar Press, 1979).

Adorno, Theodor and Horkheimer, Wilhelm, *Dialektik der Aufklärung* (Amsterdam: Querido, 1944).

d'Alembert, Jean le Rond, *Discours préliminaire de l'"Encyclopédie'*, ed. Michel Malherbe (Paris: J. Vrin, 2000).

Anderson, Lewis Flint, *A History of Manual and Industrial School Education* (New York and London: Appleton & Co., 1926).

Audi, Paul, *Rousseau, éthique et passion* (Paris: Presses universitaires de France, 1997).

Auerbach, Eric, 'Sermo humilis', *Literary Language and Its Public in Late Latin Antiquity and in the Middle Ages* (London: Routledge and Kegan Paul, 1965).

Ayer, A. J., *Hume* (Oxford: Oxford University Press, 1980).

Babel, Antoine, *Les Métiers dans l'ancienne Genève. Histoire corporative de l'horlogerie, de l'orfèvrerie et des industries annexes* (Geneva: A. Jullien, Georg & Cⁱᵉ, 1916).

Barrell, John, *The Idea of Landscape and the Sense of Place* (Cambridge: Cambridge University Press, 1972).

——, *The Dark Side of the Landscape* (Cambridge: Cambridge University Press, 1980).

Barth, Karl, *Die protestantische Theologie im neunzehnten Jahrhundert* (Zurich: Evangelischer Verlag Ag. Zollikon, 1947).

Barthes, Roland, 'Image, raison, déraison', in *L'Univers de l'"Encyclopédie'* (Paris: Les Libraires associés, 1964), pp. 11–16.

——, 'La Mort de l'auteur', *Le Bruissement de la langue* (Paris: Seuil, 1968), pp. 61–7.

Bate, Jonathan, *Romantic Ecology: Wordsworth and the Environmental Tradition* (London and New York: Routledge, 1991).

——, *The Song of the Earth* (Cambridge, MA: Harvard University Press, 2000).

Becker, Carl, *The Heavenly City of the Eighteenth-Century Philosophers* (New Haven: Yale University Press, 1932).

de Beer, Gavin, 'Jean-Jacques Rousseau: Botanist', *Annals of Science*, X, no. 3 (1954), pp. 189–223.

Benedict, Philip, *Christ's Churches Purely Reformed: A Social History of Calvinism* (New Haven and London: Yale University Press, 2002).

Berg, Maxine, *The Machinery Question and the Making of Political Economy 1815–1848* (Cambridge: Cambridge University Press, 1980).

Berlin, Isaiah, *Three Critics of the Enlightenment: Vico, Hamann, Herder*, ed. Henry Hardy (London: Pimlico, 2000).

Bernardin de Saint-Pierre, Jacques-Henri, *La Vie et les ouvrages de Jean-Jacques Rousseau*, ed. M. Souriau (Paris: Cornélie & Cⁱᵉ, 1907).

Berthoud, Ferdinand, *Histoire de la mesure du temps par les horloges*, 2 vols. (Nancy: Berger-Levrault, 1976).

Berthoud, Fritz, *Jean-Jacques Rousseau au val de Travers* (Paris: G. Fischbacher, 1881).

Besnard, Philippe, *Protestantisme et capitalisme* (Paris: A. Colin, 1970).

Besse, Guy, 'Aspects du travail ouvrier au XVIIIe siècle en France', *Essays on Diderot and the Enlightenment in Honor of Otis Fellows* (Geneva: Droz, 1974), pp. 71–103.

Blanqui, *Histoire de l'économie politique en Europe*, 4th edn, 2 vols. (Paris: Guillaumin, 1860).

Blom, Philippe, *Encyclopédie: the Triumph of Reason in an Unreasonable Age* (London and New York: Fourth Estate, 2004).

Blunt, Wilfrid, *The Art of Botanical Illustration* (London: Collins, 1950).

Bok, Sissela, *Lying: Moral Choice in Public and Private Life* (London: Quartet, 1980).

Boswell, James, *On the Grand Tour: Germany and Switzerland 1764*, ed. Frederick A. Pottle (Melbourne, London and Toronto: Heinemann, 1953).

——, *The Journal of His German and Swiss Travels, 1764*, ed. Marlies K. Danziger (Edinburgh: Edinburgh University Press; New Haven and London: Yale University Press, 2008).

Brewer, Daniel, *The Enlightenment Past: Reconstructing Eighteenth-Century Thought* (Cambridge: Cambridge University Press, 2008).

Broome, J. H., *Jean-Jacques Rousseau in Staffordshire, 1766–1767* (Keele: Keele University Library Occasional Publications, I, 1966).

Brown, Jane, *The Pursuit of Paradise* (London: HarperCollins, 1999).

Brunetti, Franz, 'De la mécanique à l'histoire', *Dix-huitième Siècle*, 16 (1984), pp. 123–36.

Bürger, Thomas, *Epilogue to Maria Sibylla Merian: New Book of Flowers* (Munich, London and New York: Pressel, 1999).

Calmann, Gerta, *Ehret, Flower Painter Extraordinaire* (Oxford: Phaidon, 1977).

Cameron, David, *The Social Thought of Rousseau and Burke* (London: Weidenfeld and Nicolson, 1973).

Cantor, David, 'The Metaphysics of Botany: Rousseau and the New Criticism of Plants', *Southwest Review*, 70 (1986), pp. 362–80.

Cardinal, Catherine, *The Watch from Its Origins to the XIXth Century*, trans. Jacques Pages (Thornbury: Artline Editions, 1989).

Carruthers, Mary, *The Craft of Thought: Meditation, Rhetoric, and the Making of Images* (Cambridge: Cambridge University Press, 1998).

Cheyron, Henry, ' "L'Amour de la botanique." Les Annotations de Jean-Jacques Rousseau sur la *Botanique* de Régnault', *Littératures*, 4 (1981), pp. 53–95.

Chisick, Harvey, *The Limitations of Reform in the Enlightenment* (Princeton: Princeton University Press, 1981).

Churton Collins, J., *Voltaire, Montesquieu and Rousseau in England* (London: no publisher, 1908).

Clark, William, Golinski, Jan and Schaffer, Simon (eds.), *The Sciences in Enlightenment Europe* (Chicago and London: University of Chicago Press, 1999).

Clarke, Katherine, *Making Time for the Past: Local History and the Polis* (Oxford: Oxford University Press, 2008).

Clegg, Arthur, 'Craftsmen and the Origin of Science', *Science and Society*, XLIII (1979), pp. 186–201.

Cole, Arthur H. and Watts, George B., *The Handicrafts Of France as Recorded in the 'Description des Arts et Métiers', 1761–1788* (New Haven: Harvard University Press, 1952).

Coleman, Roger, *The Art of Work: An Epitaph to Skill* (London: Pluto Press, 1988).

Coppola, Sylviane Albertan and Chouillet, A.M., eds., *La Machine et l'homme dans l'Encyclopédie': Actes du colloque de Joinville, 10–12 juillet 1995* (Paris: Klincksieck, 1998).

de Corancez, Olivier, *De Jean-Jacques Rousseau* (extracts from *Journal de Paris*, nos. 205, 251, 256, 258, 259, 260 and 261, and VI).

Cradock, J., *Literary and Miscellaneous Memories*, 4 vols. (London: no publisher, 1828), I.

Cranston, Maurice, *Jean-Jacques: The Early Life and Work of Jean-Jacques Rousseau 1712–1754* (Chicago: University of Chicago Press, 1982).

——, *The Noble Savage: Jean-Jacques Rousseau 1754–1762* (Chicago: University of Chicago Press, 1991).

——, *The Solitary Self: Jean-Jacques Rousseau in Exile and Adversity* (Chicago: University of Chicago Press, 1997).

Crawford, Matthew, *The Case for Working with Your Hands* (London: Penguin/ Viking, 2010).

Crosby, Alfred W., *Ecological Imperialism: The Biological Expansion of Europe, 900–1900* (Cambridge: Cambridge University Press, 1986).

Cummings, Frederick, 'Boothby, Rousseau and the Romantic Malady', *Burlington Magazine*, 110 (1968), pp. 159–67.

Cunningham, Andrew and Jardine, Nicholas (eds.), *Romanticism and the Sciences* (Cambridge: Cambridge University Press, 1990).

Daiches, David, *A Companion to Scottish Culture* (London: Edward Arnold, 1981).

——, Jones, Peter and Jones, Jean (eds.), *A Hotbed of Genius: The Scottish Enlightenment 1730–1790* (Edinburgh: Edinburgh University Press, 1986).

Defoe, Daniel, *Robinson Crusoe*, ed. J. Donald Crowley (Oxford: Oxford University Press, 1981).

Delany, Mary, *Life and Correspondence*, ed. Lady Llanover, 3 vols. (London: no publisher, 1862).

Delor, Michel, '"Homo sum . . .": un vers de Térence comme devise des Lumières', *Dix-huitième Siècle*, 16 (1984), pp. 279–96.

Delorme, Suzanne and Tatou, René (eds.), *L'Encyclopédie' et le progrès des sciences et des techniques* (Paris: Presses universitaires de France, 1952).

De Man, Paul, *Blindness and Insight: Essays in the Rhetoric of Contemporary Criticism* (Oxford and New York: Oxford University Press, 1971).

Deneys-Tunney, Anne, *Un Autre Jean-Jacques Rousseau. Le paradoxe de la technique* (Paris: Presses universitaires de France, 2010).

Dent, N. J. H., *A Rousseau Dictionary* (Oxford: Oxford University Press, 1992).

Deonna, W., *Les Arts à Genève des origines à la fin du XVIIIe siècle* (Geneva: Musée d'art et d'histoire, 1942).

Derrida, Jacques, *De la grammatologie* (Paris: Editions de Minuit, 1967), part II.

——, *Le Toucher, Jean-Luc Nancy* (Paris: Galilée, 2000).

Dessin et sciences XVIIe–XVIIIe siècles (Exposition Louvre 22.6–24.9 1984) (Paris: Editions de la Réunion des musées nationaux, 1984).

De Waal, Edmund, *The Hare With Amber Eyes* (London: Chatto and Windus, 2011).

Diderot, Denis, *Correspondance*, ed. Georges Roth and Jean Varloot, 16 vols. (Paris: Minuit, 1955–70).

——, *Œuvres esthétiques*, ed. Paul Vernière (Paris: Garnier, 1967).

——, *Œuvres complètes*, ed. Herbert Dieckmann, Jacques Proust and Jean Varloot, 25 vols. (Paris: Hermann, 1975–95).

Dohrn-Van Rossum, Gerhard, *History of the Hour: Clocks and Modern Temporal Orders*, trans. Thomas Dunlap (Chicago and London: University of Chicago Press, 1996).

Dormer, Peter (ed.), *The Culture of Craft* (Manchester and New York: Manchester University Press, 1997).

Dowd, David L., *Pageant-Master to the Republic: Jacques-Louis David and the French Revolution* (Nebraska: University of Nebraska Press, 1948).

Drouin, Jean-Marc, *Réinventer la nature: l'écologie et son histoire* (Paris: Flammarion, 1991).

Duchet, Michèle, *Anthropologie et histoire au siècle des Lumières* (Paris: Albin Michel, 1977).

—— and Galley, Michèle, *Langue et langage de Leibniz à l' "Encyclopédie"* (Geneva: Droz, 1977).

Edmonds, David and Eidenow, John, *Rousseau's Dog* (London: Faber, 2006).

Egerton, Judy (ed.), *Wright of Derby* (London: Tate Gallery Publications, 1990).

Eisenstein, Elizabeth, *The Printing-Press as an Agent of Change*, 2 vols. (Cambridge: Cambridge University Press, 1979).

Elias, Norbert, *The Civilizing Process*, trans. Edmund Jephcott (Oxford: Blackwell, 1978).

Elinor, Gillian (ed.), *Women and Crafts* (London: Virago, 1987).

L'Encyclopédie' entre arts et sciences: Musée d'art et d'histoire, Langres 29.6–18.11.2001) (Langres: Dominique Guéniot, 2001).

Epstein, S.R. and Prak, Maarten (eds.), *Guilds, Innovation and the European Economy 1400–1800* (Cambridge: Cambridge University Press, 2008).

Fabre, Jean, 'Deux Frères ennemis. Diderot et Jean-Jacques', *Diderot Studies*, III (1961), pp. 155–213.

Fallet-Scheurer, Marius, *Le Travail à domicile dans l'horlogerie Suisse et les industries annexes* (Berne: Imprimerie de l'Union, 1909).

Farr, James R., *Artisans in Europe 1300–1914* (Cambridge: Cambridge University Press, 2000).

Ferrand, Nathalie (ed.), *Traduire et illustrer le roman au XVIIIe siècle* (Oxford: Voltaire Foundation, 2011).

Findlen, Paula, 'Jokes of Nature and Jokes of Knowledge in Early Modern Europe', *Renaissance Quarterly*, 43 (1990), pp. 292–331.
Fleming, Juliet, 'How to Look at a Printed Flower', *Word and Image*, 22 (2006), pp. 165–87.
Forbes, Duncan, *Hume's Philosophical Politics* (Cambridge: Cambridge University Press, 1975).
Foucault, Michel, *Les Mots et les choses* (Paris: Gallimard, 1966).
——, *Surveiller et punir. Naissance de la prison* (Paris: Gallimard, 1993).
——, *Qu'est-ce que les lumières?*, ed. Olivier Dekens (Rosny: Bréal, 2004).
Fox, Christopher, Porter, Roy and Wokler, Robert (eds.), *Inventing Human Science* (Berkeley and London: University of California Press, 1995).
Frängsmyr, Tove (ed.), *Linnaeus: The Man and His Work*, rev. edn (Canton, MA: Science History Publications, 1994).
Frayling, Christopher, *Towards a New Bauhaus* (London: Oberon Masters, 2011).
Gadd, Ian A. and Hollis, Patrick (eds.), *Guilds and Associations in Europe, 900–1900* (London: Centre for Metropolitan History, University of London, 2006).
Gauchet, Marcel, *The Disenchantment of the World*, trans. Oscar Burger (Princeton: Princeton University Press, 1997).
Giedion, Sigfried, *Mechanization Takes Command* (New York: Oxford University Press, 1948).
Gillispie, Charles C. 'The Natural History of Industry', *Isis*, 48 (1957), pp. 398–407.
——, 'The *Encyclopédie* and the Jacobin Philosophy of Science', *Critical Problems in the History of Science*, ed. M. Glagett (Madison, WI: University of Wisconsin Press, 1959), pp. 255–89.
Glover, C. H., *Dr Charles Burney's Continental Travels 1770–1772* (London and Glasgow: Blackie, 1927).
Goldschmidt, Victor, *Anthropologie et politique. Les principes du système de Rousseau* (Paris: J. Vrin, 1974).
Good, James and Velody, Irving (eds.), *The Politics of Postmodernity* (Cambridge: Cambridge University Press, 1998).
Goodman, Dena *The Republic of Letters* (Ithaca and London: Cornell University Press, 1994).
——, 'Furnishing Discourses: Readings on a Writing Desk in Eighteenth-Century France', in *Luxury in the Eighteenth Century*, ed. Maxine Berg and Elizabeth Eger (Basingstoke and New York: Palgrave Macmillan, 2003), pp. 71–88.
——, 'The Secrétaire and the Integration of the Eighteenth-Century Self', in *Furnishing the Eighteenth Century*, ed. Dena Goodman and Kathryn Norberg (New York and London: Routledge, 2007), pp. 183–203.
Gosse, Edmund, 'Jean-Jacques Rousseau en Angleterre au XIXᵉ siècle', *Annales Jean-Jacques Rousseau*, 8 (1912), pp. 131–46.
Graham, W. Fred, *The Constructive Revolutionary: Calvin and His Socio-Economic Impact* (Richmond, VA: John Knox Press, 1971).

Gray, John, *Enlightenment's Wake: Politics at the Close of the Modern Age* (London and New York: Routledge, 1995).

Green, Jeffrey E., 'Two Meanings of Disenchantment', *Philosophy and Theology*, 17 (2006), pp. 51–84.

Gusdorf, Georges, *De l'histoire des sciences à l'histoire de la pensée* (Paris: Payot, 1966).

Habermas, Jürgen, *The Structural Transformation of the Public Sphere*, trans. Thomas Burger (Cambridge: Polity Press, 1989).

Hahn, Roger, *The Anatomy of a Scientific Institution: The Paris Academy of Science, 1666–1803* (Berkeley, Los Angeles and London: University of California Press, 1971).

Hankins, Thomas L., *Science and the Enlightenment* (Cambridge: Cambridge University Press, 1985).

Hardy, Francis, *Memoirs of the Political and Private Life of James Caulfield, Earl of Charlemont*, 2nd edn, 2 vols. (London: Cadell and Davies, 1812).

Hartle, Ann, *The Modern Self in Rousseau's 'Confessions'* (Notre-Dame, Indiana: University of Notre-Dame Press, 1985).

Harvey, Simon et al. (eds.), *Reappraisals of Rousseau* (Manchester: Manchester University Press, 1980).

Heidegger, Martin, *Discourse on Thinking [1959]*, trans. John H. Anderson and E. Hans Freund (New York, Evanston, and London: Harper and Rowe, 1966).

Hill, Christopher, 'Protestantism and the Rise of Capitalism', in *Essays in the Economic and Social History of Tudor and Stuart England in Honour of R. H. Tawney* (Cambridge: Cambridge University Press, 1961), pp. 15–31.

History and Topography of Ashbourne, the Valley of the Dove, and the Adjacent Villages (Ashbourne: Dawson and Hobson, 1839).

Holloway, Richard, *Between the Monster and the Saint* (Edinburgh: Canongate, 2008).

Holmes, Richard, *The Age of Wonder* (London: HarperPress, 2008).

Honeybone, Michael, 'The Spalding Gantlemen's Society: The Communication of Science in the East Midlands of England, 1710–1760', PhD Thesis, Open University, 2001.

Hooykaas, R., *Religion and the Rise of Modern Science* (Edinburgh and London: Scottish Academic Press, 1972).

Howitt, William, *Visits to Remarkable Places* (London: no publisher, 1840).

Huard, Georges, 'Les Planches de l'*Encyclopédie* et celles de la *Description des arts et metiers*', in Suzanne Delorme and René Tatou (eds.), *L' 'Encyclopédie' et le progrès des sciences et des techniques* (Paris: Presses universitaires de France, 1952), pp. 35–46.

Huizinga, J., *Homo ludens*, first English edn, 1949 (London: Routledge, 1998).

Hume, David, *Essays*, new edn, 2 vols. (London: no publisher, 1764).

Israel, Jonathan I., *Radical Enlightenment* (Oxford: Oxford University Press, 2001).

Jackson, Donald, *The Story of Writing* (London: Barrie and Jenkins, 1981).

Jacob, Margaret C., *The Cultural Meaning of the Scientific Revolution* (Philadelphia: Temple University Press, 1988).

——, *Science, Culture and the Making of the Industrial West* (Oxford: Oxford University Press, 1997).

Jaquet, Eugène and Chapuis, Alfred, *Histoire et technique de la montre suisse* (Basel and Olten: Urs Graf Verlag, 1945).

Jeantet, A. Mathey, *L'Ecriture de Jean-Jacques Rousseau* (Le Locle: Courvoisier, 1912).

Jimack, Peter, *Rousseau: 'Emile'* (London: Grant and Cutler, 1983).

Johnson, Lawrence E., *A Morally Deep World: An Essay on Moral Significance and Environmental Ethics* (Cambridge: Cambridge University Press, 1991).

Joyce, Patrick (ed.), *The Historical Meanings of Work* (Cambridge: Cambridge University Press, 1987).

Kelly, Christopher, *Rousseau's Exemplary Life* (Ithaca: Cornell University Press, 1987).

——, *Rousseau as Author: Consecrating One's Life to the Truth* (Chicago and London: University of Chicago Press, 2003).

Kenny, Neil, *Curiosity in Early Modern Europe: Word Histories* (Wiesbaden: Harrassowitz Verlag, 1998).

King, Lester S., *The Philosophy of Medicine: The Early Eighteenth Century* (Cambridge, MA, and London: Harvard University Press, 1978).

Kippenberg, Hans G., *Die Vorderasiatischen Erlösungsreligionen in ihrem Zusammenhang mit der antiken Stadtherrschaft* (Frankfurt am Main: Suhrkamp, 1991).

Koerner, Lisbet, *Linnaeus: Nature and Nation* (Cambridge, MA, and London: Harvard University Press, 1999).

Kuhn, Thomas S., *The Structure of Scientific Revolutions*, 2nd edn (Chicago: University of Chicago Press, 1970).

Kurz, Otto, *European Clocks and Watches in the Near East* (London: Warburg Institute; Leiden: Brill, 1975).

Landes, David S. (ed.), *The Rise of Capitalism* (New York: Macmillan, 1966).

——, *Revolutions in Time: Clocks and the Making of the Modern World* (Cambridge, MA, and London: Harvard University Press, 1983).

——, *The Wealth and Poverty of Nations* (London: Abacus, 1999).

Latour, Bruno, 'Visualization and Cognitive Thinking: Thinking with Eyes and Hands', in Henrika Kuklick and Elizabeth Long (eds.), *Knowledge and Society: Studies in the Sociology of Culture, Past and Present*, 6 (1986), pp. 1–40.

Launay, Michel, *Rousseau écrivain politique*, 2nd edn (Geneva and Paris: Slatkine, 1989).

Le Goff, Jacques (ed.), *La Nouvelle Histoire* (Paris: Retz, 1978).

Lefeyvre, Frédéric, 'Jean-Jacques Rousseau. Horloger malgré lui', *La Revue (Musée des arts et métiers)*, September 1998, pp. 34–41.

Lehmann, Hartmut and Roth, Guenther (eds.), *Weber's Protestant Ethic* (Washington, DC: Publications of the German Historical Institute, and Cambridge: Cambridge University Press, 1993).

Leigh, R. A., 'Les Amitiés françaises du Docteur Burney', *RLC*, 25 (1951), pp. 161–94.

——, 'Boswell and Rousseau', *MLR*, XLVII (1952), pp. 289–318.

——, 'Rousseau's English Pension', in J. H. Fox et al. (eds.), *Studies in Eighteenth-Century French Literature Presented to Robert Niklaus* (Exeter: Exeter University Press, 1975), pp. 110–21.

Leuba, Jean-Louis, 'Rousseau et le milieu calviniste de sa jeunesse', in *Jean-Jacques Rousseau et la crise contemporaine de la conscience. Colloque international du deuxième centenaire de la mort de Jean-Jacques Rousseau, Chantilly 5–8.9.1978* (Paris: Beauchesne, 1980), pp. 11–51.

Light, Matthew and Smith, Jonathan M. (eds.), *The Production of Public Space* (Lanham, Boulder: Rowman and Littlefield, 1998).

Ligne, Prince de, *Lettres et pensées*, ed. Mme la baronne de Staël-Holstein, 2 vols. (London: B. Dulau & Co., 1809).

Lucie-Smith, Edward, *The Story of Craft* (Oxford: Phaidon, 1981).

Lüthy, Herbert, *Le Passé présent. Combats d'idées de Calvin à Rousseau* (Monaco: Editions du Rocher, 1965).

MacCarthy, Fiona, *The Simple Life: C.R. Ashbee in the Cotswolds* (London: Lund Humphries, 1981).

MacGregor, Arthur, *Curiosity and Enlightenment* (New Haven and London: Yale University Press, 2007).

Macmillan, Duncan, *Painting in Scotland: The Golden Age* (Oxford: Oxford University Press, 1986).

Malia, Martin, *History's Locomotives* (New Haven and London: Yale University Press, 2006).

Marshall, Gordon, *In Search of the Spirit of Capitalism* (London: Hutchinson, 1982).

Mason, S. F., 'The Scientific Revolution and the Protestant Reformation: I', *Annals of Science*, 9 (1953), pp. 64–87.

Masson, Pierre Maurice, *La Formation religieuse de Rousseau* (Paris: Hachette, 1916).

Maurice, Klaus, *Der drechselnde Souverän* (Zurich: Verlag Ineichen, 1985).

McMahon, Darren, *Enemies of the Enlightenment* (Oxford: Oxford University Press, 2001).

Le Ménahèze, Sophie, *L'Invention du jardin romantique en France 1761–1808* (Neuilly-sur-Seine: Editions Spiralinthe, 2001).

Merchant, Carolyn, *The Death of Nature: Women, Ecology and the Scientific Revolution* (New York: HarperCollins, 1990).

——, *Earthcare: Women and the Environment* (New York: Routledge, 1995).

de Montet, Albert, 'Mme de Warens et le pays de Vaud', *Mélanges, Société d'histoire de la Suisse romande*, 2ᵉ série, III (Lausanne: Georges Bridelm, 1891), pp. 1–254.

Mortier, Roland, *Le Cœur et la raison* (Oxford: Voltaire Foundation, 1990).

——, 'Paresse et travail dans l'introspection de Rousseau', in *Rousseau and the Eighteenth Century: Essays in Memory of R. A. Leigh*, ed. Marian

Hobson, J. T. A. Leigh and Robert Wokler (Oxford: Voltaire Foundation, 1992), pp. 125–34.

Mossner, Ernest Campbell, *The Life of David Hume*, 2nd edn (Oxford: Oxford University Press, 1980).

Mottu Weber, Liliane, 'Les Conditions d'apprentissage à Genève au début du XVIIIᵉ siècle d'après les minutes de notaires (1701–1710)', licence de la Faculté des sciences économiques et sociales, Université de Genève, 1963.

Mukerji, Chandra, *From Graven Images: Patterns of Modern Materialism* (New York: Columbia University Press, 1983).

Mullan, John, *Sentiment and Sociability: The Language of Feeling in the Eighteenth Century* (Oxford: Oxford University Press, 1988).

Mumford, Lewis, *Technics and Civilization* (London: Routledge, 1934).

Naylor, Gillian, *The Arts and Crafts Movement*, 2nd edn (London: Trefoil Publications, 1990).

Ogilvie, David, *The Science of Describing: Natural History in Renaissance Europe* (Chicago and London: University of Chicago Press, 2006).

Outram, Dorinda, *Panorama of the Enlightenment* (London: Thames and Hudson, 2006).

Ozouf, Mona, *La Fête révolutionnaire* (Paris: Gallimard, 1976).

Pannebecker, John R., 'Diderot, the Mechanical Arts, and the *Encyclopédie*', *Journal of Technology Education*, 6.1 (Fall 1994), pp. 45–57.

——, 'Rousseau in the Heritage of Technology Education', *Journal of Technology Education*, 6.2 (Spring 1995), pp. 46–58.

Papanek, Victor, *The Green Imperative* (London: Thames and Hudson, 1995).

Parker, Rozsika, *The Subversive Stitch* (London: Women's Press, 1984).

Passmore, John, *The Perfectibility of Man*, 2nd edn (London: Duckworth, 1972).

——, *The Revolt Against Science* (London: Duckworth, 1978).

——, *Man's Responsibility for Nature* (London: Duckworth, 1984).

Perry, Norma, 'Jean-Jacques Rousseau and the West Country', *French Studies*, 24 (1970), pp. 14–22.

Petroski, Henry, *The Pencil: A History of Design and Circumstance* (New York: Knopf, 1992).

Picon, Antoine, 'La Vision du travail des Encyclopédistes', *Recherches sur Diderot et sur l'Encyclopédie*, 13 (1992), pp. 131–97.

Pirsig, Robert M., *Zen and the Art of Motorcycle Maintenance* (London: Corgi, 1974).

Pitassi, Maria-Cristina, *De l'orthodoxie aux Lumières. Genève 1670–1737* (Geneva: Labor et Fides, 1992).

Plan, Pierre-Paul, 'Jean-Jacques Rousseau aviateur', *Mercure de France*, 1910, pp. 577–97.

Plumwood, Val, *Feminism and the Mastery of Nature* (London and New York: Routledge, 1993).

Porter, Dennis, *Rousseau's Legacy: Emergence and Eclipse of the Writer in France* (New York and Oxford: Oxford University Press, 1995).

Powers, Richard Howard, 'Rousseau's "Useless Science": Dilemma or Paradox?', *Past and Present*, 29 (1964), pp. 450–68.

Prendergast, Christopher, *The Order of Mimesis* (Cambridge: Cambridge University Press, 1986).

Prestwich, Menna (ed.), *International Calvinism 1541–1715* (Oxford: Oxford University Press, 1985).

Proust, Jacques, 'De l'*Encyclopédie* au *Neveu de Rameau*. L'objet et le texte', in Jacques Proust (ed.), *Diderot et l'Encyclopédie* (Paris: A. Colin, 1962), 273–340.

——, *L'Objet et le texte. Recherches nouvelles sur quelques écrivains des Lumières* (Geneva: Droz, 1972).

Quest-Ritson, Charles, *The English Garden Abroad* (London: Viking, 1992).

Le Refuge huguenot en Suisse. Catalogue du Musée historique de l'ancienne évêché (Lausanne: Éditions du Tricorne, 1985).

Riskin, Jessica, *Science in the Age of Sensibility* (Chicago and London: University of Chicago Press, 2002).

Ritter, Eugène, *Magny et le piétisme romand. Mélanges, Société d'histoire de la Suisse romande, 2ᵉ Série*, III (Lausanne: Georges Bridel, 1891), pp. 257–324.

——, *La Famille et la jeunesse de Jean-Jacques Rousseau* (Paris: Hachette, 1896).

——, 'Notes diverses sur Jean-Jacques Rousseau', *Annales Jean-Jacques Rousseau*, III (1907), pp. 175–221.

Robinson, Eric, 'The Derby Philosophical Society', *Annals of Science*, 9 (1953), pp. 359–67.

Roche, Daniel, *Le Siècle des Lumières en province. Académies et académiciens provinciaux (1680–1789)*, 2 vols. (Paris and The Hague: Mouton, 1978).

Roddier, Henri, *Jean-Jacques Rousseau en Angleterre au XVIIIᵉ siècle* (Paris: Boivin et Cⁱᵉ, 1950).

Roger, Jacques, *Les Sciences de la vie dans la pensée française du XVIIIᵉ siècle* (Paris: A. Colin, 1963).

Rolston, Holmes, III, *Philosophy Gone Wild: Essays in Environmental Ethics* (Buffalo, New York: Prometheus Books, 1986).

Roney, John B. and Klauber, Martin I. (eds.), *The Identity of Geneva: The Christian Commonwealth, 1564–1864* (Westport, and London: Greenwood Press, 1998).

Rouquet, Jean-André, *État des arts en Angleterre* (Paris: Charles-Antoine Jombert, 1755).

Rousseau, Jean-Jacques, *Œuvres complètes*, ed. Bernard Gagnebin and Marcel Raymond, 5 vols. (Paris: Gallimard, 1959–95).

——, *Correspondance complète*, ed. R. A. Leigh, 52 vols. (Geneva, Madison, WI, Banbury, Oxford: Voltaire Foundation, 1965–89).

von Sachs, Julius, *History of Botany*, trans. H. E. F. Garnsey (New York: Russell and Russell, 1890).

Safley, Thomas Max and Rosenband, Leo N. (eds.), *The Workplace before the Factory* (Ithaca and London: Cornell University Press, 1993).

Saint-Amand, Pierre, *The Pursuit of Laziness*, trans. Jennifer Curtiss Gage (Princeton and Oxford: Princeton University Press, 2011).

Schiebinger, Londa, *Nature's Body* (London: Pandora, 1993).

Schmidt, James and Miller, James, 'Aspects of Technology in Marx and Rousseau', in *The Technological Imagination*, ed. Teresa de Lauretis, Andreas Huyssen and Kathleen Woodward (Madison, WI: Coda Press, 1980), pp. 85–94.

Scott, David, 'Rousseau and Flowers', *SVEC*, 182 (1979), pp. 73–86.

Scrase, David, *Flower Drawings* (Cambridge: Cambridge University Press, 1970).

Scruton, Roger, *Beauty* (Oxford: Oxford University Press, 2009).

Sénéchal, A., 'Jean-Jacques Rousseau secrétaire de Madame Dupin', *Annales Jean-Jacques Rousseau*, XXXVI (1966), pp. 173–288.

Sennett, Richard (ed.), *Classic Essays on the Culture of Cities* (New York: Appleton-Century-Crofts, 1969).

——, *The Fall of Public Man* (Cambridge: Cambridge University Press, 1977).

——, *Flesh and Stone: The Body and the City in Western Culture* (London: Faber and Faber, 1994).

——, *Respect* (London: Allen Lane, 2003).

——, *The Craftsman* (London: Allen Lane, 2008).

Sewell, William H., Jr, *Work and Revolution in France* (Cambridge: Cambridge University Press, 1980).

Sharr, Adam, *Heidegger's Hut* (Cambridge, MA: MIT Press, 2006).

Simmel, Georg, *On Individuality and Social Forms*, ed. Donald N. Levine (Chicago and London: University of Chicago Press, 1971).

Skinner, Quentin, *The Foundations of Modern Political Thought*, 2 vols. (Cambridge: Cambridge University Press, 1978).

Slaughter, M. M., *Universal Languages and Scientific Taxonomy in the Seventeenth Century* (Cambridge: Cambridge University Press, 1982).

Smart, Alastair, *The Life and Art of Allan Ramsay* (New Haven and London: Yale University Press, 1952).

——, *Allan Ramsay: Printer, Essayist and Man of the Enlightenment* (New Haven and London: Yale University Press, 1992).

Smith, Pamela H., *The Body of the Artisan* (Chicago and London: University of Chicago Press, 2004).

Sonenscher, Michael, *Work and Wages: Natural Law, Politics and the Eighteenth-Century French Trades* (Cambridge: Cambridge University Press, 1989).

Soper, Kate, *What Is Nature?* (Oxford: Blackwell, 1995).

Spary, E. C., *Utopia's Gardens: French Natural History from Old Regime to Revolution* (Chicago: University of Chicago Press, 2000).

Spink, John S., *Jean-Jacques Rousseau et Genève* (Paris: Boivin, 1934).

Spufford, Francis and Uglow, Jenny (eds.), *Cultural Babbage: Technology, Time and Invention* (London and Boston: Faber and Faber, 1996).

de Staël, Germaine, *De l'Allemagne*, ed. Comtesse Jean de Pange and Simone Balayé, 5 vols (Paris: Garnier, 1958).

Starobinski, Jean, *L'Œil vivant II. La Relation critique* (Paris: Gallimard, 1970).

——, *Jean-Jacques Rousseau. La transparence et l'obstacle* (Paris: Plon, 1971).

Bibliography

Starobinski, Jean, *Le Remède dans le mal. Critique et légitimation de l'artifice à l'âge des Lumières* (Paris: Gallimard, 1989).

Stewart, Philip, *Engraven Desire: Eros, Image and Text in the French Eighteenth Century* (Durham, NC, and London: Duke University Press, 1992).

Stroud, Barry, *Hume* (London: Routledge and Kegan Paul, 1977).

Sumi, Yoichi, *'Le Neveu de Rameau'. Caprices et logiques du jeu* (Tokyo: France Tosho, 1975).

Sutton, Geoffrey V., *Science for a Polite Society* (Boulder, CO: Westview Press, 1995).

Tatou, René (ed.), *Enseignement et diffusion des sciences en France au XVIIIᵉ siècle* (Paris: Hermann, 1964).

Taylor, Charles, 'Heidegger, Language and Ecology', in *Heidegger: A Critical Reader*, ed. Hubert L. Dreyfus and Harrison Hull (Oxford: Blackwell, 1992), pp. 247–69.

——, *A Secular Age* (Cambridge, MA, and London: The Belknap Press at Harvard University Press, 2007).

Thériault, Serge A., *Jean-Jacques Rousseau et la médecine naturelle* (Montreal: Editions Univers, 1979).

Thomas, Keith, *Religion and the Decline of Magic* (Harmondsworth: Penguin, 1973).

Tilgher, Adriano, *Work: What It Has Meant to Men Over the Ages*, trans. Dorothy Canfield Fisher (London: Harrap, 1931).

Tissot, Samuel, *De la santé des gens de lettres* (Lausanne: François Grasset, 1768).

Trevor-Roper, Hugh, *Religion, the Reformation and Social Change*, 2nd edn (London and Basingstoke: Macmillan, 1972).

Trilling, Lionel, *The Liberal Imagination* (London: Secker and Warburg, 1955).

——, 'Freud: Within and Beyond Culture', *Beyond Culture* (Harmondsworth: Penguin, 1967).

——, *Sincerity and Authenticity* (Oxford: Oxford University Press, 1972).

Troeltsch, Ernst, *Protestantism and Progress* (Philadelphia: Fortress Press, 1986).

Trousson, Raymond and Eigeldinger, Frédéric, *Dictionnaire Jean-Jacques Rousseau* (Paris: Champion, 2006).

Tunstall, Kate E., *Blindness and Enlightenment: An Essay* (London: Continuum, 2011).

Uglow, Jenny, *The Lunar Men* (London: Faber, 2002).

——, *Nature's Engraver: A Life of Thomas Bewick* (London: Faber, 2006).

Vallette, Gaspard, *Jean-Jacques Rousseau Genevois*, 2nd edn (Geneva: A. Jullien, Paris: Plon, 1911).

Veblen, Thorstein, 'The Theory of Business Enterprise', *Collected Works*, 10 vols. (London: Routledge/Thoemmes Press, 1994), II.

——, 'Instinct of Workmanship and Irksomeness of Labour', *Collected Works*, 10 vols. (London: Routledge/Thoemmes Press, 1994), X.

Verey, Rosemary, *The Scented Garden* (London: Maxwell Joseph, 1981).

Vernes, Paule Monique, *La Ville, la fête, la démocratie* (Paris: Payot, 1978).

Voisine, Jacques, *Jean-Jacques Rousseau en Angleterre à l'époque romantique* (Paris: Didier, 1956).

Voltaire, *Correspondance complète*, ed. Theodore Besterman, 107 vols. (Geneva: Institut et Musée Voltaire, 1953–65).

von Wagner, F., *L'Ile Saint-Pierre, ou l'île de Rousseau* (Berne: no publisher, 1815).

Wajcman, Judy, *Feminism Confronts Technology* (Cambridge: Polity Press, 1991).

Wallmann, Johannes, *Der Pietismus* (Göttingen: Vandenhoeck and Ruprecht, 1990).

Watelet, Claude-Henri, *Essai sur les jardins, 1774*, ed. and trans. Samuel Danon (Philadelphia: University of Pennsylvania Press, 2003).

Watt, Ian, 'Robinson Crusoe as Myth', *Essays in Criticism*, I (1951), pp. 95–119.

Weber, Max, *Wirtschaftsgeschichte* (Munich and Leipzig: Duncker and Humblot, 1923).

——, *The Protestant Ethic and the Spirit of Capitalism*, trans. Talcott Parsons (London: Allen and Unwin, 1930).

——, *Essays in Sociology*, ed. and trans. H. H. Gerth and C. Wright Mills (London: Routledge, 1998).

Werner, Stephen, *Blueprint: A Study of Diderot and the 'Encyclopédie' Plates* (Birmingham, Alabama: Summa, 1993).

Wiebenson, Dora, *The Picturesque Garden in France* (Princeton: Princeton University Press, 1978).

Wildblood, Richard, *What Makes Switzerland Tick?* (Lewes: The Book Guild, 2007).

Williams, Elizabeth A., *The Physical and the Moral* (Cambridge: Cambridge Unversity Press, 1994).

Williams, Raymond, *The Country and the City* (London: The Hogarth Press, 1993).

Winckelmann, Johannes, 'Die Herkunft von Max Webers, "Entzauberungskonzeption"', *Kölner Zeitschrift für Soziologie und Sozialpsychologie*, 32 (1980), pp. 12–53.

Wind, Edgar, *Hume and the Heroic Portrait* (Oxford: Oxford University Press, 1986).

Wirszubski, Charles, 'Cicero's *cum dignitate otium*: A Reconsideration', *Journal of Roman Studies*, 44 (1954), pp. 1–13.

Witte, John and Kingdon, Robert M., *Sex, Family and Marriage in John Calvin's Geneva* (Cambridge: Eerdmans, 2005).

Wollstonecraft, Mary, *A Vindication of the Rights of Woman*, ed. Sylvana Tomaselli (Cambridge: Cambridge University Press, 1995).

Wyke, John, *Catalogue of Tools for Watch and Clock Makers*, facsimile edn, ed. Alan Smith (Charlottesville: University Press of Virginia, 1978).

Yardeni, Myriam, *Le Refuge huguenot. Assimilation et culture* (Paris: Champion, 2002).

Zaretsky, Robert and Scott, John W., *The Philosophers' Quarrel: Rousseau, Hume and the Limits of Human Understanding* (New Haven and London: Yale University Press, 2009).

Zimmerman, Michael E., *Heidegger's Confrontation with Modernity* (Bloomington, Indiana: Indiana University Press, 1990).

Zonnefeld, Jacques, *Sir Brooke Boothby* (Voorburg: Uitgeverij 'De Niewe Haagsche', n.d.).

Index